How to Manage Growth and Maximize Profits in Outbound Telemarketing

Steven A. Idelman

Grady L. Dobbs

PRENTICE HALL
Englewood Cliffs, New Jersey 07632

Prentice-Hall International (UK) Limited, *London*
Prentice-Hall of Australia Pty. Limited, *Sydney*
Prentice-Hall Canada, Inc., *Toronto*
Prentice-Hall Hispanoamericana, S.A., *Mexico*
Prentice-Hall of India Private Limited, *New Delhi*
Prentice-Hall of Japan, Inc., *Tokyo*
Simon & Schuster Asia Pte. Ltd., *Singapore*
Editora Prentice-Hall do Brasil, Ltda., *Rio de Janeiro*

© *1989 by*

PRENTICE-HALL, Inc.
Englewood Cliffs, NJ

"This publication is designed to provide accurate and authoritative information in regard to the subject matter covered. It is sold with the understanding that the publisher is not engaged in rendering legal, accounting or other professional service. If legal advice or other expert assistance is required, the services of a competent professional person should be sought.

. . . *From the Declaration of Principles jointly adopted by a Committee of the American Bar Association and a Committee of Publishers and Associations.*"

10   9   8   7   6   5   4   3   2   1

Library of Congress Cataloging-in-Publication Data

Idelman, Steven A.
　　How to manage growth and maximize profits in outbound
　telemarketing / Steven A. Idelman, Grady L. Dobbs.
　　　　p. cm.
　　ISBN 0-13-400813-8
　　　1. Telemarketing—Management.　　2. Telephone selling—Management.
　I. Dobbs, Grady L.　　II. Title.
　HF5415.1265.I34　　1989
　658.84—dc20　　　　　　　　　　　　　　　　　　　　　89-23135
　　　　　　　　　　　　　　　　　　　　　　　　　　　　　　CIP

ISBN 0-13-400813-8

PRENTICE HALL
BUSINESS & PROFESSIONAL DIVISION
A division of Simon & Schuster
Englewood Cliffs, New Jersey 07632

Printed in the United States of America

Steve's Dedication and Acknowledgments

This book is *personally* dedicated to my wife Sheri, my daughter Ali, my mother Gloria, my late father Jerry Idelman and my late Uncle Jerry Cassman, my inspirations and motivations in life, day after day. Also to my sister Susan, my brother George, and papa Marty. I love you all.

This book is *professionally* dedicated to my business partners Sheri Idelman, Wes Belew, (who gets extra-special thanks for his contributions to the Appendix). Don Prohaska, Dale Broekemeier, Dan Hybner, Denise Robertson, Kathy Lee, Chris Livingston, and all the other wonderful people of Idelman Telemarketing Inc.; to Jerry Glazov, who taught me the basics of telephone selling and to Grady Dobbs, without whom this book would never have been completed.

To Sheri, Ali, Jerry . . . to the others listed above and to some I probably should have mentioned but didn't . . . THIS ONE'S FOR YOU!

Grady's Acknowledgments and Dedication

I would like to acknowledge just a few of the people who have helped me in various ways: Wes Belew, Jr., for contributing much of the material contained in the appendix of this book; Lee Van Vechtin, for valuable advice during the preparation of the manuscript; Rudy Oetting, for reading the entire first draft and giving excellent advice (including the advice to completely re-write it!); Phil Immergluck, Mike Applebaum, and Steve Idelman, for special personal friendships, as well as professional support and guidance; Galen and Ilya, for their exceptional love, support, and patience beyond all reasonable expectation while Dad was working all hours of the day and night on his book; and especially to the couple to whom this book is dedicated . . .

To my parents, Harold and Martha Dobbs,
whose support and belief in me has never wavered,
even when I have doubted myself.

Contents

Introduction:
The Growth Challenge

Telemarketing growth does not have to be the uncontrolled or uncontrollable experience many managers believe and fear it will be. Growth can be brought under control with proper management of change and a persistent commitment to quality and value. If you don't believe that can be accomplished, you should make a choice now. Either put down this book or prepare to alter your beliefs.

THE TELEMARKETER'S CHALLENGE

Telemarketing has become an integral and vital force in the American business community in the last decade. It is now a key part of the marketing strategies of at least 90% of the Fortune 500 companies. As telemarketing has moved into the boardrooms of America's corporations, the era of the "seat of the pants" manager has passed.

Telemarketing remains a unique field with its own rules and requirements. Yet the outcomes *any* organization should strive for are clear: high-quality, cost-effective results produced by people who maintain strong commitment and a tightly knit team spirit. Quality growth management in telemarketing requires an extensive knowledge and understanding of effective planning, financial controls, sales and marketing strategies, recruiting and hiring, management development, and human behavior. The challenge is not the *existence* of rapid telemarketing growth but the successful *management* of it while *maintaining* high standards throughout the growth process.

The Telemarketing industry will be brought to full recognition and power by a new breed of managers. These managers have the specialized knowledge and expertise required to balance traditional business values with the unique requirements of fast-paced, high-quality production in an innovative growth environment.

IS THIS BOOK FOR YOU?

This book is for you if you are:

- An in-house or service agency telemarketer who recognizes that being able to handle only the operational needs of today restricts you to a very limited future;
- A telemarketer strongly in favor of—or opposed to—growth;

- A founder, owner, executive, financial administrator, personnel administrator, marketer, manager, or supervisor involved in building a larger telemarketing operation . . . or if you aspire to be;
- A telemarketing supervisor or manager who wants to better understand, manage, and survive the demands of the growth process;
- A skilled and experienced manager who feels overloaded with the responsibilities and changes involved in growth management;
- A non-telemarketing executive who wants a better understanding of the requirements of quality growth management in your telemarketing center;
- A telemarketing client who desires greater insight into telemarketing;
- An executive who would like assistance—and supporting source material—in communicating the realities of growth to your people.

This book is directed primarily to telemarketers who currently have an outbound operation of 20 or more phones and the desire to grow. But even if you have only a few phones and your target is 20 or more phones, the same concepts of planning, structuring, development, and management from the perspective of hands-on experience can be extremely valuable. The principles are the same, whether you want to go from 2 to 20 phones or from 200 phones to 2,000. The only significant differences are in the size of your dream and in your specific application of the principles.

WHAT THIS BOOK OFFERS

This book is not a scholarly study of theory and abstract concepts. Nor is it solely a "how to" book, although a great deal of "how to" is included. Instead, we focus on your needs and on the critical issues that individual companies and the industry face as a result of telemarketing's rapid growth. This book focuses on application and action, on practical and purposeful steps to take, and on the experiences involved. We concentrate on the why, what, how and when of planning and execution, of staffing and structure, of training and compensation, and of risks and rewards.

Our book addresses the problems that managers of growth must face, giving step-by-step instructions and practical hands-on examples of how growth management works in real life. We also explore many hard questions, such as:

- How can you be sure you are ready to grow, how quickly, and by how much?
- What are the essential considerations in the financial planning of growth?
- What are realistic margins and rates of return?
- How can you know if you are keeping your organization lean but efficient?
- What are the best structuring systems to implement for growth?
- Where and how can you best recruit and develop our labor force?
- What can you do to reduce turnover in the labor force?
- How is employee resistance to growth and change best managed?
- How should you establish your market niche?

- How can you deal with the competition?
- What should you do to assure continuing client and program development?
- How do you keep your costs in line while increasing the value of your services?
- What policies and practical actions will allow your organization to grow constructively?
- What steps can you take to keep the growth active, yet under control?
- How do you stay ahead of growth *and* maintain quality and profitability?
- What will your future challenges be, and how can you prepare for them?

Our goal in writing this book has been to create a valuable telemarketing growth management resource, filled with specific answers, insights, guidelines, and techniques developed for outbound telemarketing applications. We hope to help you meet the challenges of growth regardless of the types of programs you manage.

This book assumes you possess certain basic levels of knowledge about telemarketing. If you lack that knowledge, we urge you first to tackle the challenge of learning to be an effective telemarketer. Then come back and read this book.

OUR OBJECTIVES

Our book is intended as a working resource for the practicing manager. We hope to reach you, to open your eyes, to challenge your beliefs, to stimulate your thinking, to prod you to action . . . and to make you see results. We want the book to be a useful guide that saves you time, prevents expensive mistakes, and improves your results. The daily grind of managing growth creates enough hardships and headaches; we hope we can help you learn some lessons in a more pleasant and less painful way.

Poorly managed telemarketing growth not only hurts the company involved—it adversely affects the entire industry. We hope to be a part of your education, maturation, and growth.

Quality is never an accident; it is always the result of high intention, sincere effort, intelligent direction and skillful execution; it represents the wise choice of many alternatives.   —*Willa Foster*

Chapter 1

Five Keys to a Strong Growth Foundation for Your Telemarketing Operation

In the heart of a dramatically growing industry, those who lead in-house telemarketing operations and telemarketing service agencies must confront the increasing reality of managing growth. Many greet that reality with enthusiasm and seek to capitalize on the additional opportunities as quickly as possible. For them, the prospect of growth is seductive. They see growth not as an alternative, but as an imperative. "Who wouldn't want growth?" they ask. Aren't the extra size, recognition, and money a big part of what they have been working so hard for? Isn't growth a vital part of what business is all about . . . to become as big as you possibly can? Aren't the excitement, challenges and rewards of rapid growth desired by everyone?

Not necessarily. Those ideas do not excite everyone. In one way or another, many telemarketing managers feel that the potential rewards are not worth the increased efforts and risks that come with growth. Some approach the management of growth as an annoying obligation. They see it as a trying necessity, required to meet the unrealistic expectations of "the people in charge." Others face the situation with feelings of reservation, resistance, or hostility. To them, growth offers the unwelcome prospect of unpleasant change, increased demands, and overburdening responsibilities. In many cases, rapid growth creates a fear of the unknown and the specter of unjustified risk. Their cry of protest is "It's too much, too fast. We're just not ready!".

Their concerns simply may be expressions of the normal resistance to change. Yet

1

the fears of uncertainty are real and, in some cases, may be justified. Thus, management of any telemarketing company must consider those feelings before embarking on the journey into new levels of growth. Managers need to assure themselves *and* their people that the company's foundation for growth is—in fact—solid, secure, and sufficient to bear the additional demands.

Sales volume, by itself, it not a reliable indicator of the quality of a telemarketing company's performance or prospects for future growth and success. Growth can create a severe strain on the company's management and resources. Without a solid foundation for that growth, the additional sales volume may signal the beginning of a company's decline in quality, efficiency, and profitability. Without the support of a strong growth foundation, the increased weight of the expansion may weaken or topple the entire organization.

Yet, outbound telemarketing growth—even remarkably rapid growth—does not have to be an unsupportable burden for the thoroughly prepared and properly managed company. Growth can be exciting and rewarding, and it can be managed effectively and profitably if you have a solid foundation built on:

- a realistic approach to growth;
- productive purposes for growth;
- precisely defined goals;
- clearly communicated philosophy and values; and
- a firm commitment to excellence.

THREE GROWTH MANAGEMENT APPROACHES

You should determine your overall approach to growth management *before* you start the process of extensive new growth. Top management of any telemarketing company should take the time and effort necessary to make certain the expansion will bring the desired results. This is important whether you are involved in the initial growth of a start-up telemarketing venture or in the expansion and redirection of an established company . . . and whether the company is an in-house operation or a service agency.

There are three approaches to growth management:

1. Growth for growth's sake,
2. Growth for immediate profitability and survival, and
3. Controlled management of growth.

Only one of these approaches, Controlled management of growth, is valid, however. The following paragraphs explain why.

Growth for Growth's Sake

The approach of growth for growth's sake assumes that bigger is better and, ultimately, that biggest is best. But biggest is *not* always best. Not if growth comes without regard for the continuance of the company's standards of excellence. Not if growth sacrifices the development of people. Not if it destroys the long-range profitability and health of the company. If the growth costs too much in terms of the essence of the company, then bigger is not better, and the growth can easily become an uncontrolled cancer. We contend that growth for growth's sake cannot be justified, at any point, for any reason.

Growth for Immediate Profitability and Survival

While not ideal, growth for immediate profitability and survival may be acceptable over the short term. When an immediate increase in profits or volume is needed to survive on a shoestring budget, it's hard to argue against this approach. Growth for immediate profitability and survival might also be necessary to satisfy internal personnel development needs. Experienced and talented telemarketing people are at a premium, and without them you cannot grow. Rather than lose several talented people unless they have opportunities for promotion, you may choose to grow specifically to provide the advancement that will keep them.

Whatever the reasons, this type of growth brings the danger of compromising excellence and fostering mediocrity.

Controlled Management of Growth

Controlled management of growth, the ideal approach, involves anticipating and planning growth for which the company has the financial and human resources necessary to prevent:

1. exceeding the mental and physical limits of your people,
2. causing harm to existing clients, and
3. dropping margins below levels required for good financial health.

Controlled growth requires planned, focused, budgeted efforts and execution. It requires patience and the ability to balance the short-term growth potential with the long-term qualitative needs. Proper controls allow growth with sustained health and profitability.

Key Point: *Controlled management of growth is the only viable, long-term approach to growth management. It is the one method that can always be justified; it is the ideal.*

HOW TO DEFINE YOUR GROWTH PURPOSES

The core, pragmatic purpose of any business lies outside of the business itself: the acquisition or creation of clients or customers. The essential motive behind that purpose is to make sure the business survives and thrives. Without clients or customers, the business is only a hobby (however expensive).

If your real purposes for telemarketing growth relate only to certain levels of volume and income, they likely will not stand the test of time. It is relatively easy to hit high sales and production goals if those are the only goals for which you are shooting. It is more difficult to achieve high sales and production when you combine those goals with the more comprehensive objectives of quality production, healthy profit margins, retained earnings, strong management development, and the nurturing of long-term client relationships.

Lack of a clear purpose will lead to vague or incomplete goals. Unless your purposes and goals interlock and complement each other, your success through growth is likely to be short-lived.

The question that is asked too rarely is: "What are the purposes for the desired growth of the telemarketing unit?"

Seven Purposes of Growth

Many purposes for growth are possible, but some purposes are much more common than others. Some of these are:

- To increase profits and build retained earnings
- To gain increased marketplace recognition and respect
- To be able to serve more or larger clients
- To capture increased market share
- To reduce the opportunity for the competition
- To meet investor expectations
- To provide opportunity for talented personnel

Will Growth Fulfill Your Real Purpose?

Two questions need to be asked that look beyond definition of purpose: "Will achieving our growth purposes carry the organization to greater success, and can—or should— the organization support the growth purposes in a manner that will result in their successful realization?" To the extent that the answers are yes, the purpose may be productive for the telemarketing organization.

Growth, however, may not be the best way to achieve your real business purpose. As an example, look at the first purpose on the list: *To increase profits and build retained earnings.* Growth may very well assist in achieving that end, yet it may not be the best initial route to take. An honest appraisal of the telemarketing operation might show that the lack of sufficient profits and retained earnings is caused primarily by improper pricing and insufficient margins. In that case, a decision must be made about the relative value of expanding sales markets and increasing sales volume versus the improvement of margins and rates of return. If the pricing and margin problems are severe, growth may simply increase the problems the company had hoped to resolve.

When the company's situation is appraised, other problems may be discovered, such as:

- Inefficient production
- Poorly trained salespeople, supervisors and managers
- Improper management ratios

- Insufficient quality control
- Disorganized client services administration
- Low personnel retention, requiring frequent and expensive replacement
- Confused or overcomplicated internal communication
- Poor company spirit
- Slipshod purchasing methods and policies
- Improper facilities (excess or insufficient quality or capacity)
- Inconsistent call loads
- High client turnover
- Inept account management
- Inconsistent management objectives
- Minimal financial and/or production monitoring
- Improper company structure
- Undercapitalization
- Weak cash management
- Ineffective business and financial planning
- Badly defined goals
- Poor marketing strategy
- Wavering market focus
- Lack of coordination between actual production expertise and the marketing focus
- Lack of management involvement and commitment

Any of these weaknesses could be the real cause of the problems you are trying to solve. Additional telemarketing growth may aggrevate those problems and create increased difficulties, decreased profits, and a reduction in retained earnings.

Unless the basic problems are repaired before growth is attempted, the organization may very well be unable to support the additional demands of the effort.

Caution: *If growth is intended to mask or compensate for a company's inherent weaknesses, the growth may very well cause the company to collapse under those weaknesses.*

Five Questions to Ask About Your Growth Purposes

Clearly you must examine your company's growth purposes before moving on. Determine:

1. What factors prevent our achieving that purpose at our current size and telemarketing volumes?
2. Would further expansion resolve or aggravate those factors?
3. What can be done prior to expansion to improve the situation?
4. Are we prepared and equipped to take the steps required to resolve the problems?
5. Is further growth at this time a wise choice for achieving our original purpose?

If the honest answers that come from this analysis reveal that growth is a productive solution to your needs, then you can move on to the next step, translating purposes into goals for growth.

Key Point: *Controlled management of growth requires clearly defined purposes and goals that precede any desire for growth.*

HOW TO TRANSLATE YOUR PURPOSES INTO GOALS FOR GROWTH

If a telemarketing business is not managed with clearly established goals that set and define what is desirable for the company, it will be subject to each fad in the marketplace and to every whim of expediency. In that situation, management is as likely to be pushed off course by the next wave of marketplace activity as a ship captain would be without a sextant and maps.

This is the principle behind the need for clearly integrated business and marketing plans. If you have only short-range objectives for production and survival, you will soon find that your victories—if achieved—are hollow and transient. Until you tie your goals into the development of relationships with clients and personnel, you will discover that the success of the business simply will fail to provide the personal and financial rewards which you expected.

For any service business—and especially for telemarketing—the key question is: "What is the quality of service which we wish to provide?" If you define that quality as excellence, then the real question that affects controlled management of growth is: "How do we grow *and* maintain our standards of excellence?"

Tip: *Acceptable standards of performance should be established in each area where the quality of the performance will be vital to your success.*

Those performance standards then will act as objective frames of reference for every management decision. They will guide management in making today's decisions with the intention of reaching tomorrow's goals.

Performance Standards: Ten Key Areas

The probability of reaching your goals will be enhanced if you clearly establish the parameters which will guide you. To do that, you must:

- Identify the specific and essential factors that will determine the quality of the outcome.
- Determine what is to be measured in each critical factor.
- Establish the acceptable standards of performance for each factor.

Many areas should be considered when you formulate your telemarketing company's performance objectives. The following questions can provide a starting point.

1. *Physical and Financial Resources:* What are your guidelines for an adequate supply of resources—in facilities, equipment, and cash or financing available at affordable cost—to support the goals for growth and development?

2. *Marketing:* On what type of service will you focus . . . business to business or business to consumer? What part of that total market do you want to serve? What image do you want to project to that market? Do you want to be known as a small-volume or large-volume telemarketer? What would represent an achievement of your market potential?

3. *Rates:* What compensation rates or fee schedules will you offer your marketplace? Are you going to work on a cost-per-order or an hourly basis? Do you want to be positioned as a high-quality service at the high end of the price range, a general-purpose service with prices in the mid range, or an economy service at the low end of the price range?

4. *Productivity:* What are the targeted costs per sale, per product, and per program? What levels of competitive performance do you want to maintain or achieve?

Remember: *Simply wanting to be positioned at one end or the other of the price range only works for a short while. Ultimately, your position will be that which the quality of your service defines.*

5. *Client Account Management:* How much and what types of support will be given to the client and programs? What information should be communicated, in what manner, and with what frequency? How involved should account managers be in program development, refinement, and execution?

6. *Profitability:* What margins and total profitability are sufficient to assure the cash or available financing to support your growth? What standards for cash management guidelines and policies are required?

7. *Personnel Attitude and Performance:* What are the guidelines for the intangible (but indicative) symptoms of employee satisfaction: tardiness, absenteeism, and turn-over; active involvement and participation in company improvement; persistence and dedication; company spirit, attitude and morale, etc.? What are the guidelines for employee performance: quality, consistency, and courtesy of presentations; production per hour; back-end results; improvement over time; error rates; complaint rates?

8. *Manager Performance and Development:* What are your objectives for management capability, creativity, authority, and accountability? What key traits or characteristics will typify successful employees? What are your expectations for their performance of their jobs, their contributions to the spirit of the management organization, and their part in the development of tomorrow's managers? What level of activity is necessary to assure an adequate transfer of values and the development of additional expertise which are required to support the growth planned? What minimum levels of education must you provide for managers to achieve your expectations?

9. *Structure:* What should be the quality and extent of the structure for program management and for the overall organization? What size work units are necessary?

How far ahead of growth do you want to be structured, to meet your objectives for your people and your clients, and to avoid unnecessary opportunity costs? And—when necessary—how far ahead of the structure can you grow and stay healthy?

10. *Innovation:* What additional services will you provide? What new skills will need to be developed, and what special activities will be needed to supply those services? What policy changes will be required to encourage innovation?

A lot of questions? Yes, but it's better to ask them (and more) before you start your expansion rather than to lose a client, a market, or your entire business because you failed to ask them. There is very little time to pause in the midst of battle to decide the quantity of ammunition and the quality of personnel you need to survive and win. Staying ahead of growth requires that you know how your organization should look, feel, and act as you continue to grow.

Answers to these questions can become the basic standards of performance by which your efforts are measured.

Defining Goals

The process of identifying purposes and developing standards of performance leads naturally into the process of setting goals. Then, the experience of striving for established standards of performance can build a stronger, more productive telemarketing company. Continually reaching targeted levels of achievement, moving beyond them, and setting new standards to be reached is what moves a company beyond acceptable results . . . to excellent performance. Thus, progressively exceeding your initial, short-term standards by quantified amounts acts as the basis for setting your medium-range and long-range goals.

Establishing goals in each area is relatively simple. The difficult part is making sure that the goals for each area mesh into a cohesive whole. Each area of the telemarketing firm must perform at levels and progress at rates which support and enhance the growth and development of the other areas.

Caution: *It is not sufficient for the goals to be acceptable to top management. It is equally important that the people who have to perform in each area perceive the goals as reasonable and realistic.*

There are two essential parts to a clearly defined goal.

- First: What specific results are desired?
- Second: By when should the results be achieved?

The combination of "what" and "when" provides a precise and understandable definition of specific goal achievement. One without the other allows too much latitude for vague definition and confused results.

The diversity of organizations and types of applications create more goal variations than we can possibly cover. However, the following example of translating purpose and objectives into quantified goals can serve as a guide.

EXAMPLE: ABC Telemarketing has determined that its main purpose for growth is to increase its profits and retained earnings. The company has defined its primary goal in this manner:

"The goal of ABC Telemarketing is to increase pre-tax profitability and retained earnings, through increased sales and efficiency, in order to provide greater opportunity for growth of current market areas and development of new market segments.

Goals for pre-tax profits are:
—$285,000 for the first six months of 1989,
—a total of $640,000 for calendar 1989, and
—$880,000 for calendar 1990.
Goals for retained earnings are:
—45% increase above current levels by January 1, 1990
—110% above current levels by January 1, 1991.

The secondary goals should be similarly defined. Each should include sub-factors involved in the performance of that area, as well as an overall factor which is indicative of that area's total performance. The goals should also be designed so the cumulative effect of achieving all of the secondary goals will result in the achievement of the primary goal.

As a further example: In determining their objectives, ABC Telemarketing establishes the following minimum sales performance parameters:

- 10 calls per hour (CPH),
- a 16.5% conversion rate (closing ratio, or percentage of contacts resulting in sales),
- 85% list completion,
- 1.65 sales per hour (SPH),
- an average order of $180,
- a cancellation rate of 11%, and
- a net effective production of $265 per calling hour.

Additionally, the company expects further improvement on those standards in order to achieve optimum results. The higher standards are:

- 11 CPH,
- 19% closing ratio,
- 91% list completion,
- 2.1 SPH, $195 average order,
- a cancellation rate of 8%, and
- a net effective production of $370 per calling hour.

Since the company is currently below both sets of standards, the following goals are communicated to the employees:

Initial sales production goals are as follows:

- 10 CPH; 16.5% closing ratio;
- 85% list completion,
- 1.65 SPH, $180 average order,
- order retention of 89%, and
- $265 net sales per hour.

The target date by which average performance of the sales team meets or exceeds these minimum standards is May 1, 1989.

Once the initial goals are met, the longer range goals for standards of excellence are as follows:

- 11 CPH; 19% closing ratio;
- 91% list completion;
- 2.1 SPH, $195 average order,
- order retention of 92%, and
- $370 net sales per hour.

The expectation is for these goals to be achieved by January 1, 1990.

The definition is precise and quantified, and deadlines are defined for each target factor the company has identified as critical to quality sales performance.

Key Point: *No matter what level of management the goals statement is intended for, the goals and expectations must be clear and specific.*

The experience of many executives shows that the act of writing a concise description of a problem dramatically improves the probability of finding a solution and rapidly accelerates its resolution. The same is true of written goals and their achievement. Written goals give the company specific and objective targets to focus the actions required to achieve its overall intent.

GUIDING VALUES: THE COMPANY PHILOSOPHY

While goals provide objective targets, they fall short in providing guidance in the less-tangible areas of the business's operation. It is the company's underlying philosophy which guides the way in which the goals will be set and guides the manner in which the company's people act to acheive the goals.

All of us have personal philosophies (stated or unstated) that act as the system of principles which govern our lives. In the same way, a company's philosophy is the system of principles and beliefs that govern the life and actions of the business. Just as the attitudes of individuals set the pattern for what they can accomplish, the philosophy of a company shapes its character and its pattern of achievement. The full spectrum of actions and decisions of the company will be tinted by those underlying values. A company's philosophy is the fire that warms its ethics and ignites its action.

A clearly defined company philosophy helps shape the thinking of the personnel in all of their planning and execution. The decisions they make are better based and more meaningful. The results people achieve are consistent with the actions they take, and the actions they take will be consistent with the principles that guide and support them.

How to Formalize and Communicate the Company Philosophy

The company's standards of performance, goals, and approach to growth must be in concert with the company's philosophy. That philosophy represents the underlying principles and values which guide you in managing your company's growth.

If the process of examining and establishing the company's standards of performance, goals, and approach to growth reveals a sense of unity and common ground among top management, formalizing and communicating a statement of company philosophy throughout the company is relatively easy. It is simply a matter of recording those basic tenets, organizing them into a sensible and understandable declaration, and establishing them as the principles which guide each employee.

The process may, however, reveal serious conflict between the beliefs, principles, and values of members of top management. As uncomfortable as that might seem, revealing that conflict "up front" is a valuable and important step. Disagreement at the level of the basic principles and values that govern a firm's operation will eventually guarantee dissension throughout the organization. When that disagreement exists, the development of a unified and supportable company philosophy becomes even more important.

Examining the Company Philosophy: Six Major Areas

Again, there are questions to be asked and answered. The six major areas you should consider are:

Service and Value:

- What is the basic value of the services the company expects to provide?
- Does the company (a) take a leadership role in establishing the standards, (b) follow the basic standards set by others, or (c) allow its services to seek their own level?

Top Management Style:

- Does upper management have high levels of direct, "in the trenches" involvement, or is there a more detached "view from the top"?
- How much communication of ideas and information is done through reports and memos?
- How much communication comes through one-on-one, personal contact?
- How frequent is direct communication with staff members?
- How frequent is direct communication with line managers and workers?

General Policies and Control:

- Do policies take the form of precise controls defining the boundaries of every action, or do they give the basic company mandatories and legalities and allow room for individual interpretation and action?
- Will the following of company policies provide sufficient control to assure a quality product?
- Do the actions of individual employees reflect the degree of personal initiative which the policies are intended to encourage?

People:

- Do we employ top people and compensate them with top pay rates, or do we go with the best people we can get for lower wages?
- What special incentives or forms of participation in the company's growth and profitability are provided for employees?
- Do we develop and promote from within wherever possible, or do we first look outside the company for talent?
- To what degree do managers operate by independent authority, by completion of assigned objectives, and by directed action?

The Client:

- How do we perceive the client's role?
- In what esteem are clients held?
- What will we do to carn their business?
- How far will we go to keep it?

Integrity:

- How important are our beliefs, and to what degree do our actions reflect them?
- What happens if conflicts arise between principles and opportunity?
- What promises do we make to our employees, to our clients, to our investors, and to ourselves?
- How readily do we make those promises, how well do we keep them, and how important is it to us to keep them?

Maintaining Your Integrity

The final point, integrity, is critical to the harmony and the success of the telemarketing operation.

A part of controlled growth is maintaining your honesty and integrity. Do not try to hide mistakes from the client. And do not try to mislead them. Only a fool believes he can deceive people on a continuous basis. It may work a couple of times, but people eventually will catch on.

Note: *Whether you are in-house or a service agency, you have a client or several clients. You must act with integrity toward your client, whether that client is a product division of your own firm, or the client is another firm which you represent.*

As former heavyweight boxing champion Joe Louis said, "You can run, but you can't hide."

If your only objective is to grow a large telemarketing company, you're in trouble.

Key Point: *A telemarketing organization without integrity—regardless of how productive it might be—will lose the positive word-of-mouth references that are critical to continuing growth and success.*

However, if you build a company that offers the best possible service of its kind, it's going to grow—whether you want it to or not. It's inevitable, because word-of-mouth advertising is what telemarketing and any service industry is all about.

Do you want to be known as a company that goes for the quick volume, or one that is a dependable service source? You must make that decision before you start expanding. Then you have to be able to stay with the courage of your convictions in your values, philosophy, and plan.

Everyone—sooner or later—faces the decision between principles and greed, and we are all vulnerable to temptation. We may momentarily forget our principles if a large enough opportunity presents itself.

Warning: *The opportunity for short-term profits may be enticing, but no opportunity is worth taking if it comes at the expense of your image in the marketplace and your long-term success.*

Submitting to the temptation is not just a moral weakness; it is also a poor negotiating strategy. You may find yourself in a position to make a "power move" with a negotiating statement that is inconsistent with your company's philosophy and track record. But the clients will know that such a statement is inconsistent with your track record and your commitment to excellence. Your existing clients will know that you won't carry through on the power move, and potential clients will question the sincerity of your commitment to excellence. You lose either way.

Remember: *It is simple honesty and integrity that inspire people's trust and develop lasting business relationships.*

If you see that something has to be done to remain true to your inner philosophy, then you do it. That doesn't mean throwing money at every problem or every situation. It just means that when your first commitment is to being as good as you can personally be, then what you do in life and for a living has to be a consistent expression of that inner striving. When that inner philosophy is expressed through a business, it has the ability to do more than affect an industry. It can have a positive and enriching effect on your life and the lives of your people.

Without that, any other recognition or success is hollow and soon loses its meaning.

Sharing the Company Philosophy and Values

When it comes to informing the company's personnel about company plans, many top managers believe in the Mushroom Theory of Management:

Keep them in the dark and
feed them enough manure to keep them happy.

That method is fine for mushrooms. However, it won't develop dedicated people who share the company's sense of values and commitment to excellence.

Unless the company philosophy is shared with all employees, the operating reality will be—to a greater or lesser extent—different than top management would like. To assure that the entire company operates cohesively and in a manner consistent with the company's values, the philosophy must be shared.

> **EXAMPLE:** In the summer of 1984, Grady was retained by WATS Marketing Outbound to assist in the development of WATS' young management and supervisory staff, to create working operations manuals and other documentation, and to help fine-tune and upgrade some policies and procedures. Additionally, some modifications in organizational structure were needed during a time of rapid growth.
>
> The project was successful, and a number of factors were important to the project's ultimate success:
>
> - The company's management had clearly decided where the company was going and the purposes and goals of the project. The scope and shape of the project were guided at all points by that clear definition.
> - Top management provided Grady with thorough briefings to give him a comprehensive understanding of the company's philosophy, its goals, and its approach to growth.
> - It was recognized from the inception of the project that the entire workforce needed to be clear about the company's philosophy and direction. The foundation for that approach was laid at the very beginning of the project.
>
> The explanation of the company's philosophy, goals, and opportunity showed management's sense of direction and vision for the company to Grady and provided a framework for the project. If Grady had not understood the underlying philosophy of the company or if he had not known precisely in what direction it was headed, he could not have made timely and appropriate suggestions for the changes that were required.
>
> Of equal importance, top management's statements and briefings also served as the basis for a written statement that was distributed to the employees. With the full understanding and cooperation of the employees, the project was given every opportunity to be successful.

Note: *Providing a written copy of your statement of philosophy, objectives, and opportunity to your employees will enhance their understanding of what your company is all about . . . and why.*

The sense of commitment and loyalty of your people will be strengthened and enhanced when they feel you care enough to share those ideas and those values with them. Their feelings of personal involvement and dedication to shared goals brings significant rewards.

If you believe in your philosophy, your objectives, and your opportunities for the future, then share them. Share them verbally. Share them in writing. Make them a part of the orientation and training of every employee. Share them by action and example. Make them a part of the everyday operation and environment.

The following example may help you get started:

IDELMAN TELEMARKETING INC. PHILOSOPHY, GOALS, AND OPPORTUNITY

Idelman Telemarketing Inc. Philosophy

Our philosophy begins with the everyday search for excellence and the full understanding that as a "people-intensive, people-oriented business" our one and only ticket to bottom-line results is through the willing cooperation of our people in taking exceptional care of our customers by providing them with superior quality and superior service . . . In other words to help each individual employee achieve the highest possible levels of excellence as individuals, while systematically, intelligently, and positively merging all such individuals into one cohesive, innovative organization that provides superior quality service to all clients. We believe:

- That if we are good to our clients, those clients will be good to us.
- If we are good to our marketplace, it will be good to us.
- In honesty, integrity and high ethics.
- That attention to small details gains us inches in the marketplace, and that constant excellence is a game of inches.
- In being a "back-end" conscious operation, delivering soft-sell, complaint-free campaigns, along with 100% order verification to each and every ITI client.
- In persistence and perseverance in the face of obstacles to achieve quality service.
- In listening, trust, and respect for the dignity and creative potential of each individual in the ITI organization.
- In innovation and the support of innovative individuals and teams.
- In "champions" who focus their attention on the project and refuse to relent until it is fully developed and implemented.
- In leaders who demonstrate, transmit, and teach the enduring values that have contributed to their achievement.

- In leaders who personally coach and develop individuals and teams to achieve their potential for excellence.
- That excellence is a full-time habit, not a part-time hobby.

Goals

- Growth of 20% annually.
- Pre-tax profitability of 20%.
- To make each and every outbound presentation of the highest quality possible.
- To represent our industry with such total excellence that marketers nationwide will consistently consider outbound telemarketing as an integral part of their overall marketing strategies.
- To be more than a "phone sales job shop," such that we want to "marry" classic direct marketing behavior to outbound telemarketing.
- To provide our service with such intensity and hands-on attention to detail that Idelman Telemarketing Inc. will redefine the industry standards for service provision.
- To develop our people as thoroughly as possible in their respective areas of responsibility.
- To build departmental staffs to the levels of "whatever it takes" to "get the job done" and get it done with excellence.
- To develop our people as outstanding community representatives of Idelman Telemarketing Inc.
- To work in sufficiently small work units so as to encourage and promote each employee's "ownership" of his/her own goals, objectives, tools, finished products and opportunities.
- To be accountable—as both an organizational whole to our clients and as individuals to our own organization—for all actions, reactions, and bottom-line performance results, whether they are good, bad or indifferent.
- To have each employee understand how his/her goals, tasks, and finished products relate to the overall performance of Idelman Telemarketing Inc.
- To promote from within and provide career opportunities for as many ITI employees as possible.
- To be successful as an organizational whole—as a committed team with common goals—rather than as a shop with a few superstars.
- To develop our physical plant to a level which implies, directs, controls, and promotes a high energy, competitive, cooperative, achievement-oriented, enjoyable work environment for all ITI employees.
- To be structured ahead of our growth at all times, to avoid paying the unnecessary opportunity costs associated with shortsightedness, while simultaneously maintaining and refining our standards of client, program and leadership selectivity.
- To become not necessarily the biggest telemarketing firm, but rather to become the standard of excellence by which any service company will be measured in terms

of the quality of employee and client satisfaction, service, productivity, innovation, opportunity, growth, profitability and organizational success. By accomplishing the above, becoming the biggest will be a natural result.

– To learn something new almost every day, and to have fun as a productive, achievement-oriented organization.

– To achieve all goals and objectives by having each employee feel a part of, and actually be an integral part of the whole.

Opportunity

Telemarketing is one of the fastest-growing industries in existence. In fact, by the year 2000, telemarketing is expected to employ more workers than any other industry, with the exceptions of the telecommunications and computer industries. ITI's opportunity is clear. We are well-positioned today to continue our growth, so that by the year 2000, our firm should employ more workers than just about any of our competition. Accordingly, individual opportunities for our work force are almost unlimited. All of this potential—as it relates to us here at Idelman Telemarketing Inc.—is perfectly realizable, provided we seriously accept the company philosophies, objectives and goals outlined above. Those philosophies, objectives and goals represent the CHALLENGES we must successfully meet individually and organizationally each and every day. To meet these challenges, it is imperative that our everyday dedication is to excellence in every aspect of the service we provide to our clients. As a final note, you will find that in order for our "leadership population" ("QARs," "TSs," "PMs," "FMs," etc.) to meet these challenges, it will be necessary—make that mandatory—for each of us to . . .

"LEAD . . .

FOLLOW . . .

OR

GET THE HECK OUT OF THE WAY!"

On behalf of the entire organization, here's to you—you and your leadership are the future of Idelman Telemarketing Inc., happening right now!

Sincerely,

Steven A. Idelman
Chief Executive Officer

MAKING . . . AND SHARING . . . YOUR COMMITMENT

Commitment is an essential word in the vocabulary of a growing telemarketing company. Gaining the sincere commitment of the entire team is a key to the company's continuing success. Unless that commitment is developed, the company's well-defined purposes, objectives, goals and philosophy will be nothing more than shimmering ideas. Without the dedication that grows out of passionate commitment, those ideas will never crystallize into the reality of achievement.

Two reasons for the success of books such as *In Search Of Excellence* are of particular importance here.

- Excellence is sincerely desired by consumers and clients.
- People are magnetically drawn—for both personal and professional reasons—to the opportunity to be associated with the achievement of excellence.

The possibility of being a part of exceptional success based upon the creation of excellent results appeals both to their highest aspirations and to their basic desires.

Will everyone make that extra effort? Of course not, but many will, if your commitment is firm and you communicate it well. A major part of the commitment to excellence is making the determined effort to find the people who believe in excellence as a way of business life. Another part is being willing to pay the price—whether in salaries, incentives, the providing of professional freedom and opportunity, or in the manner they are treated as human beings—to attract and develop the right people.

How important are those people? What difference will they make? They are the ones who will make or break your commitment to achieving excellence. The right ones can make it a day-to-day operational reality.

Although our predisposition and prejudices make us feel that significant growth should come only after excellence has been attained, size does not define excellence. Quality comes in packages of many different shapes, colors, and sizes. That's true of people, and it's true of telemarketing firms. It's not how big they are, but what they are.

Key Point: *The most important factors that set one telemarketing firm off from another are a company's knowledge and the quality of its people.*

Telemarketing, when it's done poorly, is a precarious business. There are risks to the client and to the industry. If you are to compete for business that can be good for both the client and the industry, rounded excellence is needed in all key positions in your company.

Keeping the Commitment

Developing that rounded excellence sometimes means sacrificing short-term profits in the interest of long-term quality. Entire volumes have been written about this point, but there is a great deal of valuable advice in two homespun sayings: "Never get too far from the well" and "Always dance with the lady what brung ya."

If you know that what has made you successful is:

1. a monomaniacal commitment to excellence; and
2. hands-on management by knowledgeable and talented people who shared that commitment,

then you have no choice but to stay with that approach.

Important: *If you have an exceptional opportunity to grow, but not enough of what has* *made you successful to that point, then you know it's best to forego the opportunity while you go out and get enough.*

Perhaps one of the keys to your success is 55 hours of training for new TSRs (telemarketing sales/service representatives—the people who make the calls). You're an agency, and the ABC company says "Here's 4 million calls." Or you're in-house and top management wants you to roll out two new product lines and double the staff overnight. The catches are that you can only have 10 hours of training for new TSRs, and you can't take the time to find or develop the additional, quality personnel that you need. If you try to throw the extra weight on the shoulders of your already overburdened people, you're going to take on a big part of the project, generate a lot of money, and burn out a lot of well-trained management people and a lot of TSRs who don't get the proper training.

When you do that, you have definitely gotten too far from your basic philosophy and game plan.

Note: *As fast as the best companies have grown, in many respects it has been because they turned away business when they knew they couldn't execute it with the kind of consistent quality and performance standards their commitment demanded.*

The commitment to excellence is not something to be debated. It is something to be made, to be dedicated to, and to be lived.

It makes for some hard decisions.

15 KEYS TO A STRONG GROWTH FOUNDATION

- Before committing to extensive new growth, the telemarketing firm must have a strong growth foundation. That foundation should be based on a reasonable approach to growth, honest appraisal of the reasons of growth, specific performance standards, precisely defined goals, clearly communicated philosophy, and a firm commitment.
- Sales volume is not a reliable indicator of the quality of a company's performance, prospects, or overall success. Attempting to solve a company's weaknesses or deficiencies through growth may only magnify existing problems.
- To measure the value of your growth purposes, ask "Will our motives carry the organization to greater success, and can the organization support them in a manner that will result in their successful realization?"
- The three approaches to growth are: growth for growth's sake; growth for immediate profitability and survival; and controlled management of growth. Controlled management of growth is the best choice for long-term health and profitability.
- Simply growing is no great trick. The challenge lies in how to grow while maintaining your standards.
- Specific performance standards provide a clear frame of reference for every management decision.

- A telemarketing company's probability of success dramatically improves when goals are clearly and accurately defined, written, and communicated to all management personnel.
- A business plan is the design for the operation, but the philosophy is the real foundation.
- A sincere commitment to excellence is essential to continuing success. Without that commitment, the reality of achievement will never meet the company's expectations.
- Short-term profit opportunities may be seductive, but none are worth taking at the cost of your long-term plan and your image in the marketplace.
- Business integrity is as much a practical matter as it is a moral issue. Over the long term, the success of any service business—including telemarketing—depends upon it.
- Make the commitment to meet the client's needs. What the client believes the value of your service to be will decide what the telemarketing operation produces and whether it will be successful.
- The most important factors that set one telemarketing firm off from another are a company's knowledge and its people.
- A written statement of philosophy, objectives, and opportunity shapes the attitudes, planning, actions and style of the organization. Such a statement should clearly show the staff the direction and vision of the company and provide a framework for all action.
- If your people believe the company's commitment to excellence is real, they will provide the effort, persistence, innovation, and dedication required to achieve it.

**The quality of a person's life
is in direct proportion to their commitment to excellence,
regardless of their chosen field of endeavor.**
—Vince Lombardi

Luck is what happens when preparation meets
opportunity. —*Elmer Letterman*

Chapter *2*

Planning for Growth in Outbound Telemarketing

Productive growth doesn't just happen by accident; it is the result of careful planning. Without that plan, your actions cannot be properly focused. A thorough business plan is critical to the successful management of growth in telemarketing.

There are two primary reasons for effective and thorough upfront planning:

1. to make sure that your telemarketing firm will initially develop and survive as effectively as possible with the resources available; and
2. to create an initial design which will readily accommodate future expansion.

Remember: *Before you plan for growth, plan to survive.*

Without a comprehensive business and financial plan, what you hoped would be the fascinating and rewarding challenge of managing day-to-day growth may become a much less enjoyable day-to-day struggle for survival.

When that happens:

- Your creativity will have no room to flourish.
- You will lose your focus on the commitment to excellence.
- You will soon find that the game is over.

That may sound bleak, and it is. Yet it is all too often the reality of inadequate knowledge and the lack of patience required to construct a plan that will work.

Key Point: *Without proper initial planning, you will never have the opportunity to deal with the joys and headaches of growth.*

Preparing for Telemarketing's Unique Challenges

How you will handle specific telemarketing challenges in a number of areas should be decided when you construct your business plan. For example, in the personnel area, here are some issues to consider:

- In a traditional business environment, the labor force is composed primarily of full-time employees who earn the vast majority of their income on that job. That rarely is true in consumer telemarketing, and often is not the case in business-to-business telemarketing.
- The lack of formal telemarketing training in the nation's educational institutions makes hiring and development of telemarketing managers difficult.
- For TSRs (telemarketing sales/service representatives—the people who make the calls), the frequency of rejection and the intensity of the work contribute to a high burnout factor.
- Telemarketing's people and the industry as a whole are quite young and have relatively little business experience.

In addition to those "people" issues, other issues in telemarketing involve legal structures, finances and credit positions, target markets, market position, production standards, service rates, projected profit margins, rate competition, and the absence of long-term contracts. Each must be addressed in the process of thorough planning.

IN-HOUSE OR SERVICE AGENCY?

In-house operations and service agencies are alike in many ways, and at first glance, these telemarketing operations appear to be identical. Both are involved in the marketing of products or services by telephone. Each represents a client in the marketplace. Clearly, the service agency serves clients who are external companies. But—whether or not it is designed to act as an independent profit center—the in-house operation serves as a service agency to its own organization.

As a result, few differences exist between them at most of the essential levels, once they are up and running.

In some areas, however, in-house operations and service agencies differ dramatically, and each type of operation has its own particular challenges.

Three Reasons for Wage and Salary Differences

Wage and salary structures for in-house operations are generally higher, although the difference is narrowing. Factors involved are:

1. More in-house telemarketing is business-to-business, with higher-ticket and higher-margin products and services than consumer work.
2. While the service agency basically has a one-time shot at selling and making a profit

on any given list, the in-house operation is able to build a proprietary data base for related product sales and renewal sales.

3. Many in-house shops are designed to operate as a production center or service arm of the parent company, rather than as a separate profit center. These operations are often "break even" shops, structured as a "cost of doing business" to increase the overall company's profits by selling more product and service.

Result: *In-house operations are often in a position to pay somewhat higher wages, using some of the money that a service agency would need to retain to stay healthy.*

The Problem of Program Variety

The second significant area of difference between in-house telemarketing firms and service agencies is in the number of clients they represent. The in-house operation usually is more one dimensional, in that it is marketing one product or a line of products from only one company. This brings more continuity in the educational process and the expected learning curves of the TSRs and supervisors.

Although the service agency may have a limited number of clients at a given time during the early stages of development, increasing growth brings a great deal more complexity. The sheer magnitude of the variety of programs and the resulting additional demands on the service agency level can be overwhelming, because—with that many programs—it is not possible for any single TSR or supervisor to know all of the different program characteristics and demands.

> **EXAMPLE:** Wats Marketing Outbound billed $3.5 million in its first full year, 1982. Of the $3.5 million, 90% was with one client. Because the people were well grounded in the project, new supervisors and managers who were promoted from the phones could readily be brought into the flow of the growth. That kind of situation might be typical of an in-house shop.
>
> The business grew to $7.5 million by 1984, and billed about $17 million in 1985. However, unlike 1982, the business came from more than 50 clients, with more than 150 different programs. The sheer number of clients and varied programs created entirely different challenges.

Note: *The continuing development of and training for new programs brings more stress for the service agency.*

In massive growth situations, the talent available to be promoted often will not be familiar with the programs where the help is needed. The amount of new development work required by program development grows exponentially. And the training required to adequately handle those clients and programs can be staggering, a fact that service agencies should take into consideration when doing their planning.

CRITICAL GUIDELINES FOR THE IN-HOUSE START-UP

The difficult part for the in-house telemarketing operation is not just in the mechanics. Many factors enter into the determination of whether it really is better to start an in-house operation or go with a service agency. Books have been devoted to the start-up of in-house operations. Our intent is to focus on growth rather than to provide a comprehensive guide in this area. However, some critical guidelines for the in-house start-up are in order.

Call Load: a Key Factor

One of the first considerations is the consistency of the call load. Unless the call load is consistent, with a minimum of 9 months (and as close as possible to year round), going in-house can be a disaster. Continuing seasonal layoffs of telemarketing personnel can create serious image problems for your company. The often-repeated mistake of trying to pull personnel from other areas of the company on a sporadic or seasonal basis has consistently proven ineffective. In addition, the fixed-cost investment for an in-house telemarketing operation which runs on a non-consistent basis can easily wipe out the cost differential of working with a service agency. When this is added to the inconsistent results that normally accompany inconsistent call load patterns, contracting with a service agency may be the wiser decision.

The Challenge of Finding the Right Person

A key consideration when starting up an in-house telemarketing operation is: "Who is going to run it?" Should you choose internally or look for talent outside?

While someone from inside the company may know much about the product and the way it has been sold, telemarketing is an entirely different keg of worms. The cost, time, and difficulty involved in training that individual to be an effective CEO of the telemarketing division can be prohibitive. And selecting an individual who already has the education and experience to handle the operational and financial management of the division—while fully coordinating with the balance of the corporate structure—removes a valuable asset from the existing structure of the company. There are important questions, too, about the inclinations, expertise, and training of the internal candidates. The issue of coordinating the telemarketing efforts with the balance of the corporate structure—which probably has little telemarketing expertise or understanding—should be a major consideration. Unfortunately, many corporations ignore this concern until the problems become all too apparent and a lot of money has been wasted.

Perhaps you can see why the company might instead opt for hiring outside talent. But that choice also is not as simple as it might first appear. Selecting that person demands more than the standard interviews and resume checks. Unless you also check with the accounts the individual has managed, you will have too limited an understanding of the external candidate's capability.

External candidates must have the core telemarketing knowledge and experience required. Otherwise, why go outside? Other questions must be answered, however.

- Do they have the education and experience to fully handle the operational and financial management of the division?
- Can they handle those duties while fully coordinating with the balance of the corporate structure?

- What additional training will be necessary to develop the required product knowledge?
- How well can they handle the sensitive coordination of the telemarketing efforts with the balance of the corporate structure?

EXAMPLE: The president of a large service agency had a client who was impressed by the way he managed their account. The client had a good base of comparison. Telemarketing played a significant role in the client's business—including the use of several large-volume services agencies.

When the service agency president resigned, the client quickly hired him as a vice president and as one of the highest-paid executives on staff. His responsibility was to select quality service agencies to represent the client, to place the business in those shops, to provide them with lists, and to monitor and manage their quality . . . from the client's perspective.

Yellow Flag: *The company's priorities were 180° opposite the new V.P.'s experience and training.*

His whole frame of reference and perspective of telemarketing priorities came from a service agency background. His training, knowledge, and expertise were in serving clients—as opposed to being the client and getting groups to serve him. He possessed neither the knowledge of the company's internal workings nor the willingness to bend to the company's differing needs and priority rankings.

Red Flag: *Rather than learning the company's approach, he insisted on forcing his personality and his approach into the job.*

The company failed—in short order—to execute on all of its projected call volumes. It soon lost one of its key third-party endorsers because the new vice president contracted the work with a vendor who was unable to deliver sufficient call volumes and call quality.

The loss of volume caused damage to the company, and—since it was publicly held—management wound up with some egg on their faces on Wall Street.

The "brilliant match" soon lost its luster. Although the V.P. had exceptional telemarketing knowledge, his focus and use of that knowledge were very different from what his new employer needed. He soon left the job . . . at the company's request.

Key Point: *The outside candidate's failure to understand the needs and philosophy of his employer resulted in his failure and the reduction of the company's effectiveness.*

You can reasonably expect to find an experienced person who can handle the job of supervisor/manager/department head. The right individual must have exceptional skills in dealing with all types of people who know nothing about telemarketing. He or she will also be the source of guidance, training, and growth for the entire effort.

Expect to pay very well for that talent. The cost for a relatively talented person who can handle all of the telemarketing management needs of a small operation (up to 30 phones) is a least $30–35,000 in 1989 dollars. If you plan to grow the business into more than a small operation, the cost will be dramatically higher; that person will be able to command 30–40% mcre. Operations of 100 phones and up can push the salary into six figures.

Coping with In-house Resistance

Third, in many in-house start-ups, the first venture into telemarketing is met with a great deal of doubt and resistance from conservative, old-line factions and from those who perceive the telemarketing operation as a threat to their security. The high salary of the "telemarketing CEO" frequently adds fuel to those fires, causing further jealousy and bad feelings.

This resistance is not limited, however, to the management ranks. One of the most common problems for an in-house operation is the concern of the field sales force. Telemarketing is often perceived by them either as a waste of time and money or as a threat to their existence.

Caution: *Either perception can lead to actions that range from lack of cooperation, to overt hostility, to the sabotage of the program.*

Each of these issues must be anticipated and dealt with. Once these points have been handled, there aren't many issues that differ in the management of in-house or service agency operations.

Key Point: *The work that is required to make a program successful is defined more by the program* than by where the program is being managed.

Making the Wise Choice for Your Company

Starting up an in-house telemarketing shop is not a simple process. Yet, in many cases, taking your telemarketing efforts in-house can and should be done.

Most companies should do at least some telemarketing work in-house. You may find that it is best to contract with a service agency and have a small in-house control group. In other situations, you may want to use a service agency as an outside control group. Even if the company is jobbing out the bulk of its calls to a service agency, the in-house work helps the company better understand and appreciate what is required to get the job done right. The better the in-house shops do the job, the more they force service agencies to stay on their toes and strive to excel.

Keep In Mind: *Even when the decision is to put the majority of work in-house, a good service agency can help in the initial testing, building, and refining of the in-house shop.*

The interaction, cooperation, and education that comes through such use of service agencies has helped improve the quality and increase the success of many in-house programs.

The In-house Start-up Checklist

The following checklist covers key points from the initial evaluation of in-house tele- marketing to the hiring of the TSRs. The experiences of existing (and no-longer-existing) companies demonstrate that, if you lack the in-house telemarketing expertise required to go beyond this basic checklist, you should contract with a professional telemarketing consultant or service agency to assist you in the start-up phase. To start up an in-house operation, you should:

- [ ] Conduct initial evaluation of purpose, goals, and approach for telemarketing.
- [ ] Determine markets, applications, and lists to be used.
- [ ] Establish projections for volume and consistency or seasonality of operation.
- [ ] Conduct evaluations (including tests through service agencies) to determine whether to operate in-house, through a service agency, or with a combination.
- [ ] Decide whether the existing sales force will be used for telemarketing or if a new staff will be developed.
- [ ] Decide whether telemarketing management will come from internal candidates, external candidates, or a combination of both.
- [ ] Establish work location, staffing and facility requirements, and costs.
- [ ] Develop the financial plan.
- [ ] Set the internal marketing strategy for integrating telemarketing into the existing culture and for dealing with normal internal resistance.
- [ ] Appoint/hire a project manager who will move you into telemarketing.
- [ ] Appoint/hire personnel for all supervisory, management, and staff positions.
- [ ] Finalize plans and set schedules and target dates for hiring line personnel.

THE QUESTION OF CONTROL

The fast-paced, intensive nature of telemarketing demands that the company, however large, must operate in a boutique-type atmosphere. Further, the "person at the top" needs to have the capability to function well in that more intimate environment and also be able to communicate the sense of urgency and vision throughout the company.

One definition of a genius is this: Someone who aims for something no one else can see . . . and hits it! Sometimes, in telemarketing, those special people need unusual freedom to hit the goal. They can't be shackled by bureaucratic red tape, minority stockholder rights, and other possible distractions. To avoid creating those problems, excellent foresight in legal and financial planning is required.

Critical Factor: *It is still the aggressive and visionary* individual *who sets the tone of the business and the business plan itself.*

Questions About the Legal Structure

The planning process is affected by how the form of the business—as a legal entity— affects the company's operation and growth. The legal structure will play a major role in determining how quickly and effectively the company can respond. Yet there is no single answer to "What is the best legal structure for a telemarketing operation?"

We will not attempt to cover all the options and pros and cons of sole proprietorships, partnerships, and corporations. Determining which legal structure will be best for your situation is a key planning decision to make with your accountant and your attorney, once you have determined the amount of control you want . . . or can realistically get. However, the following questions should be discussed with your advisors.

- Is the in-house shop a department or division within the company's corporate structure, or is it a separate subsidiary?
- Is it a sole proprietorship, a partnership, or a corporation?
- If it is a corporation, what is the nature of the stock distribution? Is the corporation public or private?
- Is it a straight "C" corporation or a "Sub-S"?
- How many stockholders are involved?
- What is the distribution of the stock and of the voting rights?
- In what ways does the legal structure restrict or limit financial and management decisions and actions?
- What changes, if any, could be made to allow the company to be more effective in planning for, and executing, growth?

Key Point: *The financial and legal structures of the organization must be flexible enough that the people who started the company are free to pursue their visions and dreams.*

A telemarketing company founded with plans for rapid growth might structure an employee-owned corporation with several equity holders who bring specific talents and knowledge to the venture. But that is a binding—and expensive—commitment. Spreading the equity between 6 to 10 "hands on" management partners sows the seeds of the organization: rapid growth becomes a requisite part of the plan in order to support the initial overhead and to achieve the levels of financial success that all the shareholders expect.

However, the distribution of stock and voting rights can also make a dramatic difference in how smoothly the company will operate and how effectively it will achieve its objectives.

> **EXAMPLE:** In most states, corporate law requires two-thirds of the common voting shares of stock to elect a board of directors. If one individual holds two-thirds or more of the common stock and voting rights, the planning decisions and the day-to-day decisions are less complex, because one person holds the power.

In other states, such as Delaware, 51% of the common voting shares are needed to control the election of the board.

How to Assure Your Vision Will Be Followed

As a telemarketing company becomes larger, it develops a larger and more complex structure. In any business, there needs to be some sort of a court of final authority. But, especially in telemarketing, that final authority has to be able to make decisions quickly.

Since each member of the board of directors has one vote, a tie vote at any time may seriously hinder the company's ability to act. To eliminate stalemates in the initial stages of the company's development, an odd number rather than even number of board members is needed. A one-member board of directors would assure that there will be no ties and that the principal stockholder controls the votes, but that is only a temporary solution to the control issue.

The Board of Directors

A small telemarketing operation may be able to operate effectively with that limited kind of board. But if you expect to achieve growth, you need to surround yourself with an excellent group of management advisors. Be *very* selective in choosing them. They should be people other than your co-workers, peer group, and employees, because you will need people who can bring a neutral, third-party perception, as well as additional knowledge from different experiences. An ideal place for those people is on the board of directors.

A board of directors can help you grow or dramatically limit your growth. The board of directors is charged with the overall direction of the corporation, as opposed to the day-to-day operation. But a simple majority vote of the board of directors will carry any issue.

So the first consideration may be for the principal stockholder (generally the person who put up the majority of the equity) to be able to control the election of a board of directors. In that case, the corporation can be structured under the laws of states that allow a 51% majority stockholder to maintain that control.

Key Point: *The makeup of the board of directors can have a profound effect on the management and growth of the corporation.*

A good board of directors can act as an advisory council which provides information, contacts, suggestions, expertise, and assistance to guide the top management of the company in achieving its objectives. When you plan for growth, that group of people is invaluable. While they may not always agree with you, they can provide important perspectives and reminders of reality to which you may be blinded by your position and by your closeness to the situation.

Remember: *The majority stockholder can control the election of the board of directors and make sure that the company is guided by a group of friendly advisers. This is neither good nor bad . . . it's simply a fact to consider.*

HOW TO DEVELOP YOUR MARKETING PLAN

Before you establish the full business plan and try to set the structure of the telemarketing organization, you need to:

- Identify what part of the market you will target.
- Decide what your position in that marketplace will be.
- Design your plan to appeal to that market segment.

The Big Corporation vs. the Small Entrepreneur

Big corporations are quickly stepping into telemarketing, because the marketplace is hot, and they have the deep pockets to afford it. That does not mean they will control the industry. But they have discovered telemarketing's power and potential.

Interesting Point: *Despite the entrance of larger corporations into the field, outbound telemarketing is still dominated by the entrepreneurial "boutique" companies and is fueled by their spirit.*

The reason why is not really surprising. Telemarketing demands fast response and flexibility, and entrepreneurial businesses tend to be better able to meet those needs.

The day is fast approaching when entrepreneurs will be able to match all the bells and whistles of the deep-pocketed corporations.

Prediction: *In the long run, it's going to be the telemarketers who are the most flexible, innovative, and fastest responding service businesses who will establish themselves as the industry's leaders.*

The Importance of Finding a Niche

One telemarketing company may very well be the best for particular applications and particular client needs. But another company may be the best in other situations. Perhaps one company will become the best in all areas through a lot of hard work and diversified development. But it's unlikely.

Warning: *A company that fails to focus on providing quality service to distinct and segmented areas of the general marketplace is a company run by fools.*

Only a fool tries to be all things to all people. You *can't* be all things to all people. That's what finding a niche is all about. That niche may grow or change or be modified, but it determines the basis for the balance of your planning.

What Is Your Niche?

How do you determine that position? What process do you use to identify and determine that niche? Those are key questions that are not easy for most people to answer. Some of the most successful people seem to do it by instinct. But that doesn't help the person who hasn't yet developed that instinctive ability. Fortunately, instinct is not solely an inherited, God-given talent. The ability can be developed through the process of trial and error. The important thing is to shorten the trial and reduce the error!

Whether you are in-house or a service agency, ask yourself the following questions to help reduce your errors:

- Who would our first client/couple of clients be?
- What type of clients are they?
- What markets do they serve?
- What are their previous experiences with telemarketing?

- What are their expectations?
- Are they only rate-conscious, or are they primarily concerned with quality?
- Will the client use our services exclusively, or will they place business in multiple locations?
- What is our probability of succeeding for the client?

For the service agency, there are other special considerations regarding clients:

- Do they represent a legitimate, quality product or service that we will be proud to include as a reference?
- Can we count on them for the long term, or are they offering a short-term, quick-hit program?
- Does working for the client mesh with our long-range goals?

EXAMPLE: If your first account is a distributor selling in the business-to-business computer industry, and your second account is selling travel clubs, and your third client is selling magazines, it's difficult to focus your plans and draw a bead on a single market segment. With that early mix of clients, it will be next to impossible for your company to become known as the telemarketing group of choice for any given industry.

Tip: *Don't expect to become* the *telemarketer for any single industry. It is extremely unlikely that any telemarketer can achieve complete domination of an entire market segment.*

Your Niche . . . and the Competition

As attractive as the "hot" or "high visibility" markets might seem for the short run, you have to size up the overall marketplace. That includes looking at the competition and where they are in the marketplace. You then identify what part of that marketplace you can hang your hat on. Be careful that your chosen niche is one which is good for more than the near future.

Critical in Planning: *Don't overlook potential long-term markets that will provide long-range opportunities for consistent volume and financial health.*

Identifying your market is a major step toward success in telemarketing. But to be successful, it may not be enough for you to do well. Someone else may have to fail. When a new business starts out in large volume in an established industry, rarely does it simply turn over new markets and develop them. That usually happens after it sets up a strong base. The competitive reality of telemarketing today is that the solid base usually comes at someone else's expense.

Checklist: How to Identify Your Market

☐ Consider the specific industry background in which your skills and experience have been gained, and related industries in which your skills and experience may be of value.

☐ Analyze what exists in the marketplace today, both at the level of client needs or demands and at the level of competitive activity.

☐ Determine who the competition is and what type of industries and accounts they work.

☐ Determine what the competition is doing and the what specific skills they have; what are their strengths, and what are their weaknesses?

☐ Isolate what demands in the marketplace are
   – being satisfactorily met,
   – being met only partially,
   – not being met at all.

☐ Evaluate what particular traits, skills, or areas of expertise you and your company have which can meet one or more of the marketplace needs or demands.

☐ Decide what skills you have that will provide a competitive edge . . . and how hard you are willing to work to develop the additional skills that can expand your opportunity.

☐ Determine what size telemarketing unit—and what depth of management strength—you will present to the marketplace, and, accordingly, what size programs (how large or small of a volume) you can accept. (Rather than overextending your capabilities and failing on large volume programs, you are much better served to start with smaller-volume programs, develop a reputation for success, and gradually grow into being able to accept and succeed on larger-volume programs.)

☐ Eliminate markets in which you have little chance of succeeding or markets that you don't want to work.

☐ Determine where you can successfully attack the competition at its strengths.

☐ Decide what methods you will use to introduce your company to the new marketplace.

How to Identify the Competition

Knowing the things to do to identify the market isn't enough. It's also important to know how and where to get the information. Some telemarketers—especially those newer to the business—are unsure where to look. Here are some suggestions of how and where you can start.

• Telemarketing industry publications and directories:
   – *Telemarketing Magazine's Annual Buyers Guide*
   – *Direct Marketing Magazine;* at the back of the magazine is "Direct Marketing Marketplace"; a listing of companies by type of direct marketing service provided
   – *The DMMP (Direct Marketing Market Place)*
   – *Target Marketing*
   – *Who's Who In Direct Marketing* (annual)
   – *Inbound/Outbound Magazine*

- Join national telemarketing associations. The largest of the national groups are:
    - The American Telemarketing Association
    - The Direct Marketing Association
    - The Telephone Marketing Council of the DMA
- Attend national and regional telemarketing conferences. The larger of these are:
    - The Annual Direct Marketing Association Convention
    - The Spring DMA Conference
    - TBT East (Telemarketing & Business Telecommunications)
    - TBT West
    - The Telemarketing Expo conventions (held regionally)
    - The American Telemarketing Association annual convention
    - The American Telemarketing Association spring conference
- If you have identified one or more specific industries or industry segments to which you may want to market, find and join those industries' trade associations. Attend their meetings and ask around to find out who are the major suppliers and users of telemarketing services in those industries.
- If you plan to market locally only, join the local chapters of marketing clubs and attend their local and regional direct marketing meetings.
- All of these gatherings provide good opportunities to do a lot of creative fact finding and investigation, but simply attending the meetings will not provide you with all the information that is available at them. You need to ask good questions about who your competition is likely to be and what those companies specialize in.
- Call your clients and ask what other telemarketing companies have contacted them, how frequently, and what other companies your competitors claim as references.
- Call prospective clients in the industries you have targeted. Ask if they are currently utilizing the services of an "outside telemarketing agency." Ask if they have used one previously and if they plan to do so in the future. If any of those answers is "yes," then ask what telemarketing companies they are using, have used, or expect to use.

ESTABLISHING THE MARKETING STRATEGY: A CASE STUDY

When I started my first telemarketing company, the fund-raising industry was the most likely ticket to success because it was the area in which he had the most experience, and where I had a good reputation that was based on more than one account. More important, it was the only industry in which the marketplace really knew me at all.

However, the first thing I did was size up the entire marketplace. I saw a lot of people at a lot of different companies going after a lot of big-name accounts. But there weren't many major, big-name corporations being approached and marketed to properly. My study showed:

- relatively few high-quality services that were conscious of truly applying successful direct marketing axioms and principles to outbound telephone marketing;

- an absence of strong concern with the back-end;
- the industry appeared to be concerned more about a quantity labor market than about a quality labor market;
- the one or two companies in the field that had good reputations were relatively expensive; and
- the client marketplace was one that sorely needed education because it was so new to telemarketing.

Look for an Opportunity to Serve

That analysis revealed openings to serve the market better by:

- applying successful direct marketing axioms and principles to the telephone;
- developing and applying methods and techniques that would improve the back-end performance of programs;
- cultivating and developing a higher-quality labor force;
- bringing more of an educational and consultative approach to the marketing and selling of telemarketing services to the target universe of prospective clients.

Seeing an uneducated marketplace was a significant key. That information could be translated into specific steps of an action plan:

- recognize the power of knowledge, and continually build on the existing knowledge base;
- provide meaningful and realistic education to the marketplace as a part of the marketing and selling of the company's telemarketing services;
- demonstrate the power of knowledge by performing very well on the clients' programs.

The expectation was that, by diligently and successfully executing the plan, I would be able to create the image and the reality of my company being recognized as a credible source of knowlege and productivity in outbound telemarketing.

Key Point: *Careful identification of the supply and demand factors—and how well they were being fulfilled—were matched with the new company's capability to satisfy specific areas of unfulfilled demand.*

Setting the Company's Long-Term Goal

The long-term goal set for the company was to become known as a first-class outbound telemarketing business, serving companies in both the business and consumer markets. Since the better-known firms were fairly expensive, there was an opportunity to successfully market a high-quality service at a reduced price. Since I didn't want the company to be known as a "cheap price" competitor, I picked a rate that put us at the upper level, but noticeably below the most expensive rate. The company entered the marketplace at $28 an hour when the industry average was $25, but the most reputable firms were at $29 to $32. By the fifth year of operation, the company commanded an average rate of $31 an hour.

Core Strategy: *The company was positioned as a "Rolls Royce" type of service, consistent with the founder's underlying values and philosophy from the beginning of the marketing effort!*

How to Carve Your Niche in Telemarketing

For years, marketing in this country has been perceived as needs-oriented . . . or at least the marketing gurus have told us that it is needs-oriented. Yet our belief is that the market is at least as much competition-oriented as needs oriented.

It's awfully hard to dislodge the "King of the Hill" when the King of the Hill has:

- a clear reputation as "#1"
- a long-term successful track record
- an excellent image
- deep financial resources.

The typical marketing approach to overcome those advantages has been to:

1. run focus groups, to determine marketplace needs, and;
2. try to develop strategies to meet those needs.

> **EXAMPLE:** Burger Chef spent a lot of that time and energy running focus groups on what the marketplace wanted and needed. But McDonald's could spend millions more than Burger Chef every year to uncover the same things . . . and more. The difference was that McDonald's had established a dominant market share and the finances to protect it. The result is that McDonald's is still firmly entrenched in the #1 position, and you may never have heard of Burger Chef.

We subscribe to the Ries and Trout "Marketing Warfare" philosophy* of carving a niche out of the market:

- If you're the leader, you play defense;
- if you're #2 or #3, you attack the leader by playing dead-straight offense;
- if you're a little farther down than that, you play around the leader's perimeter by creating other markets;
- if you're just beginning or an "also ran," you play guerilla warfare and carve out a piece of territory small enough to defend, and hopefully too small for the competition to even want to attack.

The respect for the strategy comes from previous experience. As a brand new

* *Marketing Warfare* by Al Ries and Jack Trout; © 1986, McMillan & Company

player in the market in 1981, Steve hadn't heard of "Marketing Warfare," but he followed the rules by:

- analyzing the general marketplace,
- sizing up the competition,
- defining *where* the competition was least likely to care about making it impossible for him to succeed.

As the "new kid on the block," taking those steps was essential to assuring his small start-up company's survival!

How to Attack the Competition's Strengths

If you're a competitor and we can find out what your weaknesses are, you'll just go out and shore up your weaknesses . . . if you've got enough money. But if we can find weaknesses inherent within your strengths, you've got a problem . . . no matter how much money you have.

If you want to enter telemarketing with the optimum chance of success, look for a place to attack at the points of vulnerability in the competitor's strengths by:

- analyzing the strengths and weaknesses of other telemarketing companies;
- finding the weaknesses and points of vulnerability within their strengths;
- analyzing what strengths you have that can slip through at their points of weakness; and
- devising a plan of attack accordingly.

> **EXAMPLE:** In 1981, one of the strengths of the telemarketing competition was that they were located in major metropolitan areas, close to the clients, with access to large labor markets that would drive for high front-end productivity. Steve saw a weakness in that apparent strength.
>
> In what appeared to many to be a foolish move, I located in a rural labor market away from all of the accounts. I chose Omaha's low-key, accent-free, soft-sell labor market—the home area of Johnny Carson, Walter Cronkite, Dick Cavett, Tom Brokaw, et al. Why? One of the major reasons was the region's neutral accent, one that would enable TSRs to appeal to the whole gamut of demographics nationwide.
>
> **Marketing Strength:** *A neutral accent enables TSRs to communicate with essentially equal effectiveness to all regions of the country.*
>
> The company then focused on marketing and selling its service as being soft-sell and accent-free. The benefits marketed to the clients were image protection, image enhancement, and image projection through accent-free soft selling.
>
> A good competitor might have countered with "Do you really want people from laid-back, sheltered Omaha trying to communicate with the street-smart,

major metro population?" Had the competition used that approach very early on, they might have made it more difficult by attacking what could have been perceived as a weakness in the soft-sell and accent-free strength.

Fortunately, partly because the competition didn't see the "upstart" company as a significant threat, none of the competitors used that tactic in the early stages of the game, and—by the time they tried that approach—those "laid back, sheltered" people had proven that they could really perform!

Gaining Recognition Through Innovation

The 19th century essayist, Ralph Waldo Emerson, noted the power of uniqueness and individuality when he observed that "Imitation is suicide." That maxim has particular meaning when we market our services. Yet, the telemarketing industry—in which creativity is highly respected and desired—is full of sameness in marketing approaches and advertising.

That sameness makes it easy to get lost in the crowd. Unless you have an established name, sameness is unlikely to get you the recognition you want. Sometimes you have to innovate and be different to gain recognition. You can discover productive areas to be different by evaluating the methods and techniques of the competition and finding areas to do things differently.

EXAMPLE: Another major strength of the competition was that they were closer to the clients' offices. That made it more convenient for the clients to make personal visits and observations of the operation in action. That convenience was a strength, but it was vulnerable to being sold through to a greater strength.

When we would run into the objection that another company is a lot closer, we would say "That's O.K. We have installed a remote monitoring system. So you are as close as a phone call, and you can monitor the quality of the calls no matter where you are. You can monitor from your office or wherever you are on the road anytime you like . . . without taking any time out to make a special trip."

(*Note:* Today, most reputable telemarketing services provide remote monitoring capability, which neutralizes that particular advantage. However, the fact that the competition had to go to remote monitoring to remain competitive shows how real a strength the innovation of remote monitoring offered!)

The Strength of Back-end Telemarketing

Prior to 1981, telemarketing service agencies marketed their services by stressing front-end response rates and the ability to perform large call volumes within short time frames. Everyone was selling the front-end response rates which far exceeded those of traditional direct mail. However, the back-end cancellation rates were also dramatically higher than those clients had learned to expect from direct mail. Analyzing that situation, we recognized the inherent weakness and a potential market demand for an offsetting strength.

We went in and said: "We might sell less! That's right, we might sell less . . . but we will sell the right amount. We make it pay, and we make sure the people we sell to are willing to do repeat business."

The clients were delighted; here was a new company that recognized their needs and was effectively concentrating its marketing and selling thrust on back-end tele-marketing. Although it is an essential part of telemarketing today, it was a relatively untapped and unsold approach then. The new company was able to present a viable and attractive alternative:

- a central location that appealed to all markets country wide,
- planned, quality front-end efforts with back-end results that made sense to each clients' bottom line.

Key Point: *Attack the weaknesses in the competition's strengths and offer an alternative to fill the gaps the competition has left open.*

The emphasis on front-end telemarketing was a particularly good area to attack, because:

- The back-end emphasis appealed to a very real and sensitive concern of the marketplace; and
- The whole telemarketing industry is labor-intensive, and the competition could not react quickly enough to make dramatic change in that area.

If telemarketing had been a software-intensive industry, the competition could have responded to finding a weakness in their software by simply rewriting their own software. And they could have done so relatively quickly. But telemarketing is people-intensive, and the competitors' strengths and weaknesses existed—to a great extent—within their work forces.

Since people are resistant to change, meeting any competitive challenge regarding large-scale changes in how those people work could not be accomplished by mandate. The competition couldn't retrain their people overnight. Had they tried, they would have wound up not only having to retrain them, but would also have had to turn over a large percentage of that "front-end ingrained" labor force. In effect, they would almost have to start all over. And the hardest part of all for the competition would be in the leaders convincing themselves of the need to change. It would require them to move out of their own comfort zones.

That was the key advantage to a company that was starting a fresh operation with a labor market that had no significant outbound telemarketing habits to break. If people wanted to work in outbound telemarketing, the labor market had one large-volume choice—the Idelman way! It wasn't necessary to retrain bad habits and sell through opposite mind sets. Nobody came in saying "I've worked at XYZ Company, and they did it another way." It was simply a matter of finding the best communicators possible and training them to follow the Idelman system.

Keeping Your Sights on Your Long-Range Goals

An important step is taking a realistic look at the market and the experience you can bring to it. Our analysis was fairly simple: "We're a brand new start-up company, we don't have a lot of cash, and nobody has really heard of us." It wasn't encouraging, but it was based in reality.

My biggest successes up to then had been in fund-raising markets. I had represented several fund-raising accounts and had established an excellent reputation with them. I had an opportunity to be introduced to virtually every major political, and charitable fund-raising organization in America. But I said no.

Why? I recognized that the deeper a reputation the company developed in the fund-raising industry, the more money it would make in the first couple of years. But that would be a short-term view. After the first couple of years of generating lots of cash and capital, the company would have been a telemarketing organization that knew nothing but how to raise funds. Since fund-raising is perceived with some negative connotations by traditional product and service direct-marketing companies, the telemarketing firm would have developed an image and reputation that would have made it difficult to be accepted by the more traditional—and larger—direct-marketing community.

While the company started primarily with fund-raising accounts, the overall focus remained on the larger goal: to become a first-class outbound telemarketing business, serving direct-marketing organizations in both the business and consumer markets. The key question was: "How do we make the transition?"

Since fund-raising is a list industry, the best opportunity for transition was to become known as a telemarketing support service for list-intensive direct marketing accounts. With good references from the fund-raising accounts, the company picked up a couple of accounts in other fields that required the same list-based telemarketing expertise.

Transition Key: *Examine your background and experience to identify your strengths that can move you beyond limited immediate opportunity to greater long-term potential.*

EXAMPLE: One of the company's first accounts that was not a fund-raiser came through an introduction to a fund-raising program. The client was in the fund-raising list business and also in the travel club business.

The client wanted to use telemarketing for the fund-raising but not for the travel business, because of previous bad experiences with telemarketing on the travel account. After getting to know the client well and earning respect by doing a good job for them on the fund-raising, the company earned a shot at their travel business.

The beginning of that program wasn't particularly auspicious. It started with a 100-hour test on a third-party bank list for their travel account. But, through careful handling and aggressive application of the lessons learned in handling list-intensive, demographic-based telemarketing, the project developed into an account that provided more than 750,000 names and phone numbers a month. It also became the company's longest-term account.

Any success involves a certain amount of "luck" or good breaks, but that type of success doesn't happen by accident . . . nor does it happen without painful lessons that are learned along the way.

EXAMPLE: After opening in April, 1981, the company grew for the first 90 days, largely working fund-raising accounts. After the projects were complete, the company went dormant and almost everyone was laid off because the company had so little business. In fact, the company nearly went out of business!

What had happened? The marketing director (and only salesperson), the C.E.O., the training manager, and the director of operations were all the same person. Since that one person was totally occupied with the daily operation, virtually no time had been spent on marketing the company's services.

Once marketing activity was reestablished, several new accounts soon were signed on. The company was fortunate to survive, and several important lessons were learned in the process.

Lesson Learned: *Planning too closely for time and money needs is a big mistake . . . and one that easily can be fatal.*

What can you do to survive that kind of situation?

- Reset priorities.
- Recognize and clearly determine the short cash position.
- Take the cash management actions that are required for immediate survival, and:
- Make the time to get out and do the marketing to get some business in the door.

Key Point: *Partial planning and wishful thinking aren't enough. Thorough planning and the ability to modify the plan to respond to changing conditions are vital to long-term success.*

For the process of establishing a successful marketing thrust, what then are the most important planning steps?

1. Identify what is in the marketplace, what is good, and what isn't.
2. Determine the nature of the prime competition. In the previous example, the two major companies in the field which had good reputations were, by and large, on the fence, and they were relatively expensive.
3. Set a fee schedule that positions the company properly from the beginning; high enough to be a quality service, but low enough to be very competitive.
4. Emphasize the importance of knowledge, expertise, and hands-on involvement.
5. Focus the marketing strategies on areas that attack competitors' strengths which are not quickly or easily changed or defended.
6. Be innovative in developing approaches and techniques which would provide the

marketplace with attractive—and distinctive—alternatives to the existing services.

7. Focus on markets that can be long-range winners, rather than going only for the short-term gain.

8. Execute according to the business plan . . . with appropriate moves to revise that plan as experience shows it is necessary.

PLANNING THE QUALITY OF THE TELEMARKETING OPERATION

However well it is conceived, the marketing plan of a service business ultimately is only as good as the service you offer. In telemarketing, that quality is shaped in great part by the quality of your labor market. In addition, labor is both the single greatest revenue generator and the single largest cost center in an outbound telemarketing business.

As a result, doing a labor market analysis is imperative. You must make sure that the talent you will need is available. Otherwise, serious consequences could occur as you grow.

The Labor Market Analysis: Four Important Points

When performing a labor market analysis, make sure:

1. there is a ready and qualified labor pool that will fit your plans;
2. that the labor pool is large enough to meet your expansion plans;
3. that the local accents will not cause problems with the customers you will be calling; and
4. that you can afford the pay scale in the marketplace.

Whether you are new to a labor market or very experienced in it, doing a labor market analysis makes a lot of sense. If possible, look at labor markets all around the country before you make your final decision on where to locate your business.

Keep in Mind: *Your choice of a particular location and labor market can make a dramatic difference in your operation, as well as in its long-term structure and success.*

There are good, logical reasons why cities like Omaha and Des Moines have become—far out of proportion to their size—centers of telemarketing activity. Many companies have found a labor pool that meets their requirements and matches their own philosophies. They have found not only the neutral accents, but also a population that has the work ethic they want. The people aren't pushy, but they are persistent. They aren't afraid of hard work. And the cost of living is such that the hourly rate for TSRs could fit into a competitive pricing plan.

That's not a blanket suggestion that everyone in telemarketing should move to the Midwest. Beyond being impractical, it's not right for everyone. Additionally, Omaha is virtually a saturated labor market today, and other Midwestern cities are rapidly moving toward saturation.

Determining your labor market, however, is essential to understanding your potential for growth. The nature of that labor market—and the quality of those people—will play a significant role in your growth. The right people make all the difference.

The supply of those people in any given community will be the best determinant of whether your telemarketing growth can be centralized or will need to be decentralized with branch offices in multiple labor markets. Decentralization creates an entirely different set of problems, the most significant being the need for that many more qualified profit-center managers.

Key Point: *Do a labor market analysis to find which labor market most suits your operation, provides the opportunity for growth, and gives you the best opportunity to succeed.*

SIX CRITICAL POINTS IN MAKING FINANCIAL PLANS

In all businesses, managing growth is more than just managing the people, the clientele, the fixed plant resources, the expansion capability, the working relationship with your suppliers, quality accountants and attorneys, and all of the daily operational requirements. It's also managing the financial resources and having a good supportive relationship with a bank or other dependable money source. Capital resources are critical.

Making your financial plans for growth includes making sure you have the proper financial structure to provide the ability to expand as required to meet your goals. The process of revising your financial plans and structure to accommodate your expansion plans largely will mirror and build on (and perhaps modify or correct) the steps that were taken in designing the financial plans during the initial start-up phase or subsequent growth planning.

Of particular importance is your financial history, experience, track record, and growth plans:

- Have you established and maintained good working relationships with your financial partner or partners and banks and/or financial investors?
- If those financial partner working relationships are good, is there any reason why the financing of the projected growth can't be handled much the same way as it has been handled in the past?
- Have your previous financial plans included sufficient retained earnings for the expansion you are considering?
- What is the magnitude of your expansion plans as a percentage of current volume?
- Where is the growth coming from?
  - Existing clients?
  - New clients?
  - Current market segments?
  - Newly targeted market segments?
- What are the payment terms vs. the real expectation for payment? Does the client (or clients) you are expanding with intend to have your company, in essence, help

finance their growth by trying to require you accept payment terms of net 90? (In fact, that happens a lot in the direct marketing industry.)

Key Point: *An existing company that is expanding rapidly must go through many, if not most of, the same steps as a start-up firm. If either doesn't plan properly, the chances of running out of cash are good.*

Whatever your situation or your plans, significant expansion is not a quick and effortless process. Expect the financial planning and securing of funds to consume a significant amount of time and energy. Then double your estimate of the time required, and you are more likely to be accurate.

When you prepare the financial part of your telemarketing business plan, there are six major considerations:

1. What is your business's financial situation?
2. Are you sufficiently capitalized?
3. Where will you get financing, and at what cost?
4. How are you going to handle cash flow?
5. Is your pro forma accurate and realistic?
6. Have you—to be safe—figured high on expenses and low on income, or have you left yourself very little margin for error?

Number one on that list—your business's financial situation—is an overriding consideration. You must have clear answers to a number of questions:

- Are you part of a large corporation with ready access to significant amounts of capital at relatively low cost?
- If so, what is your telemarketing unit's charge or mandate from the corporate level?
- Are your superiors overly concerned about short-term profits, or are they willing to cover your financial needs so you can manage for long-term opportunity?
- If you are in your own business, what is your cash and credit position?

There are some financial bottom lines. If you're in your own business, you have to make sure you can survive before you can grow effectively. You have to manage your cash flow and the financial matters. When you are part of a large corporation, cash flow is not as great a concern, and financing is usually available at interest rates lower than those available in the open market.

Note: *Whatever your financial situation, your pro forma (your company's financial packaging) is going to be your guide.*

If you can maintain at least the projected cash flow projections of the pro forma, the corporate office or the investors will be happy. Their concern is for the protection of, and return on, their investment. If the business is yours and has been started with your cash reserves, the pro forma is your own protection. (See sample pro forma in the appendix.)

Being undercapitalized has always been a major cause of failure of new business operations, and it can be equally devastating to an existing company embarking on major expansion. Your business plan and pro forma must make sense and be realistic. A cash flow commitment of two years is an absolute minimum safety margin. Otherwise, you're not free to manage for growth; much of your time will be spent worrying about what happens if you don't make it.

Warning: *If you structure a plan and pro forma to fool the bank and get less than the real cash requirements, you'll end up fooling yourself.*

There are ways to reduce the actual needs you will have as compared to the pro forma projections. First, always figure high on expenses, low on income. Then you might accomplish lower cash needs by having better-than-projected performance. You might have less-than-projected costs while keeping near the projected levels of performance. You may improve your cash flow position by assuring that the clients pay within 30 days rather than the projected 60 to 90 days.

Reminder: *If you want to stay free to focus on the management of your growth, solid capitalization is needed.*

If you have established a $250,000 line of credit for start-up or expansion and use only half of it to do the job the bank expects, you have $125,000 available for additional expansion. That's a nice situation, but first you have to get the commitment for the money. For most small businesspeople, that's the concern.

(*See* "Financing a Telemarketing Business" in the appendix.)

With an established operation or a large corporate expansion, the job is a little easier, but only in the short run. In the long run, the larger the initial investment the greater the return that is ultimately expected. And with those increased expectations comes increased pressure.

When to Involve Your Financial Backers . . . and How to Keep Them in Your Corner

It's especially wise in telemarketing to get the financial supporters involved in your operation very early. Here are several helpful steps:

- Have your financial supporters visit your facilities.
- Demonstrate that your operation is much more than the "boiler room" concept they may still envision.
- Explain the company's operational structure.
- Show your professionalism; guide them through the basic process of how the operation works and the internal coordination and controls you have built in.
- Let them meet your key people.
- Show them how their money has been—and will be—put to good use!

Typically, they will be pleasantly surprised that you have created a sophisticated business structure and environment "just to make phone calls." They will be amazed at how much intricate and detailed planning and coordination goes into the making of just one outbound call. And they will be impressed with how hard everyone works.

As you start meeting your objectives of having them really understand the value and the potential of your operation, talk to them further about your ideas for growth. Educate them on the importance of having additional space available, and on the value of the opportunity cost represented by not having it.

Tip: *Make allowances in your financial plans for phones and facility beyond your immediate projected needs.*

Before you need to ask for it, give them some ideas of what you could do with additional cash. It's better to let the backers know in advance what is happening and what you would like to happen. They're going to find out sooner or later, anyway. Nobody likes surprises, and bankers particularly despise them!

Key Point: *Developing the right relationship with your financial backers can mean the difference between struggling for survival and prospering through growth periods.*

Remember that your first job is to make sure you're budgeted for survival. Then make advance plans for the resources you will need to grow beyond that. You have to know that the projected figures can be met closely enough to keep the financial backers happy while still leaving you with enough room to make the financial commitments required to build the organization.

Cost/Revenue Planning for Growth

If you're selling a commodity of any sort, one of the most poignant rules is that if it will cost you "X" to bring the product to market, you'd better sell it for "X" plus something. No matter how creative you may be, thinking you can buy it for "X" and sell it for "X" minus just won't work!

That's cost/revenue relational planning in the simplest of terms. If all of your costs are $14, you can charge less than if your costs are $19. (We're talking higher mathematics and economics here!)

Finding out how much the "plus" should be isn't that hard. More challenging is the trick of determining the real cost. That's where a lot of managers fall apart. They think they have put the pro forma together with every possible cost category and contingency. Then, month after month, they say to themselves: "Gee, it would have been a better month if we hadn't had that unusual expense."

Without a Real Financial Plan . . .

It's easy to forget about things such as a brochure expense. It's not a recurring monthly activity, but it *is* a monthly expense, once the cost is amortized, and it has to be included in the budget. If you aren't thorough when you do the initial projections, you will discover—12 months a year—*unusual* expenses of that kind have not been included in the budget. Unexpected expenses happen to everyone, but good planning reduces the number of surprises.

A lot of telemarketing companies that failed never had a chance, simply because they had no real financial plan. They went into the business and decided they would charge 22 bucks an hour. While they lasted, they had a fair amount of business, but they went under because they determined their hourly rate and sold their product before they knew their costs.

Red Flag: *It's suicide to just do the marketplace analysis, create a marketing model, and start selling. You must also have a thorough financial plan.*

There is no one way you have to do it, just so long as you decide which way you want to do it, and then go ahead and do it.

You can first profile your costs, determine your rates, and then decide on the appropriate marketplace. Or you can decide which market you want to enter, learn what rates will appeal to it, determine the fair profit margin for existing businesses providing service to that market, and then structure your costs to fit your formulas.

Note: *Either way, you eventually have to recognize that your minute-to-minute cost of doing business decides what you have to charge the client for each minute.*

The Key Financial Factor: Profitability

It's essential to keep clear on your profitability goal. Is it 6%? 10%? 15%? 25%? What's realistic? Your expansion will affect those figures as you work to stay ahead of growth. But growth only affects those things negatively if you fail to build enough room into your start up pro forma to do what you need to down the line.

Once the data is gathered, it's a matter of learning the formulas, the terminology, and doing the "number crunching." But getting to the bottom line is simple.

- You have a total cost factor.
- You want a certain profit factor.
- With your identified costs, you find that you will have to charge $29 to attain your desired profit margin of 15%.
- If your plans call for entering a market where the going rate is $23, you either have to:
  1. reduce your costs,
  2. convince the market your service is worth more than the going rate, or
  3. stay out of that market!

Otherwise, you will be struggling with a different issue: whether you have the cash and the time to survive, let alone grow!

The Dangers of Undercapitalization

Without a comprehensive plan and pro forma, the chances are excellent that you'll soon find yourself in the position of saying "We've got to get this out and we've got to get this done . . . but the money just isn't there." That is often followed by this kind of story:

> We were so close. We almost had it, but we ran out of money. We could have done it, but we just ran out of cash. It was because of things beyond our control. Inflation hit us, and the interest rates went so high that it would have been almost impossible to afford money from the bank. Besides, they got so tight with their money and became so restrictive in their loan guidelines that they wouldn't give us any more.
>
> If we had just had a little more money to be able to expand when that 60-phone opportunity came along, we wouldn't have gone under when we lost that 110-phone program we thought was so solid. If we could just have weathered that losing period for another month or two, we could be running that new 'no brainer' program that's so successful now at XYZ Telemarketing.
>
> Why did they get it when we were more productive? I guess that it's just that they're still around.
>
> Boy, what could have been!

If you don't cross all your t's and dot all your i's, your story can easily become a very similar one. And the number one reason for those storied failures? Undercapitalization. The most common reason why businesses fail is they were undercapitalized—either because the financial analysis was faulty or because the results of the financial analysis were ignored.

Even the "overnight successes" had to do their homework and learn the financial lessons. The public rarely sees the background they have, the hours of working on the phone, the experience gained in managing at other companies, and the lessons they have learned from their failures. With those many years of practical hands-on telemarketing management experience, the "overnight success" they reap is simply the harvest from an eight- or ten-year period of planting that is finally bearing fruit.

The experience of those people shows that anyone going into the telemarketing business is well advised to be budgeted and financed for a minimum of two years . . . with five years preferable. And the bigger you enter the marketplace, the longer your commitment to making it has to be.

(*See* "Sample Financial Plan" and related information in the appendix)

A Final Recommendation

A real key to remember is that there is no one way of planning for growth, because there's no one "right" budget, no exclusively "perfect" business plan, no single "correct" target marketplace, no "ideal" marketing strategy. Many telemarketers have had business plans that could be outlined quite simply:

- sell as much as they can,
- execute as well as they are capable,
- beg for money if they need to,
- work as hard as necessary, and
- survive.

Some have survived . . . but many more have found that such a simplistic plan was a formula for failure.

Telemarketing can be very rewarding, but in today's marketplace, the payoff comes to those who have the willingness to do the planning and preparation—and the ability to execute their plans. Telemarketing is not the same business that it was in the 1970's and early 1980's. It is more competitive. Competition is stronger. Clients are more sophisticated and more demanding. Successful operations that start on vague plans and shoestring budgets are no longer the norm; instead, they are the rare exception. Thorough planning maps out your road to success.

Can you succeed without doing the planning? Yes, you can . . . but don't expect anyone else to bet on it.

Remember: *If you don't know where you're going, any road will get you there.*

26 KEYS TO PLANNING FOR TELEMARKETING GROWTH

- Before you plan for growth, build a plan to survive. That is essential if you are to reach the point where you can concern yourself with growth.
- The business growth plan must include allowances for the major changes that come with growth in volume, number of programs, and number of clients.
- There are both strong similarities and distinct differences between in-house operations and service agencies. The biggest differences are in the initial planning and start-up phase.
- Factors that are particularly critical in the initial in-house evaluation and planning are the call load, selecting the right project manager, and overcoming internal resistance.
- The in-house telemarketing unit must make plans to deal with resistance from internal management and from the field sales force.
- In-house operations are often in a position to pay somewhat higher wages, using some of the money that a service agency would need to retain in order to remain healthy.
- The continuing development of and training for new programs, large numbers of clients, and varied programs creates more stress for the service agency.
- Even when a company makes the decision to put the majority of its telemarketing work in-house, a good service agency can help in initial testing, in building, and in helping to refine the in-house shop.
- The financial and legal structures of the organization must be flexible enough for the people who started the company to be free to pursue their visions and dreams.
- Despite the entrance of larger corporations into the field, telemarketing is still dominated by the entrepreneurial "boutique" companies and is fueled by their spirit.

- In the long run, those telemarketers who run the most flexible, innovative, and fastest-responding service businesses will establish themselves as the industry's leaders.

- The beginning point of your planning is establishing a niche and developing a marketing plan and strategies to serve that market segment. Your niche may grow or be modified, but it determines the basis for the rest of your planning.

- A company that fails to focus on providing quality service to distinct and segmented areas of the general marketplace is a company run by fools.

- In doing your market analysis, evaluate up your specific marketplace, size up the competition from there, and define where it is that the competition is least likely to prevent you from succeeding.

- Look for the weaknesses inherent in your competition's strengths. That is often where you will find your strongest marketing opportunities.

- Plan fresh and innovative strategies to gain recognition. If your approach is one of imitation, you may get lost in the crowd.

- Plan beyond the short-term "sure things." Keep your long-range focus on opportunities that will lead to the fulfillment of your overall vision.

- To extend your marketplace niche, examine your strengths to discover what can move you beyond immediate applications into new opportunities with greater long-term potential.

- A labor market analysis is essential to understanding your potential for growth. The nature of that labor market—and the quality of those people—plays a significant role in your growth.

- An existing company that is expanding rapidly must go through many, if not most of, the same steps as a start-up firm. If either doesn't plan properly, the chances are good that the company will run out of cash.

- In preparing the business plan, an overriding consideration is your business's financial situation. Your financial planning should begin with the development of a comprehensive pro forma as a financial guide.

- A cash flow commitment of two years is an absolute minimum safety margin; five years is ideal. Otherwise, continuing concerns over cash flow will not leave you free to manage for growth.

- Developing the right relationship with your financial backers can mean the difference between struggling for survival and prospering through growth periods. Get them directly involved early and often.

- Cost revenue relational planning, in the simplest of terms, is this: If it will cost you "X" to bring your service to market, you'd better plan to sell it for "X" plus something.

- Your minute-to-minute cost of doing business decides what you have to charge the client for each minute; this is true whether you are in-house, charge on a per-sale basis, or charge an hourly rate.

- Partial planning and wishful thinking aren't enough. Thorough planning and the ability to modify the plan to respond to changing conditions are vital to long-term success in telemarketing.

Make no little plans;
they have no magic to stir men's blood
and probably will not be realized.
Make big plans; aim high in hope and work,
remembering that a noble,
logical diagram once recorded will not die.
—*Daniel H. Burnham*

How do you eat an elephant? One bite at a time.
—Harold O. Dobbs

Chapter *3*

Structuring the Telemarketing Business for Growth

Telemarketing companies thrive and grow with a large variety of structural combinations. There are sound reasons for that variety. Each company has its own personality, its own resources, its own founding vision, its own challenges. Each company also has its own unique situation in terms of the number of programs, number of rooms, number of floors, and number of facilities involved in the structure. The combination of all those factors, more than a particularly popular or currently accepted corporate organizational system, determines the best structure for the company.

Keep in Mind: *The telemarketing organization's structure must be flexible enough to allow the company to change—or the structure will inhibit the company's growth.*

The company's underlying philosophy and concepts determine its nature and the course it will take. The philosophy and concepts set the tone for the vision. The vision then shapes the plan. And the plan guides the structuring of the vision into an operational reality.

In the same sense, organizational clarity guides you in the overall structuring process. Intelligent growth-structuring decisions can be made by acting from your philosophy, objectives, resources, and the particular challenges you must meet.

The growing telemarketing organization needs two kinds of structure in place. The first is the overall organizational structure that determines the chain of command and the reporting sequences. This type of structure is common to all businesses, with basic areas of division of responsibility and duties. The second kind of structure is more specific to the primary business of the telemarketing company. This is the portion that addresses the structuring of the project management group.

HOW TO FORM YOUR ORGANIZATIONAL STRUCTURE

Discussing how to structure a telemarketing company is not quite like giving the recipe for making a two-layer vanilla cake with chocolate icing. It's difficult to say "These are the ingredients for the structure, here are the proportions, and this is how long it takes." Structuring a telemarketing company is not that precise and not that clearly defined.

Just as a given service may be best for Client A and may be the worst possible service for Client B, a structure that may be best for Company X may be the worst possible structure for Company Y.

Despite the variety of combinations of departmental structure that may be used, the internal organizational structure of a telemarketing company can be divided into five primary areas. They are:

1. Finance and Administration—(General management, facilities maintenance, collections, cash management, purchasing, receivables, and payroll)
2. Marketing—(Bringing in business and new clients)
3. Account management—(Operationally manages and works with the clients)
4. Operations—(The phone production operation itself, materials control, and quality assurance)
5. Client Services—(Handles all verification, audits, and fulfillment)

Personnel services and training may be included within either Finance and Administration or Operations; payroll may be put into either Personnel or Finance and Administration; or either department may be structured as a separate and independent area. The number of people involved in each area will be determined by the size of the operation and the applications involved.

Your evaluation of the choices of structure should help you determine whether or not they will allow you to grow:

- in a smooth and effective manner;
- in the directions that you anticipate;
- at the rates you have projected; and,
- through incremental additions and modifications, rather than through comprehensive restructuring.

How Your Company's Size Affects its Structure

Two telemarketing companies may look and sound a lot alike in what they are doing and how they conduct their business. They even could have been developed initially by the same person. But the circumstances of their founding, their point in the process of maturing, and their current situations may dictate totally different structures.

> **EXAMPLE:** Consider the differences in the structures of a multibillion dollar international bank, a $150-million regional bank, and a local $10-million bank. The structure of each is vastly different, yet there remain consistent similarities.

If you are going to call on the person handling marketing for the bank, you'll see different people based upon the size of the bank. You will wind up with the president at a small bank. At the $150-million bank, you'll meet with the vice president of marketing. At the largest banks, you will talk to the product line managers. They're all banks, and they're all successful. But each will have different business plans, different markets, different responsibilities . . . and different structures to accommodate those differences.

In the same sense, the needs are different for a 20-phone operation than they are for a 100-phone operation. What you could do alone in the smaller shop you can't do alone in the larger shop. As an operation grows from 100 to 200 phones, then to 1,000 to 1,200 phones, the needs change even more dramatically.

The experiences of many telemarketing companies of different sizes demonstrate that the organizational needs change as the organization becomes larger.

EXAMPLE: A small company needs a good trainer to conduct initial classroom training and additional ongoing training. That trainer may also participate in hiring and floor supervision functions.

A moderate-size company needs a good training development *manager* who can develop and conduct training programs for TSRs, supervisors, and trainers . . . while doing the administrative scheduling and work to supervise and develop the department.

In a large company, the training development manager also may have to develop and participate in the conduct of the training programs for operational sales managers and for the various supervisors and managers of other departments.

A very large organization needs a training *director* to oversee training managers who hold separate responsibilities for the development and conduct of training programs for each department within the company.

A very small "Ma and Pa" operation with a limited budget has different needs and different challenges than larger telemarketing organizations. The basic approach is to recruit a bunch of good helpers that will work hard. "Ma and Pa" are in the phone room making it happen on 10 to 25 phones and out marketing the company's services and managing the shop, and—most likely—handling most of the fulfillment activities, if not client services, as well! Everyone else in the company focuses on the direct telephone production work.

The organizational chart of such a small shop might be best represented in the following manner shown in Chart 1, page 54.

In this kind of an operation, it's not unusual to find that there is absolutely no structure. The owner just works in the trenches as long and as hard as is necessary to get everything done.

Personal experience has shown us that a one-man shop is fun for a while. But it becomes increasingly stressful, makes future growth very difficult, and it gets old real quick!

The best guidelines for structuring are rules of commitment, communication, standards of excellence, the provision of service, and the creation of opportunity. The

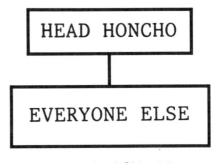

Organizational Chart # 1:
The "Ma and Pa" Shop

Chart 1

specific structure comes out of those guidelines. All telemarketing firms—including start-up companies of any size—that have plans for growth would be wise to have certain positions that are filled "out of the gate" and other positions in the budget. If you expect to grow much past 25 phones, you need to design a structure that allows you to concentrate your time and energies on the achievement of different priorities. And it should allow you to meet your predetermined standards of quality for your service.

Key Point: *The size and the nature of the company's operation and of its key people will help determine the best structure for the company.*

Individual Considerations that Shape the Structure

Beyond the smallest shops, the nature of telemarketing helps define the company's structure. You need someone doing the marketing, someone running the operation, someone managing client services, someone who does the training, and so on—even if each area is a one-person department. But it is really impossible to give the "correct structure"—or even the "three correct structures"—for a telemarketing business, because structure depends on so many variables, including:

- the growth stage of the company;
- the skills of the people available to fill the positions in the company's structure;
- the number of skilled people the budget can support;
- the number of people available to fill in the positions in the company's structure;
- the role of the top person in the company.

The last of these points is especially important in a small telemarketing company. If you are the key executive, the kinds of people you need to fill the structure of the company depend on your role and your goals. What are you going to do, and what do you want to accomplish?

Note: *The process of structuring returns you to your original vision, your business philosophy, your commitment, and the plans you have for shaping the company.*

When you set about defining the particular positions that are needed in the structure, first define your role and your needs. Analyze your areas of knowledge and experience and the areas where you are weak or deficient. If you know you don't like, or don't do, a particular job function well, recognize the need to create a position and fill it with someone who can and will do it well. Ask yourself some very practical questions:

- What is top management going to do? (Not just today, but tomorrow and the tomorrows thereafter.)
- What is your management style?
- What are your strengths and weaknesses?
- What type of people do you need to complement you where you are weak and to support you where you are strong?
- Do you have the people who can fill those needs?
- What are the aspirations of the people you have available to move into positions of expanded responsibility? Do their strengths and abilities match their aspirations?
- How quickly can you develop those people to the point that they can assume those positions?
- What kind of talent is available in the open labor market, and at what cost?

The process of determining positions that need to be filled immediately and the ones that should be planned and budgeted starts with identifying the skills and preferences of the top person in the organization.

If the primary skills, strengths, and preferences of the head of a small telemarketing organization lie in the sales and marketing area, it will be a mistake to create a small organizational structure that attempts to force the top person to focus the bulk of time and effort on administrative duties. A better structural design for a company with such a person at the top might be an organizational chart as illustrated by Chart 2, page 56.

The elementary structure that has been created reflects the individual needs of the organization, based on the initial premise that it is essential to have the top person focusing on the sales and marketing specialty. From that premise, departments can be developed that allow for differentiation of duties and provision for specialized needs and activities.

However, that organizational chart is not practical if the strengths and preferences of the C.E.O. of a small company—rather than being sales- and marketing-oriented— are in the general management, financial, and administrative areas. That company will need a structure that allows positioning people and departments to complement the top executive in other areas. See Chart 3, page 57 for such an organizational chart.

As a company grows in size and complexity, the variety of personnel needs—and the organizational chart—take on a greater complexity, with increased departmental structure. A medium-sized telemarketing company, because of the demands of its increased size, requires increased level of specialization. Additional departmental specialization must occur, with more separate positions that carry responsibilities for specific segments of the operation . . . and the interactive relationships between them.

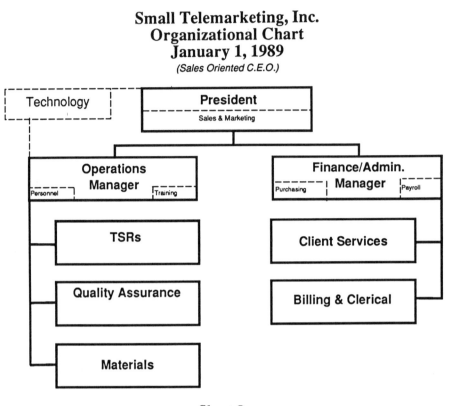

Chart 2

The organizational chart for the medium-size organization is illustrated in Chart 4, page 58.

As the organization continues to grow and becomes a large telemarketing company, it brings a great deal more of that type of specialized segmentation and differentiation. Chart 5, pages 60 and 61, might represent the organizational chart for a large, multibranch, multi-application telemarketing operation.

There are tremendous structural differences between the last four charts. Which of the organizational structures is the *right* one?

None of them.

Key Point: *There is no one right structure for all telemarketing organizations. Simply selecting and implementing one structure because it looks good is not a realistic approach.*

One telemarketing company may be deep with talent and be in a situation where it has to create and deal with extremely rapid growth. Its situation may require it to be structured only barely ahead of growth.

Another company may be in a consolidation or retrenching phase. It may be short on talent and need enhanced structure to help them compensate. It may be preparing for a major marketing thrust. Those situations may call for the company to be structured quite far ahead of its projected growth.

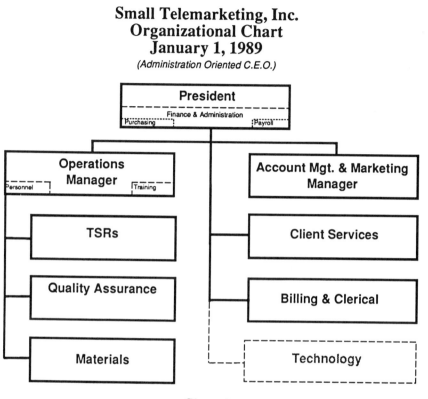

Small Telemarketing, Inc.
Organizational Chart
January 1, 1989
(Administration Oriented C.E.O.)

Chart 3

The structures of the two companies may be very different, with both being correct for each company's specific needs.

The key is in analyzing the particular needs of your company and designing a structure which will support those needs.

How to Combine Two Critical Structuring Elements: Business Plans and People Resources

It's a good idea to watch what other companies are doing. Even if you don't respect, or agree with, their overall approach to business, you will find things that they are doing well that you can apply to your situation.

However, whatever the competition is doing, your decisions about structure cannot be isolated from your hopes for the future and the reality of available personnel.

Remember: *Planning for the growth of the structure means you have to consider both your current and future people needs and people resources.*

Your visions will be nothing more than pipe dreams unless you deal with the reality of the need for quality people who can grow with the structure that you have planned.

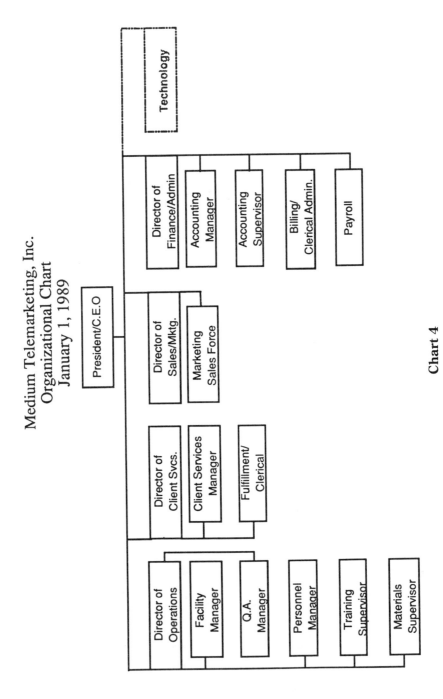

Medium Telemarketing, Inc.
Organizational Chart
January 1, 1989

Chart 4

EXAMPLE: If you are considering creating a position of Director of Operations, you have to look into the qualifications of the individual being considered and into your plans for the structure you will need in the future. You have to consider:

- whether your vision includes eventually needing a Vice President of Operations;
- whether the individual being considered has the capacity to grow into the next position; and
- whether the structure you are creating will help or hinder that process.

If your plans do not include eventually having a Vice President of Operations, your decisions can be based more upon your current needs and the basic qualifications of that individual. But if you will be needing a Vice President of Operations, it's not a great idea to believe you can eventually hire in another person as the Vice President over the individual you would promote to Director today, at least not without the probability of significant repercussions.

Again, a combination of your vision and your current situation will shape your decisions. When you know both where you are and where you are going, finding the right path becomes a much simpler task.

CREATING A POWERFUL TELEMARKETING ACCOUNT MANAGEMENT STRUCTURE

The second of the two parts of structure a telemarketing company must consider is the structure for the management of specific clients and projects. There are two different approaches to developing that structure. The first is the traditional or old-school approach; the second is the service agency approach.

The Old-School Approach

The old-school approach is taken when one entrepreneurial person who is at least relatively well versed in telemarketing sets up what is essentially a one-man shop. The founder/owner/president is the source of all expertise and has hands-on control of every aspect of the operation. The structure is very simple. The owner is in charge of all the areas, with a lot of helpers filling in the details and doing the production work. Everyone is hired, trained, and supervised directly by that top person. The boss also takes care of marketing and everything that requires specific knowledge and skills, other than the actual selling on the phone. Most important, anything having to do with the development and management of the client's program is in the hands of the boss.

The Problems of the Old-School Approach

You can recognize an old-school telemarketing firm easily. It's the one that charges $19 to $24 per hour. The larger services can't compete with the rates because of the old-school firm's core financial advantages:

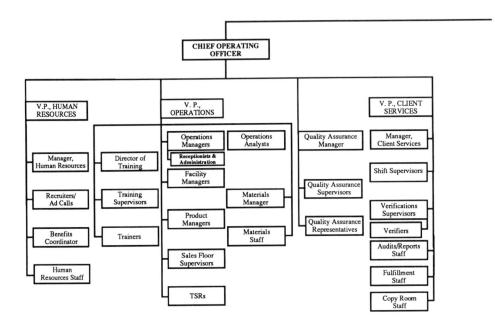

- bare-boned fixed costs
- minimized (rather than optimized) variable costs
- minimal management costs

While their financial advantage is real, the old-school companies do have a major weakness; they are not deeply structured. If the Head Honcho is out because of illness, marketing trips, or vacation . . . well, good luck!

Please understand that we're not damning the old-school bureau. That structure may work very well for a small telemarketing organization, but we know the problems the old-school approach can cause an aggressive and growing company—and its clients—because we've been there.

EXAMPLE: I used the old-school approach when I had 45 phones in 1981. I was the source of knowledge and handled everything in the company. Being so occupied with the operation, I had no time to market and wound up having to go with almost no business for a period of time, while I went out and sold new

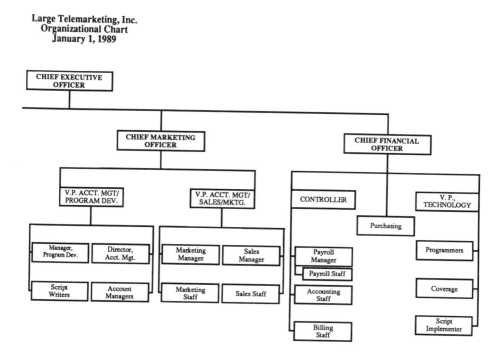

**Large Telemarketing, Inc.
Organizational Chart
January 1, 1989**

Chart 5

accounts. You would think I saw the handwriting on the wall then, but I was stuck in the old-school approach.

Fortunately, we sometimes grow in spite of ourselves.

A year later, the company had 200 phones in operation. The company had continued to grow, but had made very little change in its structure. One night, we made a slight mistake.

We were selling magazine renewal subscriptions for a major publishing firm, and acquiring new card holders for a major travel card company. That fateful night, we called approximately 1,000 of the magazine's renewal customers for the travel card company, and 1,000 of the travel card company's proprietary list for the magazine renewal client.

The results were *not* what anyone could call excellent.

When I discovered what was happening, I contacted the clients, told them what had happened, let them know the programs would be down for a couple of days, and promised to make up for the loss in production.

I closed down the entire operation for 48 hours. The entire support staff was brought in to re-inventory and reorganize the materials and to completely restructure the materials systems and procedures to assure that mistakes like that would never be repeated.

The lack of planning time and low management levels that were dictated by the old-school approach had taken their toll. It was an expensive lesson for everyone involved.

Lesson Learned: *The old-school approach to the structuring and operation of a telemarketing company fails to meet the principles of controlled management of growth.*

The growth of a company (and the success of its client's programs) can be made or broken by the company's choice of which way it will structure: old school or service agency. Yet the old-school approach is still in wide use by companies that profess a desire for growth with professionalism and excellence.

They just haven't learned the lesson yet.

The Service Agency Approach to Account Management

The Service Agency approach is very different. Controlled management of growth and the service agency structure for project management fit together hand and glove.

In the service agency system, there is a structured account management team environment in which:

- Teams of individuals are developed to handle delegated responsibilities for each of the specific segments of the client's project.
- Account management teams are created, each composed of:
  - an account executive
  - an account manager or managers, depending on the complexity of managing each specific account
  - a client services representative
  - an operations team, including
    - a program manager
    - telemarketing sales supervisors
    - telemarketing quality assurance representatives
    - telemarketing sales representatives

The agency structure creates an entire team of talented specialists working in concert to assure proper development of, and execution on, each program. The process also includes detailed, daily communications between the agency and its clients.

Note: *By definition, the agency approach calls for a major emphasis on education and training programs that are maintained on an ongoing basis.*

The account management team works toward the success of that program from the moment it comes in the door, and it continues to work together to improve the program throughout its test phases and its rollout. The agency structure provides for a strong focus of talent and commitment to the success of each program.

Result: *The agency structure allows for planned and anticipated growth patterns and for excellent execution on the programs of the clients who make that growth possible.*

How Your Client/Program Mix Affects Account Management Staffing Requirements

The makeup of your client/program mix will have a great deal to do with how you structure your account management team, particularly at the operations level. After you have developed a clear understanding of the kind of telemarketing expansion you want and how it fits into the marketing plan, you should consider your particular applications and the difference between the capabilities of your organization and those of others. Your role in the marketplace will help determine the structure that will work best for you.

What kind of programs do you perform?

- Are you working for one primary client or for a number of different clients?
- Are you working all business-to-business, all business-to-consumer, or a mixture of each?
- Are you working with a single program or with multiple programs?
- If you are working with multiple programs, are they all similar or do they vary dramatically?
- Are you working with tangible products (such as computer hardware), intangible products (such as computer software), or services?
- Are you gathering information, performing pre-selling actives, or actively closing sales over the phone?

There are six primary types of telemarketing applications which you might be doing. Although each can stand alone in any telemarketing effort, two or more of the applications may be combined on any project to meet the needs of the client.

The areas of application are:

1. Market research/survey/information capture
2. Lead generation
3. Lead qualification
4. Appointment setting
5. Fundraising
6. Direct selling of a product or service

Just as each project application will require varying types of telemarketing techniques, they will also affect how your structure needs to take shape. If you are working with telecommunications projects, travel-related programs, financial services, and insurance programs, each type of project will require differing expertise and slightly different account management structure to best support that expertise.

Even when a company uses the agency structure, it may not always be used to the same extent on each program. Some accounts require only one account manager, while accounts with more complicated and/or varied projects will requrie more than one account manager. Other accounts will not need the same complexity and depth of account management.

Note to In-house Operations: *An in-house operation may do quite well without a full-fledged agency approach because of the focus on a single product or product line. But aggressive, growth-oriented in-house shops will be well served to create modified or simplified versions of the agency approach for their account management structures.*

The service agency structure dramatically increases the company's probability of success by providing the depth of talent and the focused expertise that those accounts demand.

If you are planning for growth and you want to be a major force in telemarketing, how do you do it? It's an easy answer. You do it with a service agency structure and comprehensive account management teams.

You can start with the old-school system, but if you're going to grow, you have to be ready to recognize when one or two people just can't do it all any more.

How do you know when it's time?

- You may know from experience.
- You may know from instinct.
- Or—most likely—from a little bit of both.

If you're smart, you'll know because the structure you have planned for begins to need to be filled in. But if you want to grow successfully, you've got to recognize when the handwriting is on the wall. And you need to recognize that fact *before* you discover that far too many mistakes are being made.

HOW TO STRUCTURE AHEAD OF GROWTH

As important as planning structure is, it is not enough; you must also make sure that you structure *ahead* of growth. The only way to get structured ahead of growth is to do it. In both the organizational structure and the project management structure, that means planning for change, planning for the costs involved, and taking the advance structuring actions required to meet your projections. The tougher part for most managers is to actually *spend* the money on the new structure *before* it is needed.

How To Create a Structure for Modular Expansion

You can start by building modules. It's very much like automating on 100 phones and making sure that the system will accommodate the company as it expands to 500 CRTs. If you automate, the key is to look for a system that you can gradually expand in increments by adding on additional modules of the same system. It makes no sense to set up an automated system that you have to discard whenever you need to grow.

The same is true for any part of your organizational structure. You want a clearly defined, expandable organizational system that fits your particular needs. You should set up systems that get the job done at existing levels of production, but that can expand as needed by adding on additional modules of the same system. Then you simply have to decide how much of that predetermined system you need, at any given time, to handle your existing volume levels and to accommodate your growth plans for the business.

To determine these structures:

1. Define your existing strengths and weaknesses in:
   - training
   - marketing
   - personnel
   - operations
   - account management
   - financial administration
2. Structure the models for those areas.
3. Determine what needs to be done in each area to fill in the structure and begin to evolve your structure accordingly.

Part of the process of designing modules which allow progressive and necessary structural changes is to look back at your origins and your history:

- What has shaped you to this point?
- How has your vision changed and how is it likely to change in the future?
- How have you adapted the structure in the past to adjust to growth and change?
- What key structure elements have remained both strong and flexible?

You need to answer the historical questions that provide you with a frame of reference; the answers can give you a better perspective from which to work. Review the lessons you have learned and your current level of knowledge. Your plan for further structuring must take those things into account so you can integrate where you have been, where you are, and where you are going. You have to take the whole of what you are and create the new structure so you capitalize on and extend the best of what you have. Take all the resources and energies and personalities involved and combine them in a way that will create a model for progressive growth and expansion of your structure.

Expansion Capability Projections

When you begin to structure ahead of growth, you:

- Determine what you can handle from a growth standpoint;
- Establish the structure and personnel requirements to achieve those growth levels;
- Take actions that allow you to grow in structured modules as the company's growth calls for additional personnel to adequately fulfill those roles;

- Refuse to accept any amounts or types of business that will exceed your ability to handle them at your expected standards of performance.

If a telemarketing company wants to stay ahead of growth, it starts by determining its expansion needs and capabilities, remembering its maximum limits.

EXAMPLE: XYZ Telemarketing has 240 phones currently in place, with 195 in regular use. The current "Not to Exceed" limit is 335 phones. The company's management has projected short-term growth from current levels to 290 active phones within six months, with plans to increase the "Not to Exceed" limit to 380.

In structuring for the projected expansion, the company must plan for all the additional facility and equipment expansion capabilities that will be required, but that is neither enough nor the first priority. If they find themselves with the additional facility, but without the personnel to manage and supervise it, the additional physical capacity will be unproductive.

Growth Key: *The company's first priority for expansion is to develop the additional* personnel *required to manage and supervise the expansion.*

Since they know that the first step in expansion is an additional 100 active phones within six months—and they operate under a 1 : 8 supervision ratio—management has determined that they cannot delay in beginning to develop, promote, and train the following additional personnel:

- four quality assurance representatives,
- six sales supervisors, and
- two program managers.

They also need to plan for the additional reserve capacity to bring their total number of phones to 360 within six months.

Recognize that you will be cutting profitability temporarily while you build your facility and personnel beyond your current day-to-day needs. If your next increase is going to be 100 phones, you should hire close to the full complement of management and supervisory people you will need at the new facility, while running the current facility.

Important: *You can then train them under the closer control and observation capabilities you have with the existing situation.*

That is especially good if you've been growing very fast. Using the existing situation gives a little bit of rest to a lot of people who have been taxed with a heavy work load during the development stage of that new business. It's the ideal place and time to train. In addition to the greater availability of time for classroom training, the newer people get strong support in their OJT (on-the-job training) from experienced personnel.

Key Point: *With the extra people on staff, no one has to fly by the seat of their pants or be overtaxed by the extra training and added effort that is caused by the growth.*

The Importance of Avoiding Restrictive Overstructuring

Sometimes bigger than the problem of structuring ahead of growth is making sure you aren't structuring too far ahead. It's a delicate balance. If you implement fixed structure too far ahead of anticipated growth, your bottom line will disappear. Yet you can't be structured behind the growth or precisely at your present volume levels. You have to start with the minimum amount necessary to stay slightly ahead of growth, then add to the structure as you grow.

Not only is there no one right structure, but what is right for you today may not be right for you next year. If you think that success is just a matter of doing your planning and structuring once and then executing, you're going to be very surprised. It is an ongoing process.

It's important to not overstructure from more than a budgetary standpoint. It's better to have your key players putting out that extra effort and remaining a little lean in your structure to maintain the flexibility to adjust the structure as needed. Maintaining adaptability during rapid growth periods is a major challenge. As you develop more momentum, the systems themselves become more restrictive.

It is all too easy to let the structure dictate the activity of the organization. That is exactly the opposite of how it should operate. If you allow the structure to decide what your company can and cannot do, the structure will soon have the company in a squeeze that will strangle its ability to act innovatively. Structure—like policy—should be a guideline, not a girdle.

Remember: *The purpose of the structure is to allow the people who* are *the company the flexibility to operate most effectively and productively.*

How to Avoid "Double Jeopardy" Structuring

In the early stages of growth, your budget may not be able to support hiring or promoting separate individuals into distinct positions handling relatively one-dimensional tasks. During this period, the multi-talented individuals will be critical to your growth and development. As much as you appreciate them at that time, however, you must provide them—and the company—with backups who can assist them during heavy-load periods and fill in when they are absent.

Tip: *In the early stages of development, look for multi-talented people who can handle more than one area while developing the required personnel to promote when the need arises.*

Caution: *Although the initial structuring for growth will almost certainly demand that a number of key people* are *multi-talented, it is important that you do not create weak points in the structure.*

> **EXAMPLE:** It might seem tempting from a cost standpoint to have the director of operations also be the head of training. But the reality of the situation is quite the contrary. Among other things, if that one person leaves the company or is out sick, you've lost two key positions. That's called double jeopardy, and it's not a fun game to play.

You can avoid the potential problems of double jeopardy, but doing so requires clear insight and careful planning—combined with patience on your part and on the part of your staff in the early stages of the process.

Depending on your budget, your inclinations, and the potential backup talent available, two approaches may be taken:

1. Formally hire the backups on a part-time basis as assistants, while they continue in actively productive positions in closely related areas of the company.
2. Informally appoint the backups to provide support and learn the job before making the position official.

The first option is more traditional, more risky, and more expensive. Aside from the cost of wages, neither you nor the individuals in the backup roles know—however thoroughly you have screened them—if they will be happy and effective in their duties. If the backup role doesn't work out, they may feel they have no alternative but to leave the company if they have to resign the position or are removed from it.

The second option, while unconventional, offers several advantages:

1. The arrangement allows for a test of the need for, and value of, the position.
2. It provides a test of the person filling the role before making the position a formal one—whether part-time or full-time.
3. If the person isn't capable of handling the job on an ongoing basis, or if he or she doesn't like the work, it is easy to let the person resume full-time activity in his or her other position without shame or loss of face.
4. If the person does work out and the budget later limits you to increase it to an official part-time position, the person still feels that it is a reward;
5. The second option provides an opportunity for developing and hiring people from within the company.
7. When the demands in the area require additional support, expansion is much easier and more comfortable.

Will your people accept the idea? They will if you handle it properly. Make sure you let them know:

- That the company is growing and that additional growth may require more support and additional positions in the future;
- That you are thinking about a new support position, but you are not ready to budget for it or to make it a formal part of the company structure;
- That you are considering an informal test of position;
- That you are considering them for the test, by having them devote part of their time in the new area . . . at no increase in compensation;
- The reasons why you are considering them, including the strengths you see and what you feel they might bring to the job;

- Precisely what you would expect of them in their current position and in the additional role;
- That you see the situation as a growth opportunity for the company and for them that it could lead to the formal creation of a position.

As you conclude the discussion, remind them that it is an exploratory conversation, and that you are not ready to make a decision. Ask them to think about the possibility, and if they decide they might want to try it, ask them to specify:
- What value they feel the position could bring to company;
- How they feel they could handle current work if some of their time is being devoted to other areas;
- What they feel they could bring to the work.

When people actively start assisting in an area, make the announcement informally to those people who they will be involved with in the work. It is enough to say that the person has offered to help out in area for a while.

Remember: *No matter which route you choose to take, those backup people must then be thoroughly trained.*

Your purpose is neither to give the appearance of providing backup support nor to cut expenses. You are working to establish true depth of support in the organization and to manage costs. Unless the backup personnel are given comprehensive training, you are kidding yourself and your people. They will have very little chance of developing their potential talent so they can truly become the valuable backup support you want them to be.

HOW TO BUILD AND MAINTAIN A TELEMARKETING TALENT POOL

For telemarketing companies that wish to grow, the biggest problem remains the same: finding excellent people who are already telemarketers and ready to be promoted . . . or even finding excellent people who are willing to make a career in telemarketing.

Amid all of your hopes and dreams for expansion *now,* you may have no choice but *not* to grow if you can't find enough people.

If you are not in the position to bring on a lot of top talent:

- Target talent for a couple of key positions that *must* be afforded.
- Be prepared to work your tail off while you get into the position of being able to afford the additional talent.
- Focus on identifying, training, developing, and promoting the very best talent from within.

Reminder: *The need to "home grow" leadership personnel automatically defines that you don't hire and keep your entry-level talent at too cheap a labor rate.*

The Importance of Investing in Top Talent

The most productive attitude to take toward managing growth is that it is best to pay at or a little above the going market rate so you can always select from the best in the labor market. Of course, you never want to be so high above it that your operation becomes burdened with costs that require you to charge the client more than you should have to.

There are other philosophies where people simply try to figure out ways to pay under the labor marketplace rates. But, sooner or later, they learn the meaning of "there's no such thing as free lunch." This really is a case where you get what you pay for.

Caution: *Whatever you decide to pay your entry level personnel, it's important to understand the consequences.*

A key to managing the costs of the service agency structure is the expense of the top people in the account management team. You generally need an agency structure to attract the kind of people who can handle the account management position, but there are three problems with getting those people from the outside:

1. They are expensive (and usually overpriced).
2. For quite a long period of time, they don't know your company well enough to do an exceptional job.
3. They may never fit in with your company culture and team chemistry.

As a result, you ideally want to develop those people from within the organization.

Warning: *If you're not hiring the kind of people who are capable of handling larger volume accounts as your business grows, you're just going to Peter Principle them by calling them "Account Managers."*

THE REWARDS OF EFFECTIVE STRUCTURING

Situations may arise that cause you to completely rethink your plans, even when the structure is very close to being put in place. When such a situation happens, you have to take a realistic look at the pros and the cons of the situation, examine the strength of your structure, and make the decision that is best for the business.

> **EXAMPLE:** The following situation happened several years ago when we were working on becoming automated. Our parent company was supportive of the idea, and a great deal of work had been done to prepare for the step. The automation required making some significant changes in our organizational structure, and the necessary plans had been drawn up. We had talked to our staff about doing the automation project and had gotten them excited about it. They had set the objective to become the first top-quality manual shop in the country to automate . . . and to do it under a unique structure.
>
> Just as we were about to embark on the project, a major conflict arose. We

suddenly had the opportunity to take on a huge contract with a major telecommunications company. It was a wonderful opportunity for a lot of top-quality business and a wonderful reference. And it promised to be a very profitable project, if the job was done right.

It also required a great deal of very rapid growth in our part to handle such a huge and complex program. The growth would require:

- Developing an entirely new facility.
- Hiring and training hundreds of new TSRs.
- Crosstraining many of the existing TSRs.
- Promoting and training many management and supervisory people.

Although the new opportunity was going to stretch the company to the limit of its operational capabilities, management knew they could do the job and do it well if we mobilized all of our forces and concentrated our full energy on taking care of all of the clients, including the new one.

The company had an underlying commitment to excellence. We decided that we could not meet that commitment while starting both the automation project and the new client at the same time. We had a decision to make. Here are the factors we faced.

Comparing the Values

Automation:

- would be very helpful for securing new types of projects.
- would be very expensive.
- would take an extended period of time to complete.
- could be expected to bring some operational problems during the period of implementation.

The new client's project would provide:

- immediate growth for the company.
- new opportunities for the development of personnel.
- opportunities for new types of high quality projects.
- immediate additional profits.

We couldn't justify a position of rejecting the new growth and profitability opportunities, especially when our analysis showed that not automating wouldn't cause us any long-term difficulties in maintaining our long-range market position. As a result, we had to completely set aside the plans for the automation project and the new structure.

Management was forced to make a hard choice, and the huge success we had with the client's project proved that we made the right one. Had we tried to continue with our plans to automate under a new structure at the same time, it would have pushed us past our capabilities. We would have failed.

A major factor in that success was the telemarketing service agency structure that had been developed previously. It was ideal to meet the situation. It brought the required depth of strength to support the dramatic growth activities that were required, yet did so by simply expanding the structure that was already in place.

It's not uncommon to hear in-house telemarketers talk about having to deal with large, unexpected projects or hear telemarketing agency people talk about having to deal with overflow. But you can meet the challenges if you:

- really know how to manage productive telemarketing;
- are well structured ahead of growth;
- manage your labor market and bring on top talent; and,
- have developed deep management talent and reserves.

Perhaps the most important words to keep in mind in structuring are *perspective* and *flexibility*. You need a clear perspective of where you are going. You need a clear perspective of where the market is and where you fit into that market. You need the perspective of your organizational resources and how best to structure them to channel those resources most effectively. And you must have the flexibility to make the changes necessary to revise that structure as new situations and opportunities call for change.

Key Point: *If you're properly structured ahead of growth, you really shouldn't have to turn away significant growth opportunities.*

Realistically, there is no way to do the ideal advance structuring, so that you are completely prepared to take advantage of extremely large program opportunities that may present themselves. Programs of exceptional size, complexity, and urgency usually can't be taken on gracefully without extending yourself and the company. Yet, if you have a deep enough structure of talented and dedicated people, you can meet the challenge.

24 KEYS TO STRUCTURING FOR GROWTH

- It is the combination of a specific telemarketing company's unique factors, more than a particularly popular or currently accepted corporate organizational system, that will determine the best structure for the company.
- The telemarketing organization's structure must be flexible enough to allow the company to change—or the structure will inhibit the company's growth.
- The growing telemarketing organization needs to make sure two kinds of structure are in place: the overall organizational structure and the project management structure.
- Companies of different sizes require different structures. The needs are different

for a 20-phone operation than they are for a 100-phone operation, and those needs change even more dramatically as a firm grows to 200, 500 or 1,500 phones.

- Companies of the same size, but with different growth objectives, may require very different structures.
- The process of structuring returns you to your original vision, your business philosophy, your commitment, and the plans you have for shaping the company.
- The process of identifying, planning, and budgeting for positions that have to be filled immediately and the ones that will be needed with growth starts with identifying the skills and preferences of the top person in the organization.
- Determining your needs includes clear and honest appraisal of your particular strengths and weaknesses and your developmental plans for the company.
- Planning for the growth of the structure includes taking into consideration both current and future personnel needs and resources.
- The growth of a company (and the success of its client's programs) can be made or broken by the company's choice of which way it will go for account management structure: old school or full agency.
- The old school approach to the structuring and operation of a telemarketing company fails to meet the principles of controlled management of growth.
- The service agency structure allows for planned and anticipated growth patterns and for excellent execution on the programs of the clients who make that growth possible.
- By definition, the agency approach calls for a major emphasis on education and training programs that are maintained on an ongoing basis.
- The makeup of your client/program mix will have a great deal to do with the structure of your account management team, particularly at the operations level.
- In-house operations may do well without a full-fledged agency structure, but growth-oriented in-house companies can benefit from modified versions of it.
- Planning structure is not enough; you must also make sure that you structure ahead of growth with an expandable, modular approach.
- Start with the minimum amount of structure necessary to stay slightly ahead of growth, then add to the structure as you grow.
- The company's first priority for expansion is to develop the additional personnel required to manage and supervise the expansion.
- The structuring process is more than doing your planning and structuring once and then executing; it is an ongoing process.
- It is important not to overstructure; it's better to have your key players putting out extra effort and remain lean and flexible in your structure.
- It is all too easy to let the structure dictate the activity of the organization. That is exactly the opposite of how it should operate.
- Although the initial structuring for growth will almost certainly demand that a number of key people are multi-talented, it is important that you do not create weak points in the structure.

- The rate of pay you set for entry-level people will have a dramatic effect on the quality of talent you have available internally to draw upon to flesh out your structure as the company grows.
- If you're properly structured ahead of growth, you really shouldn't have to turn away significant growth opportunities.

Success obsoletes the organization that created it.
—Esping & Masterson

Cost is the Father and Compensation is the
Mother of Progress.   *J. G. Holland*

Chapter *4*

Money Matters

When dealing with financial management, there are two different viewpoints to consider. They are explained well by Nido Qubein, a premier speaker and management consultant. Asked what $1 + 1$ equals, he answers in this way: "It depends; am I buying or am I selling?"

The quality of the financial management of a growing telemarketing company can easily spell the difference between continuing prosperity and fiscal failure. With growth and increased size comes increased costs. Growth brings the need for more people and for more talented people who will be better paid. Added people means more training and increased training staff. Growth brings more physical plant, equipment, and phone lines. Growth may require additional locations in a single labor market or going into multiple labor markets. You may have to upgrade to an automated environment. These additional costs must be well managed.

When one telemarketing CEO first became involved in the financial end of telemarketing—including the questions about facilities expansion, automation versus manual systems, telecommunication options, depreciation, amortization, and the rest—he called his old college economics professor and asked if there were any simple solutions to financial management. The professor answered: "Yes sir, there is. Get an M.B.A.—a Monster Bank Account."

That CEO has long since discovered that even a Monster Bank Account can dwindle to nothing unless you take control of the financial management of the company, starting from Day 1.

The three greatest cost centers to evaluate and keep under control for effective financial management in outbound telemarketing are:

1. Variable labor cost
2. Fixed labor cost
3. Variable phone cost

These three items typically consume about 60% of a healthy outbound telemarketing firm's revenue. Phones and labor, on the financial side, are what this business is all about. How both are managed will help determine just how healthy your telemarketing business is.

The temptation is to keep the costs at absolute minimums in each area. That is not always the best approach. Expenses need to be kept in line while considering the potential impact—both positively and negatively—of each lowered cost. You can simply try to operate at low costs, but it is more important to diligently manage reasonable costs.

Key Point: *Careful cost* optimization *is more important than sweeping cost reduction.*

There is no standard or ideal wage that must be paid to phone personnel. The average wage in Omaha for an outbound business-to-consumer TSR in 1989 was about $6.50 an hour. Some firms pay a guaranteed $6.00, some pay $7.00, and some pay $7.50. Idelman Telemarketing pays up to $8.25 guaranteed, and—with sales bonuses and profit sharing—our top producers can, over the course of a year, earn as much as $10.00 per hour.

To the best of our knowledge, all of the companies referenced above are financially healthy. The key is not simply what any one company is paying, but how that cost relates to the revenue generated per unit of measure.

Note: *Calculating all revenues and costs on a "per billable hour" basis allows you to readily compare major cost centers to revenues.*

Revenues come from billable hours in an hourly rate shop. Even if you work on a compensation-per-sale program, it is wise to translate that revenue per sale into revenue per hour by multiplying the rate per sale by your actual sales per hour. You may not bill the client that way, but it is the best way to keep internal tabs on your costs of doing business.

If all other things are equal, a company paying $7.50 per hour to TSRs and generating $29 in revenue for that same hour will be more profitable than a company that pays $6.00 but generates just $23. The fact is that the $7.50 is only 25.86% of $29.00, while the $6.00 is 26.09% of $23.00.

That's an example of cost/revenue relationship, and . . .

Key Point: *The effective management of the cost revenue relationships is the key to keeping an outbound telemarketing business financially healthy.*

ESTABLISHING COST/REVENUE RELATIONSHIPS

In your early financial planning, you must establish your initial costs and cost/revenue relationships. The first step in that process is to understand what the guideline for those relationships should be.

The Ideal Financial Model

When working up your financial model, you should start with a simple but critical rule:

If it costs you "X," you have to sell it for "X" plus.

The actual amount of the "plus" will be critical to maintaining a healthy profit level.

The key guideline to live by is to achieve a 40% contribution to margin (the amount of gross profit before the fixed expenses are deducted). Normally, fixed expense should be no more than 15 to 25% of revenue, such that net (before tax) profit equals 15 to 25%.

Financial Model: *Gross profit at 40% and fixed expenses at 15 to 25%, leaving a 15 to 25% margin.*

That's the ideal model for a healthy telemarketing service company. Of course, in-house operations can—and often do—look at this issue quite differently.

Not only is that higher margin fair for a telemarketing service company, but—more importantly—it defines the ongoing health of the organization. Furthermore, since the industry needs more and better people, telemarketing companies must have the ability to pay for them.

With good breaks and a steady volume flow, a telemarketing company can survive and even thrive on a 10% to 12% margin . . . but 20% is the goal to shoot for.

Key Point: *A 20% margin gives a company the wherewithal to attract, train, and retain quality personnel; to spend some money on R&D; to forge ahead with new innovative ideas.*

Determining the Fixed/Variable Budget Ratio

A basic but important concept confuses many people:

Fixed expense varies per billable hour as the volume changes, while variable costs remain relatively stable per billable hour throughout volume changes.

Once that is clearly understood, you should also understand that the method for determining the best budget mix of variable and fixed expenses may vary. You can establish more positions as variable, with minimal fixed expense. That is the approach often taken by smaller firms and startup companies with limited cash resources. Or you can make fixed expenses a higher portion of your budget. As you grow, doing so is almost essential.

EXAMPLE: In 1982 our average billable rate was $24.88, the variable phone costs were $6.75, and total variable costs were just under the budgeted $15. That gave a 40% contribution to margin, which was right at formula. The fixed expense was only 11.6%. The founders were the only fixed management expense. The company had just one account and all of the economies of scale associated with that fact. Although the result was a 30% profit margin, there was not enough fixed expense to build a healthy company.

Then the company began to experience significant growth. By 1985 the variable labor costs had increased from $7.75 to $11.60. Since the phone costs were still $6.75, the total was up 31% to $18.35, and this accounted only for the variable phone and labor costs.

How does such a dramatic change in costs come about? There are two reasons:

1. When you're small, you can maintain lower fixed expenses by operating with a lot of hourly people and just a couple of managers who perform multiple duties. As you grow, the economies of scale of the smaller and less-diversified company do not hold.
2. As you grow in size and substance, both fixed and variable expenses increase. Depth is required in management positions, in marketing, in training and in account management. A management team is needed for each account, whatever the number of hours the account is running.

Survival during such significant growth depends on:

- constant awareness of the changing expense ratios;
- refinement of the budgeted allowances; and
- adjustment of rates to reflect the changes.

Tip: *Have a healthy respect for fixed expenses, but don't fear increasing them.*

Without the careful addition of fixed expense in the areas required to support the growth, the telemarketing company can collapse like the proverbial house of cards.

There are two methods for setting up a financial model in this area.

- One is to start with your profit margin goal and work backwards, calculating what fixed and variable costs can be set to achieve the desired margin.
- The second method works in reverse sequence, first determining what the realistic budget for variable wages will have to be.

We prefer to work with the second method. If you use it, too, first determine what costs will be classified as variable.

- Will the cost for TSRs be there if volume goes away?
  No, because they won't be on the phones if there is no phone work.
- Material handlers?
  They will have only a few days of inventory and housecleaning before they're gone.
- The manual clerical and keypunch costs? Programmers?
  Variable, because the amount of work for them drops with the volume. If the volume gets too low, client services supervisors and management personnel can handle the audits.
- Verifications and security?
  Variable again, because the amount needed depends on production levels.
- Supervisors?
  Variable, because as volume shrinks, supervisors become TSRs in very quick fashion.

The Worst Case/Best Case Formula

As you grow larger and larger, you must put on increasing amounts of fixed expense . . . and not just more absolute expense. During very rapid growth periods, you may find that nearly 100% of what would have been profits on your additional revenues become fixed expense instead. Prior to entering that steep growth curve, it's wise to evaluate the potential impact of both "best case" and "worst case" scenarios.

The Challenge: *Measure everything against your worst-case revenue stream expectations.*

> **EXAMPLE:** By the time we had grown to 600 active phone stations, the management was comfortable that—barring an Armageddon—their worst-case situation would still allow them to run at least 300 phones. They then measured the fixed expense against the best case of 600 producing phones, and against the worst case of 300 phones. That established a "worst case/best case" range for fixed expense percentages from "X" at 300 phones to about "½X" at 600.

The range from "X" down to "½X" is considered as incremental profit. Fixed expense is the only place incremental profits can be managed. The variable expense, effectively, is fixed in relation to your billable hours. Once you know what the phone expense and the TSR and other hourly rates will be, you can—with a high degree of confidence—structure your internal salary administration around those formulas.

How to Maintain Flexibility for Changing Conditions

All of the analysis, planning, and management that is done must be tempered by one powerful business axiom: Whatever factors your decisions have been based on, expect them to change.

Warning: *Inflexibility and the refusal to recognize the approach of changing conditions has killed many companies.*

It is that principle that cuts at the heart of rate cutting strategies. It's a basic principle. Wages go up. The costs of goods go up. Even if you have a period of general price decreases or volume purchasing discounts, sooner or later those prices will go up. If you become very price-competitive by having an 8% margin at $22, what happens if the conditions that those tight margins are based on change considerably?

You can't safely assume that you won't be caught in that situation. You have to plan for it and respond when you see it coming.

As you grow and need to recruit more labor, you have to pay more for it unless you can remain the only telemarketing game in town. But you don't remain the only game in town if you do well.

> **EXAMPLE:** In 1981, we were the only locally headquartered national outbound shop in Omaha. Being virtually the only game in town had its advantages and its

disadvantages. The competition for outbound people was not fierce, but the general public had only a limited awareness of outbound telemarketing as a job opportunity or career path.

Today there are more than 30 companies hiring Omaha's telemarketing talent! Telemarketing has an enormously higher image and increased profile in the city and people are much more in tune with the medium. But Omaha is a small city. As a result, we have heavy labor market rate competition.

If part-time people with a base of $4.00 an hour have the opportunity to make a $5.00 base somewhere else, you can expect to see some percentage of those people leave. So you have to show performance incentives and merit increases to help maintain stability. That's going to affect your cost structures, and you have to be prepared to deal with the changes.

Labor and Phone Cost Guidelines

The two most significant expenses in telemarketing are the cost of labor and the cost of phones.

When either of these areas exceeds budgeted amounts and percentages, the bottom line is quickly affected. As a result, establishing proper guidelines for these two areas is critical to the success of the operation.

Total payroll costs normally represent 40–50% of the budget, including the "hidden costs" of unemployment compensation, FICA, workmen's compensation, vacation allowances, etc. The range, while relatively large, will be determined by the size of the organization and its philosophies about personnel quality. The variable/fixed payroll breakdown generally approximates the 80/20 rule of distribution. The fixed telephone costs may range from 0.5–2.0%, depending primarily on the length of the calling day/week and the amount of reserve facility maintained. Variable phone usage generally accounts for 14–18%, and total phone costs should fall into the 15–20% range.

At the equivalent of a $26.00 to $28.00 rate, the combined total of personnel and phone costs usually consumes between 55 and 70% of a telemarketing center's budget. That's an awfully big bite! If you want to achieve a margin of 20%, that leaves as little as 10% for all other expenses.

Pitfall to Avoid: *The strong temptation is to cut costs to the absolute bottom end of the ranges . . . or lower.*

For a company striving for excellence, that is a serious mistake. The rates a service bureau can charge (or the size of the budgets that in-house telemarketing shops can win) are ultimately decided by the quality and quantity of service the unit can provide. In large part, those are determined by the quality and quantity of the labor and phones. Cutting costs too deeply in these areas immediately opens the door to mediocrity.

Although labor costs are in the 40–50% range, commitment to the value of truly talented people to the achievement of excellence will mean that you can expect to be at 46% to 52% total payroll cost. Of that, 38% to 40% is devoted to variable wages and 8% to 12% is devoted to fixed personnel costs.

Payroll and Phone Cost Ranges

Fixed payroll costs:	8–10%
Variable payroll costs:	32–42%
Fixed telephone costs:	0.5– 2%
Variable phone usage:	14–18%
Total Payroll & Phone Cost:	54.5–72%

Why would companies be willing to come in at (and sometimes exceed) the high end of the range? They pay for their conviction about quality people and services. Often, you will find that their personnel—both TSRs and fixed staff—have wages at the top of the market.

Note: *The top outbound telemarketing companies not only pay at the top of the scale, they strive to stay at the top of the scale!*

Why? Because they have found that it pays big dividends. In managing growth, the additional talent they can attract and hold by taking on that extra cost helps to reduce the companies' headaches, increase their productivity, and keep the clients happier.

It's not a case of throwing money around recklessly, and you can't allow the situation to get out of hand. There has to be a balance between the wages you pay and the productivity of the labor pool.

Remember: *When you pay more, you need more productivity, and your personnel have to understand and respond to that need.*

Still, the exceptional companies wouldn't have it any other way. They will continue to invest an extra 6–10% in order to do a 20–30% better job.

HOW TO KEEP PHONE COSTS IN LINE

When you work to keep costs in line so that you can remain competitive on the rates you charge, it is tempting to focus on possible reductions in phone costs. Phone costs consume a significant portion of the total budget.

Recent developments in the telecommunications industry have created both a large number of choices and a great deal of confusion for telemarketing companies.

Caution: *Cost should be a consideration in making your decision, but it should not be the only one.*

There are many phone vendors to choose from, with varying levels of cost and quality. In addition to the cost, the quality of the service must be considered. By definition, telemarketing is phone-service sensitive.

How to Tell if You Should Use Alternative Carriers

Alternative carriers may or may not be effective for you. Most common carriers can offer cost savings at some level, but you may have to trade off transmission quality, reliability, and service or repair response time. Because telecommunications is changing so rapidly, these criteria are as subject to change as any area of consideration in telemarketing. Dozens of different common carriers and re-sellers offer traditional types of service, satellite transmission, microwave transmission, and the newest technology in fiber optics.

Depending on your applications, you may find that having a combination of carriers is of value. If one of the services goes down, you still have at least partial service available. Yet reduced loading of lines may cost you the savings you might otherwise have had, and still give you the usual problems with which to contend.

Major factors to consider in determining the potential benefits of alternative carriers are:

1. calling patterns and frequencies
2. calling times, and
3. average call length.

You may find common carriers to be particularly advantageous if you are a strictly daytime business. If you use a computerized phone switch, common carriers may provide some additional benefits. The benefits and quality will vary from one area of the country to another and also will be affected by the locations you are calling. As a result, you should test any long distance service thoroughly enough from your location to know where you can call without a significant loss of quality.

How to Analyze Alternative Phone Rates

You also need to do an analysis of the rates based on your own usage patterns. Because any information published on phone rates and comparative analysis is subject to being outdated before it reaches the public, we will not attempt to provide a "current" rate analysis here. Yet, while not current, the following information and comparative rate analysis can serve you as a guide for how to do an analysis that is current and meaningful to you.

The essence of a comparative rate analysis is the calculation of effective net rates and comparative costs for each vendor being considered, based upon your actual usage (connected time per line per hour) for the month and for each class of service for the day parts you use. You will normally have established use levels for each rate period.

> **EXAMPLE:** If you average 62% connected time (the time that your TSR's are actually "connected" during a telemarketing hour) per hour calling Monday through Thursday from 6 PM to 10 PM, you will have approximately 40 connected hours per line per month during the Evening rate period. With the same percentage of connected time and calling from 5 PM to 10 PM Monday through Friday, the figure will be approximately 60 connected hours. If you call from 5 PM to 11 PM Monday through Friday, the connected time will be around 80 hours. Businesses calling constantly from 8 AM to 5 PM Monday through Friday at the 62% connected time figure will normally use about 120 hours per line per month.

The 62% figure of connected time per hour represents an average that can be achieved with good management in most calling situations. Looser management may result in considerably less connected time. Long business presentations may result in a higher percentage of connected time per hour, and should be adjusted accordingly.

One of the first points to establish is the rates that are in effect in the area you are calling. No general analysis is accurate for all locations of the country, because the calling areas or bands differ based on the originating location of the call. Even when the comparison is only for the 48 contiguous state calling area (traditionally designated as Band 5 by AT&T), the rates will change from one area to another. Also, it is important to determine what the different designations cover. What AT&T calls "Area 5" may be called "Area 4" by another vendor.

Keep in Mind: *If you have multiple locations, simply doing one analysis comparing services is not sufficient.*

The results of the phone cost analysis often differ dramatically between geographical areas. It is possible that these geographic variations will completely reverse the cost advantages for the different services in each area.

For simplicity in explaining the study to be done and the comparative charts you might put together, we will limit our examples to the nationwide fixed bands of two different vendors in two different calling locations. They are sufficient to demonstrate the principle. The locations used in the examples are Chicago, Illinois, and Omaha, Nebraska. The companies used are AT&T and US Sprint. The comparative rates for those locations for nationwide calling during the summer of 1986 were as follows:

WATS Step Rate Cost Comparison

AT&T		(Nationwide/fixed band) Omaha, NE	US Sprint	
Day	Eve.	# Hours of Usage	Day	Eve.
15.28	10.60	0–15	12.50	9.15
14.49	9.43	15–40	11.85	9.11
12.71	8.26	40–80	12.58	9.00
12.71	8.26	80+	9.28	8.97
$7.15/hr.		Night/weekend	$6.35/hr.	
AT&T		**Chicago, IL**	**US Sprint**	
Day	Eve.	# Hours of Usage	Day	Eve.
16.45	10.70	0–15	12.34	9.33
14.66	9.52	15–40	9.53	8.30
12.84	8.36	40–80	9.52	7.36
12.84	8.36	80+	9.50	7.32
$7.25/hr.		Night/weekend	$6.75/hr.	

Daytime rates are 8 AM to 5 PM (local time) Monday through Friday. Evening rates are from 5 PM to 11 PM Sunday through Friday. The remainder of the time is Night/weekend rates. That covers the period from 11 PM to 8 AM Sunday through

Thursday and from 11 PM Friday through 5 PM Sunday. Hours are billed under the rate structure for each separate day part, and usage is accumulated separately for each.

In the example given, there are step rates for AT&T for up to 15 hours, over 15 up to 40 hours, and over 40 hours. US Sprint has an additional structure of over 40 through 80 hours. In each case, the rates are cumulative, rather than retroactive; no reduction is given on hours in each rate level as they are exceeded. Since there are step rates, with decreasing costs per hour of usage with increased use per line, the only way to find the net effect of the rate structure is to apply it to your usage patterns.

WATS Step Rate Cost Comparison

(Nationwide/**Evening**/fixed band)

Omaha, NE/ATT

Hours	Eve. Rate	Eve./40 hours	Eve./60 hours	Eve./80 hours
0–15	10.60	159.00	159.00	159.00
15–40	9.43	235.75	235.75	235.75
40+	8.26	00.00	165.20	330.40
Total/(avg. hr.)		394.75 (9.87)	559.95 (9.33)	725.15 (9.06)

Omaha, NE/US Sprint

Hours	Eve./Rate	Eve./40 hours	Eve./60 hours	Eve./80 hours
0–15	9.15	137.25	137.25	137.25
15–40	9.11	227.75	227.75	227.75
40–80	9.00	0.00	180.00	360.00
80+	8.97	0.00	0.00	17.94
Total/(avg. hr.)		365.00 (9.13)	544.50 (9.08)	725.00 (9.06)
US Sprint savings		7.5%	9.7%	0.0%

Chicago, IL/ATT

Hours	Eve. Rate	Eve./40 hours	Eve./60 hours	Eve./80 hours
0–15	10.70	160.50	160.50	160.50
15–40	9.52	238.00	238.00	238.00
40+	8.36	0.00	167.20	334.40
Total/(avg. hr.)		398.50 (9.96)	565.70 (9.43)	732.90 (9.16)

Chicago, IL/US Sprint

Hours	Eve. Rate	Eve./40 hours	Eve./60 hours	Eve./80 hours
0–15	9.33	139.95	139.95	139.95
15–40	8.30	207.50	207.50	207.50
40–80	7.36	0.00	147.20	294.40
80+	7.32	0.00	0.00	00.00
Total/(avg. hr.)		347.45 (8.69)	494.95 (8.24)	641.85 (8.02)
US Sprint savings		12.8%	12.6%	12.4%

WATS Step Rate Cost Comparison

(Nationwide/**Daytime**/fixed band)			

Omaha, Nebraska/ATT

Hours	Day Rate	Day/40 hours	Day/80 hours	Day/120 hours
0–15	15.28	229.20	229.20	229.20
15–40	14.49	362.25	362.25	362.25
40+	12.71	00.00	508.40	1016.80
Total/(avg. hr.)		591.45 (14.79)	1099.85 (13.75)	1608.25 (13.40)

Omaha, NE/US Sprint

Hours	Day Rate	Day 40/hours	Day/80 hours	Day/120 hours
0–15	12.50	187.50	187.50	187.50
15–40	11.85	296.25	296.25	296.25
40–80	12.58	0.00	503.20	503.20
80+	9.28	0.00	0.00	371.20
Total/(avg. hr.)		483.75 (12.09)	986.95 (12.34)	1358.15 (11.32)
US Sprint savings		18.2%	10.3%	15.5%

Chicago, IL/ATT

Hours	Day Rate	Day/40 hours	Day/80 hours	Day/120 hours
0–15	16.45	246.75	246.75	246.75
15–40	14.66	366.50	366.50	366.50
40+	12.84	0.00	513.60	1027.20
Total/(avg. hr.)		613.25 (15.33)	1126.85 (14.09)	1640.45 (13.67)

Chicago, IL/US Sprint

Hours	Day Rate	Day/40 hours	Day/80 hours	Day/120 hours
0–15	12.34	185.10	185.10	185.10
15–40	9.53	238.?5	238.25	238.25
40–80	9.52	0.00	380.80	380.80
80+	9.50	0.00	0.00	380.00
Total/(avg. hr.)		423.35 (10.58)	804.15 (10.05)	1184.15 (9.87)
US Sprint savings		31.0%	28.7%	27.8%

One of the first things you may notice in the analysis is that the cost advantages are very different in the two different locations. The actual Daytime rates and net costs for AT&T are significantly higher in Chicago than in Omaha. The Evening rates for AT&T are somewhat higher in Chicago. The reverse is true for Sprint; the actual rates and net costs for both Daytime and Evening are significantly lower in Chicago than in Omaha.

More important, the comparative savings are different for the two locations and for different usage levels. At the Evening 80-hour level in Omaha, the effective rates for both Sprint and AT&T are the same. For each hour beyond 80, AT&T becomes increasingly less expensive than Sprint. Without the 10% charter savings for US Sprint, which were in effect at the time the analysis was done, the AT&T service in Omaha would be less expensive than US Sprint in each Evening usage range. In Chicago, the savings on Sprint are more substantial, but the loss of the charter savings would bring the costs differences between the services to the 2.5 to 3% range.

In Nebraska, the greatest savings with US Sprint are for the Daytime usage. Again, the lack of availability of the charter savings would eliminate most of those savings. The Daytime savings in Chicago are significant and would remain so even without the 10% charter savings.

The phone cost analysis is the starting point. You must also consider your type of usage (as opposed to your amount or time of usage), including similar comparisons for issues such as the different calling bands and high frequency calling to particular LATAs.

How Call Measurement Affects Your Rates

Another part of the phone service vendor decision concerns the way the calls are measured for billing purposes. On this issue, there are two primary considerations. The first is the billing increment. The second is the accuracy of the measurement of when calls are connected.

1. Billing increments are the minimum billing measurement periods within individual calls. The length of the billing increments are set by each vendor and may vary within the different types of long-distance service each vendor offers. These increments generally range from 6 to 30 seconds. As a result, a 63-second call may be billed by one vendor as a 1.5 minute call; for another vendor, it will be billed as 1.3 minutes; for a third, it will be billed as 1.1 minutes.

   EXAMPLE: If three companies have the same rate per minute for a particular call—20¢ per minute—but have billing increments of 30 seconds, 18 seconds, and 6 seconds, your cost for the call can vary greatly. A call of exactly one minute would be billed at the same cost for all three: 20¢. However, a call of one minute and one second would be billed at three different amounts: 30¢, 26¢, and 22¢. The 30-second minimum billing increment results in a charge for that call that is over 36% higher than the charge based on 6-second increments.

Note: *This kind of variance exists not only between companies, but also between different services offered by a single company, such as AT&T's PRO WATS, Standard WATS, and Megacom.*

Reminder: *When extended over thousands (or hundreds of thousands or millions) of calls a month, the significance of the billing increments to your company's phone expense can be enormous.*

2. The second aspect of call measurement is in regard to when the call is considered to begin.

Note: *Only AT&T provides true "answer back supervision," the most accurate way of measuring connect time.*

Answer back supervision measures the connect time from the moment the party answers the phone. All the other phone companies have to use variations on that concept, and none—to date—can measure actual connect time. While they may offer "billing grace periods" of 10 to 45 seconds before time is charged, they still may measure the call from a time well before the other party answers.

If you hang up before the grace period ends, whether or not the call has been connected, you will not be charged for the call. You might get away with no charge for a small percentage of brief contact calls. But the nature of quality telemarketing is such that by the time you have identified yourself and the company you represent, asked for the proper party, and politely arranged for any later time call, you are well beyond the grace period.

The Bottom Line Result: *There may be little or no cost savings.*

In some cases, the "grace period" arrangement will cost you more. If the unanswered phone is allowed to ring a few seconds longer than normal, you wind up paying for a call that was never connected.

> **EXAMPLE:** One businessman wanted to "busy out" his hotel phone and used an alternative carrier to call his private office line across the country. Imagine his surprise when he was billed for two hours of connected time on a coast-to-coast call that was never answered!

While it is unlikely that would happen in a phone room situation, 120 unconnected calls that are billed at one-minute rates have the same effect. And that does happen.

If the vendor starts measuring the billing time 15 seconds after the number is dialed—and the phone is answered after 27 seconds—you pay for the twelve seconds of non-connected time. With the volume of calls made in telemarketing, those extra seconds and extra costs add up quickly.

Red Flag: *They can cost much or all of your savings.*

In this area, most telemarketing companies prefer to make one of two choices: either the longest grace period possible, or precise measurement of the moment the call is answered.

Advantages and Disadvantages of Other Types of Service

Foreign exchange (FX) service, tie lines, and satellite service also offer particular advantages and disadvantages. The regulations on minimum length of service, the increased costs for installation and base monthly service, and the decreasing number of cities with free local calling have reduced the cost effectiveness of these services during recent years. But if you consistently have heavy calling patterns into a metropolitan area less than 1,000 miles away, the FX line may provide good quality and be particularly cost effective—especially with the advent of the LATA system. Again, comprehensive analysis of the costs and benefits involved is required.

The need for distance-sensitive service might make a mixture of bands most effective. Some of the service vendors offer virtual banding, such as AT&T's Megacom or MCI's Prism. Virtual banding service offers one line with cumulative loading of hours, but with charges incurred for each call based upon the distance called. If your calling patterns include progressive calling across different time zones, the virtual banding usage may be a convenient and economical choice. However, make sure you consider the impact of the heavy one-time installation and/or recurring monthly fixed charges involved with those services (such as channel banks and T-Spans), which can add dramatically to the effective cost per minute used.

With the strongly competitive nature of telecommunications, other services and discount methods are continually being introduced. Special discounts have been offered for geographically decentralized, multiple-office companies. Guaranteed volume discounts—in addition to the normal discount prices on services—are now available to large users who are willing to guarantee specific minimum amounts of usage over a specified period of time.

There is an additional advantage to the availability of alternative long distance services. It's always good to have at least a few phones of an alternate company, whatever your primary choice. Although few of the telecommunications companies will admit it, having some mixture of competitive vendors' lines may provide additional leverage in negotiations for costs and service with the different companies. When that leverage works, a mixture can result in meaningful savings on miscellaneous costs and service-response time.

Using Alternative Carriers: the Opposing View

The question of whether to use the newer alternative long distance vendors or stay with the traditional carrier is a hotly contested issue. The foregoing discussion generally favors, with judicious analysis, the viewpoint that you consider all carriers.

The opposing viewpoint—with some important additional considerations— follows.

Note: *As it stands today, we consider AT&T and MCI to be the phone service vendors of choice.*

While you may save money with some of the alternative phone carriers, what you give up in transmission and repair quality often makes them a bad investment.

Reliability and sound quality are critical in the application of effective telemarketing. It's foolhardy to save 3% of your phone usage cost and try to conduct sales activities over lines that do not provide consistently clear sound quality. That will cost you sales, and it will cost you goodwill.

Key Point: *The outbound call (whether or not we like to admit it) is often an interruption for the consumer or business, and compounding that problem with poor quality sound transmission is simply unacceptable.*

In addition to the potential financial impact of the inaccurate time connect measurement, AT&T offers the added advantage of call back supervision which is the only true and ongoing way to measure the time required for your presentations and your average call length. With any other company, that measurement is only an approximation. The real time may be longer or shorter, regardless of the final cost. Virtually every other company puts you in a position of gambling that their measurement system will come out in your favor. Sometimes it does . . . and sometimes it doesn't! Our experience shows that MCI is the most accurate, after AT&T.

In our opinion, other companies simply do not give the kind of overall quality that AT&T and MCI do. The others can't give you the response and repair time you need. The newer vendors are improving, but they haven't caught AT&T or MCI.

How To Reduce Costs with Effective Day Part Mix

An important aspect of phone cost management is creating phone usage in the less-expensive day parts. If you are not operating according to a good day part mix efficiency model, the higher costs you incur may make the difference between marginal profitability and a heathy profit . . . or between surviving and not surviving.

Key Point: *A substantial portion of your calling must be done during the lower Night/ weekend rates if you are to be price competitive in consumer work.*

For the business-to-business operation, this might mean starting earlier or running later in the day to take advantage of the Night rate before 8 AM and the Evening rate after 5 PM For the consumer telemarketing firm, it means working as many hours as possible during the lowest-cost Night/weekend hours. For consumer telemarketing companies in the Eastern Time Zone, it may also mean working after 11 PM

This approach demands more thought and more effective planning of the program matrix. It requires developing management systems that will give you a good mix of calling in higher and lower phone rate times. It also keeps your phone costs down. By having a substantial part of your calling done in the lower-cost hours, you can effectively reduce your net cost per hour by several percent.

There will always be some month-to-month variation in the phone costs.

EXAMPLE: In the early 1980's, efficient consumer telemarketers knew their phone cost would be between $6.50 and $6.75 an hour.* With 10 phones, that extra 15¢ or 25¢ an hour doesn't seem like a lot. When you grow to 20,000 hours a month, you realize that a quarter an hour difference is more than a minor expense.

Note: *As of the first quarter of 1989, a savings of 1¢ per minute on phone usage costs meant a difference of more than $400,000 a year for Idelman Telemarketing, Inc.*

The Most Effective Daypart Mix Models

The key is understanding what is happening on an ongoing basis. You should use a simple monitoring system that is based on percentage distribution of phone usage at the effective hourly rates for the different day parts.

* Phone costs have become considerably lower as a result of increased competition since the break-up of the Bell System. The average cost is now closer to $5.00 per hour, but the principle is still the same.

- For consumer telemarketing operations:
  - Establish a maximum of 75% usage at Evening rates and a minimum of 25% at Night/weekend rates.
  - Shoot for a 65/35 mix as an ideal.

EXAMPLE: With the rates in effect in early 1985, we could predict what the phone cost per connected hour would be. With good line loading, the base rate Monday through Friday would be $7.55. With the sales force connected 62% of each hours (what a good manual shop will do), the effective variable phone cost for the weekdays would be $4.68. With the night/weekend rates at $5.79, the 62% connect factor meant the variable cost would be $3.59 per calling hour on weekends.

With various mixes of evening and weekend calling, management could dramatically impact the overall effective rate. The effect of the various mixes was as follows:

Mix Eve./Weekend	Effective Rate	$ Savings per hour	% Savings
100%/ 0%	$4.68	0.00	0.0%
90%/10%	$4.57	0.11	2.4%
80%/20%	$4.46	0.22	4.7%
75%/25%	$4.40	0.28	6.0%
70%/30%	$4.35	0.33	7.1%
65%/35%	$4.30	0.38	8.7%
60%/40%	$4.24	0.44	9.4%

The chart demonstrates why telemarketing operations that place all or the vast majority of their calls only during peak rate hours must give serious consideration to adjusting their day part mix.

- For business-to-business operations:
  The opportunities for working in the Evening rate period and the Night/weekend period are more limited, yet the rewards for effective utilization of those periods can be very high for business-to-business telemarketers who adopt a combination of Day, Evening, and Night/weekend rates. Assuming the primary opportunity to contact your business prospects is between 8:00 AM and 5:00 PM in the prospect's time zone Monday through Friday, a nationwide operation can establish calling hours to capitalize on those rates:

Eastern Time Zone

Calling can be done at Evening rates from:
- 5 to 6 PM to reach the Central, Mountain, and Pacific time zones.
- 5 to 7 PM to reach the Mountain, and Pacific time zones.
- 5 to 8 PM to reach the Pacific time zone.
- 5 to 10 PM to reach prospects prior to 5:00 local time in Alaska and Hawaii.

Central Time Zone

Calling can be done at Evening rates from:
- 5 to 6 PM to reach the Mountain and Pacific time zones.
- 5 to 7 PM to reach the Pacific time zones.
- 5 to 9 PM to reach Alaska and Hawaii.

Calling can be done at Night/weekend rates from:
- 7 to 8 AM to reach the Eastern time zones.

Mountain Time Zone

Calling can be done at Evening rates from:
- 5 to 6 PM to reach the Pacific time zones.
- 5 to 8 PM to reach Alaska and Hawaii.

Calling can be done at Night/weekend rates from:
- 6 to 8 AM to reach the Eastern time zones.
- 7 to 8 AM to reach the Eastern and Central time zones.

Pacific Time Zone

Calling can be done at Evening rates from:
- 5 to 7 PM to reach Alaska and Hawaii.

Calling can be done at Night/weekend rates from:
- 5 to 8 AM to reach the Eastern time zones.
- 6 to 8 AM to reach the Eastern and Central time zones.
- 7 to 8 AM to reach the Mountain time zones.

Of course, if your prospects start work earlier than 8 AM, work later than 5 PM, or work on weekends, those are additional opportunities to gain reduced-cost calling time.

Once you know your current day part rates and effective usage costs, it requires no brilliance to figure out the approximate mix you are actually getting. First, construct a similar chart using your current effective rates. To find the range your mix falls into, simply check the average cost per hour for your connected time for the month against the chart. If it is too high, you know you have gotten away from your optimum mix and that some adjustments in the scheduling of your people must be made. It is a simple but effective monitoring method.

Tip: *The telemarketing firms that are most successful in this area* require *weekend work as a part of all consumer TSRs' schedules, giving special incentives for employees to be scheduled accordingly.*

If you want to maintain peak competitiveness and profitability, you need a phone cost management system that combines the realities of the marketplace with good management skills. You have to manage, monitor, control, motivate, offer incentives, and—if you have a consumer operation—inspire your people to achieve the 65/35 mix. If you do your best and find that a 65/35 model is not realistic, you have to revise the model.

Do your absolute best to get the model to work, but don't give up on the concept if your first model doesn't conform to the reality of your marketplace. Staying with the project can pay big dividends.

HOW TO CONTROL YOUR CASH FLOW

Rapid growth eats into your cash flow. If your growth has been at an unexpectedly fast rate, you may not have enough retained earnings to handle the needs.

In large corporations, telemarketing managers usually aren't as concerned about how to manage cash flow, or what to do with with it if the cash flow is positive. Real cash management gets into what you do with the money you have available until you need it. The cash managers of the corporation take care of that. (In many cases, they actually prefer that you don't know what to do with it.)

In smaller firms, a part of growing the business is both creating and managing a positive cash flow. The full issue is quite complex, and beyond the scope of this book. Yet there are a few guidelines that can dramatically simplify the situation:

1. First, budget for all payables on a Net 30 basis.
2. Then convince your suppliers to give you terms of Net 60. (Explain that it's only important for them to do it if they want your business!)
3. Next, convince your clients of the non-negotiable need for you to be paid within 30 days. (If you can't convince the clients, then you may have to convince yourself that you were being a bit extreme when you used the term "non-negotiable"!)
4. Then budget all receivables on a Net 60 basis.
5. Finally, assume payroll is a weekly event, even if it isn't.

Simplifying the cash flow situation is really not much more complex than figuring:

- high on expenses
- low on income
- fast on payments, and
- slow on cash receipts.

If you budget in this way, there is *almost* no way you can screw up badly enough to run out of cash.

HOW TO MANAGE YOUR MARGIN

The cash flow you have available and the ability to manage the financial end of the business are also dependant on the pricing of your services and the profit margins you establish. Again, the core guidelines are simple:

- Establishing too high a profit margin results in not being competitive, and profitable opportunities are lost.
- Selling your services at rates lower than your costs means you will eventually go out of business.
- The profit margin must be competitive, yet high enough to allow you to stay ahead of growth.

Warning: *Service businesses have great difficulty surviving with low profit margins, because they are subject to wide margin swings as their volumes varies.*

The need for higher margins in service industries often is not fully understood. Manufacturing companies with long-term contracts—and cash flow that is correspondingly more stable—can survive well with lower profit margins. But service businesses of any kind—and especially in telemarketing—are subject to wide swings in volume and, accordingly, wide swings in profitability.

Key Point: *To manage a healthy telemarketing business, margins must be high enough to take volume swings into account.*

Margins of 15% to 30% give a service business the ability to survive the peaks and valleys of volume and to continue to manage for growth. Those percentages may sound high to less experienced telemarketing managers (not to mention many clients), but a 20% margin is a realistic goal for service businesses which have few long-term contracts, volatile volume swings, and the potential for seasonal shrinkage. Without margins in that range, your attempts will—at best—be filled with worry and frustration.

> **EXAMPLE:** You have done your research and investigation and determined that your rate should be around $26 per hour to be competitive in your target market. You also have decided that you want to remain 15% profitable, but find that your anticipated costs will deliver only 6% at a $26 rate.
>
> You are aware that planning on a 6% annual pre-tax profit would set you up for serious financial problems. Yet, you are working with temporary marketing costs caused by your initial entry into the market. You have included especially high costs that will go down dramatically after successfully penetrating the market . . . *and* reduced rates that will be offered for only a short term. You feel comfortable that the margin will go up after a very short while.
>
> Then, even though you have targeted the lower rate for only a short time, to be followed by a rate increase, a deep pocketed competitor drops the bid to $24. Matching their rate would mean your small margin plan becomes a money-losing plan.

"Economies of Scale" Can Be Misleading

The odds are that you won't run 400 phones at the same cost per *call* (as compared to cost per *result*) as when you're running 40, assuming the quality of your service remains the same or improves along the way. You've got more physical plant, you have to have multiple facilities, and you have to carve out multiple labor markets, even within one city. Your fixed expense will grow immediately, but your variable cost also will grow with it.

Caution: *Don't believe that "economies of scale" will cover it all.*

That might work in some businesses. But in outbound telemarketing, the larger you become, the more you will need to pay for that precious commodity, *people*. The right ones will make it possible to be competitive on a cost per *result* basis, even if you can't match the smaller shops' cost per *call*.

Key Point: *The rates you charge your clients and the effectiveness of your cost/revenue relationships will determine the quality of people you can draw.*

If you establish yourself as a rate competitor, you will limit the number of talented people you can attract and hold, the quality of your operation, and the number of programs and/or clients you can handle.

That point needs to be explained to clients. The "great deal" they get from a "rate competition" shop will deteriorate the longer they "buy by price alone." To maintain any kind of margin, the cut-rate shop has to hire less-talented people, skimp on training and education, and potentially watch the best people they have go to companies which pay what they are really worth. In most cases—if not all of them—the clients' programs will, over a period of time, suffer right along with the low rate shop.

> **EXAMPLE:** In 1982, we had a 30% profit with a $24.88 average billed rate. But the business wasn't prepared for growth. If we had been dumb enough to look at the business and congratulate ourselves on how healthy it seemed, the business would have remained small—or been out of business—five years later. Steps had to be taken to plan for growth and development.
>
> Management had to look the clients in their eye and say "We know you are used to having a $26 rate, but our costs have gone up 50¢ and we need a 10¢ contribution to maintain a 20% margin. So, although our costs have gone up 50¢, we need to raise you 60¢."

This is just working with basic math. It's not enough to raise your rates $1.00 an hour if your costs go up $1.00 an hour.

Important: *You can't possibly raise your rates by the same amount as your increase in costs without dropping your profit margin . . . and your profit margin is important.*

If you don't include the margin in your rates increases, then one day you may have to raise the rate so significantly that the increase will generate real resistance. You must protect your profit margin; it is the measure of your company's financial health. It also enables the quality and effectiveness of your service to improve over time.

> **EXAMPLE:** In 1981, our variable wages were $8.00 per billable hour (each hour billed); in 1985 they were a little over $12.00. In 1981 the average hourly rate was $24.88; by 1985 it was $30.00. There would have been hell to pay if management had kept the same rate all that time, and then tried to raise the client from $24 to $29 overnight. Instead, it was done in stages throughout that four-year period.
>
> The rate was raised from $24 to $26, and the clients said they could afford it. Gradually it was raised . . . from $26 to $27.50, from $27.50 to $29 . . . and the clients were never happier, because they got what they paid for. In fact, the clients actually experienced the same or lower cost per order at the higher rates.
>
> How? The productivity increased as a direct result of having more high-quality people—whom the higher rates had allowed us to attract, train, and develop.

Key Point: *Costs go up. When they do, you have to make rate increases to stay healthy and grow. A critical part of your job is to get the clients to understand that.*

That kind of an approach has to be taken. A telemarketing business has to be covered for possible volume swings. If volume quickly drops, the fixed costs can become devastating, and margins can be dramatically reduced.

STAYING AHEAD OF GROWTH

Growth comes to a telemarketing firm in two primary ways:

1. Through increasing and extending the success of existing programs;
2. By adding new, productive programs to your existing base.

The growth that comes through the successful development of existing programs is more gradual and predictable. You can see the rate that you are growing the program and make consistent, discrete increments in your facility and staff.

You do not always have that same luxury with the growth that comes from new project opportunities: a new client comes through the door with a rush program; an existing client insists on turning over an in-house program to you immediately; your company's marketing V.P. mentions that he forgot to tell you about the telemarketing department's involvement in a new product introduction . . . and that the mail goes out next week.

Taking on a new program is much easier when you don't have to rush to find and develop all of the new management people, the added facility, and the additional phones. A major part of staying ahead of your growth is keeping more facility than you need for your existing volume requirements.

A very important principle underlies the concept of staying ahead of growth: It is unlikely that you are going to be fortunate enough to pick up programs that require the exact number of phones that you recently lost.

Key Point: *If you fail to budget the additional expense for the reserve inventory of phones and for the development of people, you may miss a program opportunity that is twice the size of the lost volume.*

Where does the missed opportunity go? To someone who can bid competitively because they can say: "I already have the facilities in place necessary to handle the program."

Caution: *It is a delicate balancing act. Too much reserve facility and too many phones cut too deeply into your margin. Too little a reserve may prevent you from taking on significant new volume.*

If you are growing your business properly, initially all you should have to add—for all but the very large new programs—is variable wage. To accomplish that, you need enough fixed plant and fixed management to handle not only current volume, but something between that and a preplanned "not to exceed level" of volume for the year. If your fixed costs allow only for the current volume levels, then both your current and new clients and programs are hurt when you try to grow the business quickly.

At the same time, you can't afford to have the fixed costs at the "not to exceed volume" level, because it's wasted money when you are not at capacity. The level needs to be somewhere in between, so you should increase the absolute fixed expense a little whenever the volume starts to move close to the fixed capacity. Gradually, the old fixed levels become the new actual volume levels, the projected capacity levels become the new fixed levels, and new "not to exceed" levels are established, (See Chart 6).

This management approach allows for immediate growth without increasing the fixed expense per calling hour at the same pace as the increasing call volume. By doing this on a formulated basis from the beginning of your expansion, you can easily add projects that will carry you beyond the current volume levels.

Caution: *Real problems come about when the new project exceeds your current fixed capacity.*

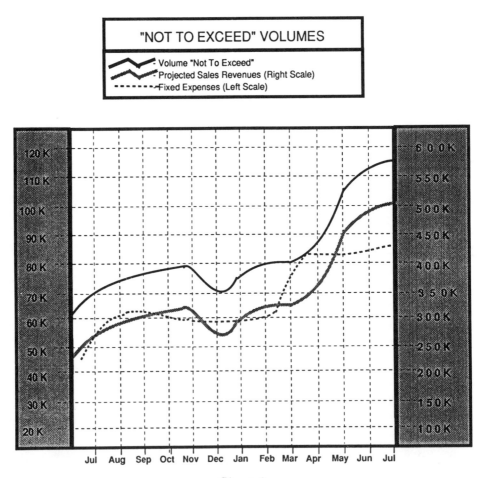

Chart 6

As you see that you are approaching the point that the fixed personnel and fixed plant are going to reach maximum, it's time to put on more fixed personnel and/or facility. That's called staying ahead of growth.

If you do that, you will usually be able to take on a new project without being under undue pressure to immediately increase the absolute fixed expense costs. If you have to pay additional variable wage for a quick-hit recruiting program for quality labor, you can still hold your rate about the same.

How to Stay Ahead of Growth in Your Facility

If you are planning for growth, you always want to have more phones—or, at least, the physical space for them—than needed to take care of the business at hand. Even with those phones just sitting there, it's not a significant fixed expense to absorb. When they are not being used, there are no variable TSR wages, variable connect time usage charges or other variable costs to worry about. Without sufficient reserve phones (or the space to install them very quickly), you may not be able to take advantage of the right kind of business when it comes along.

General reserve facility guidelines are:

- For the growing in-house unit: reserve phones and/or facility of between 10 and 15% above active levels.
- For the growing service bureau: 20% more phones and facility than are actively running to accommodate quick-hit programs.

You can physically see those phones and know they represent the amount of management you should be training to stay ahead of growth. Shortly before those phones are going to be filled on a permanent basis, bring the management people up to speed and move them in to handle the phones. Then rebuild the reserve facility and phone banks.

You may think you're sold out or at capacity on 100 phones, but in essence you need 125 phones of work today to to maintain a consistent 100. If you say "I need to run 100 phones to reach my goals", then—to do it right—you probably need 115 to 125 available phones. When all of those phones are covered, you make incremental profit gains. When they're not, the additional overhead of those unused phones cuts into the profit margin only a little.

How to Analyze the Cost of Staying Ahead of Growth

The question that quickly arises is "Can we really afford to have that reserve of extra phones?" Don't guess at the answer. Do a cost analysis and compare the cost to your ability to absorb it.

The next example and the "Reserve Facility Costs Calculation" worksheets which follow demonstrate the reserve facility cost analysis process.

EXAMPLE: Let's assume you're looking at 60 reserve phones for a 300-phone operation. First, you need to determine the cost of the phone lines. Multiply the 60 reserve phones by the monthly line charge, including taxes, of about $60 a month. That's $3,600 a month.

Next, figure the reserve space costs. This will vary, depending on your applications, their space requirements, and real estate costs in your area. A business-to-business telemarketing operation that needs room for substantial amounts of reference material for multiple product lines will require more space than most consumer telemarketing operations. Use whatever figures your plan calls for. Most operations find they can operate effectively with from 65 to 75 square feet per phone station, including the space for aisles, monitoring booths for quality assurance, break rooms, managers' offices, etc. It can be done easily in 75 square feet with good ergonomics, if you're smart about how to set it up.

For this example, we will use 75 square feet. That means you need roughly 4,500 square feet for the reserve space. Rental costs vary across the country, but an average might be around $15 a square foot. That means another $67,500 a year, or $5,625 a month. You now have $5,625 for facility plus $3,600 for phones.

If each work station can be done for $300, the work stations cost $18,000. With 5-year depreciation, it adds a $300-a-month cost. Now you are up to $9,525 additional fixed expense a month. Figure in around $4,000 more for additions to the monitoring system. With a 60-month depreciation, that adds another $66 a month. The total comes to just under $9,600. To cover contingencies and allow for variations around the country, add roughly 10% to bring the total to about $10,500 a month. That's what it will cost to have the reserve facility available.

But it's producing nothing; it's just sitting there waiting. How will that affect your bottom line?

We started this example by saying you are running 300 active phones. For a consumer operation, multiply the 300 phones by 26 shifts a month, times 4 hours per shift. That equals 31,200 hours per month. Divide the $11,000 monthly cost by the 31,200 hours a month you are running. You find it costs roughly 34¢ an hour out of your profit.

Can you afford that?

The answer depends on what your margin is. For example, if your average hourly rate is $28, 34¢ is about 1.1%.

Example Worksheet: Reserve Facility Costs Calculation

1. Calculate the base monthly cost of the reserve phone lines:
   (# lines) × (rate/mo.) = phone line cost
   [eg.; 60 × $60 − $3600/mo.]
2. Calculate the reserve facility space monthly costs:
   (# lines) × (sq. ft./station) × (cost/sq. ft./yr.) ÷ 12 mo. = facility cost
   [eg.; 60 × 75 × $15 ÷ 12 mo. = $5,625/mo]
3. Calculate the monthly (depreciated) cost of workstations:
   (# lines) × (cost/station) = (workstation cost) ÷ 60 mo. = cost
   [eg.; 60 × $300 = $15,000 ÷ 60 mo. = $300/mo.]

4. Determine the monthly cost of monitoring system additions:
   (Additional system cost) ÷ 60 mo. = cost of monitoring additions.
   [eg.; $4000 ÷ 60 mo. = $66/mo.]

5. Determine the total monthly cost
   (add 1 − 4) = Total Monthly Reserve Cost; Round upward 10% to be safe.
   [eg.; $3600 + 5625 + 300 + 66 = $9591 × 1.1 = ~$10,500]

6. Calculate the overall cost effects of inactive reserve facility and phones, based on active production:

   a. Calculate the total monthly sales hours (active phones) × (shifts/mo.) × (hrs/shift) = (sales hrs/mo.) [eg.; 300 × 26 × 4 = 31,200]

   b. Calculate the cost/hour:
      (reserve cost/mo.) ÷ (productive hrs/mo.) = (cost/hr.) [eg.; $10,500 ÷ 31,200 = 33.65¢; round to 34¢]

   c. Calculate the percentage cost of total revenues:
      (cost/hr.) ÷ (billable hour rate) = cost as a % of revenue [eg.; 34¢ ÷ $28.00 = ~1.2% of revenue]

Reserve Facility Costs Calculation Worksheet

1. Calculate the base monthly cost of the reserve phone lines:
   (# lines) × (rate/mo.) = phone line cost
   (_____) × (_____) = _____

2. Calculate the reserve facility space monthly costs:
   (# lines) × (sq. ft./station) × (cost/sq. ft./yr.) ÷ 12 mo. = facility cost
   (_____ × _____ × _____) ÷ 12 mo. = _____

3. Calculate the monthly (depreciated) cost of work stations:
   (# lines) × (cost/station) = (work station cost) ÷ 60 mo. = cost
   (_____ × _____) = (_____) ÷ 60 mo. = _____

4. Determine the monthly cost of monitoring system additions:
   (Additional system cost) ÷ 60 mo. = cost of monitoring
   (_____) ÷ 60 mo. = _____

5. Determine the total monthly cost
   (add 1 − 4) = Total Monthly Reserve Cost; (Round upward)
   (_____) + (_____) + (_____) + (_____) = (_____)

6. Calculate the overall cost effects of inactive reserve facility and phones, based on active production:

   a. Calculate the total monthly sales hours
      (active phones) × (shifts/mo.) × (hrs./shift) = (sales hrs./mo.)
      (_____) × (_____) × (_____) = (_____)

   b. Calculate the cost/hour:
      (reserve cost/mo.) ÷ (productive hrs./mo.) = (cost/hr.)
      (_____) ÷ (_____) = (_____)

   c. Calculate the percentage cost of total revenues:
      (cost/hr.) ÷ (billable hour rate) = cost as a % of revenue
      (_____) ÷ (_____) = (_____)

That 1.2% cost is really not a lot. Not for the opportunity it creates. If you have an 18% margin, it makes sense to target 1% or 1.2% to stay ahead of growth. In a business that calls for the capacity to put large numbers of people and large amounts of facility into action on short notice, there is no doubt that the reserve capacity is a good investment.

Do you feel that's more than you can afford? Then figure out what is affordable to you. That's where you have to look at your margin. If you have lower margins and can do very little to increase them, work backward in the process. Start with the percentage you can afford to take from the margin to stay ahead of growth, and work back to the amount of reserve you can afford to have in place.

You may resist adding the reserve. That's fine. Just don't be upset when your growth is exceeded by those telemarketing operations which make the investment to have it available. Staying ahead of growth allows you to build on your momentum.

How to Handle the Significant Growth Opportunity

Not all growth opportunities come in comfortably manageable sizes that can be inserted into the reserve facility. If you are a 40-phone shop and the new program adds 50 phones, your company is taking on a whole new shape. If a new program requires adding 100 or 200 phones, you're starting a program that is bigger than the large majority of tele-marketing companies in existence. It's not unlike starting a whole new venture, although you do have the significant advantages of:

- proven operating systems and procedures
- experienced personnel
- established revenue stream
- retained earnings
- established banking relationships

Yet the changes that come with large programs are significant and the challenges are similar. Those areas must be considered in evaluating the impact of the program on your overall margin.

The larger a program and the less prepared you are, the harder it is to take the program on a competitive basis that is healthy for your company. That means you have to work to constantly stay ahead of your growth . . . and take additional steps before accepting large programs that will bring dramatic volume increases.

Before you take on the increased volume, make sure you know what the financial impact of the program will be. Do a financial analysis on the cash flow required for the program. Do revised cash flow and profitability analyses for the program based on the cost revenue relationships of the program. Doing the analysis properly actually requires putting together a new business plan and pro forma, just as if you were starting a new business. (See Appendix).

Depending on the results of your revised analyses and projections, you will be faced with one of three choices:

1. Accept the project, recognizing that it will be sufficiently profitable and manageable enough to warrant taking on the program and all of the extra work required;

2. Decline the project, recognizing that it will not be profitable enough to warrant taking on and/or that the program is so large that taking it on will overtax your fiscal, physical, and personnel resources;

3. Accept part of the project, recognizing that—while it will be profitable—trying to taking on all of the program is beyond your fiscal, physical, or personnel resources.

Each choice is a reality of the telemarketing business. Declining a project that has the potential of being successful and profitable may be less pleasant than taking on part or all of the project. But the work you have done is to discover whether you can handle the program successfully.

Warning: *The worst problems come not from which choice your company needs to make, but from emotional decisions to ignore the results of the analyses and take on more than you can handle.*

You can avoid those problems. Keep your emotions in check when you do your planning. If you find that—realistically—you can take on only a part of the program . . . or even none of it . . . get your ego out of the way and recognize the importance of what you have learned. Rather than jeopardize the client's program and your reputation, make the honest decision and start taking the steps required to put you in position to take advantage of the next large opportunity that presents itself. The steps are:

- Fully and realistically analyze and your financial situation;
- Re-evaluate your costs, rates and margins;
- Structure the financial end of the business on a basis of strong capitalization and sufficient retained earnings;
- Establish sufficient reserve facility to give yourself an extra edge in future opportunities.
- Prepare systems that will help you manage your costs efficiencies and maintain your targeted margin.

If you do those things consistently, you can have a very enjoyable and profitable operation that grows in size and respect.

HOW TO MONITOR AND MANAGE EFFICIENCY

Once you have made sure your cost/revenue relationships are structured properly, it is vital that your operation continues to function in a manner that keeps your actual operating costs in line. Unless you can manage the operation in a way that maintains the planned margins, your efforts in developing the financial plans for growth will have been virtually wasted.

Your success in this area will be determined by your ability to monitor the day-to-day expenses, and by how effectively you make adjustments when deviations from the financial model show they are needed. That is where your monitoring systems and activities come into play.

The Critical Measurement

The most effective method for monitoring and analyzing the financial criteria is one that is similar to the monitoring and measurement done to determine program results. In the same way, the company's profitability can be managed through the effective use of tools which measure overall and individual component operational efficiencies.

It's important to run estimated data on a daily basis. With a good system, it only takes a few minutes and it's extremely important to the company's continuing health. The numbers won't lie, but the story they tell will depend on your ability to perceive what they are saying. This is an area where your experience and comprehensive knowledge of telemarketing play major roles in determining your level of success. What you learn and gain from the numbers depends on your understanding, your perceptiveness, and your ability to accurately and objectively analyze the numbers.

Key Point: *It is essential to monitor and manage your operational efficiencies so you can control your costs as growth changes your economies of scale.*

How to Create a Variable Cost Master Control Sheet

A fast and effective system to monitor efficiency is one which measures the number of hours billed out as a percentage of total payroll hours. That percentage acts as an efficiency rating. The ideal efficiency rating occurs when your billable hours are equal to roughly two thirds of all variable wage or "time clock" hours.

Yellow Flag: *When an outbound telemarketing shop is running under 65% efficiency, the operation has a problem.*

What is the problem? In most cases, it's simply what is best described as bureaucratic, red tape, slow reacting, "Fat Cat" inefficiency. At other times, it may not be "Fat Cat" laziness, but indications of specific weaknesses in the organization. Whatever the reason, it is critical to find out the problem's source.

To be able to quickly monitor and analyze the costs, you need an efficiency guidelines worksheet which shows all the fixed and variable categories and the percentage of revenue each category should take. This becomes your master control sheet, providing you with the data needed to monitor your variable costs. (See page 103.)

How to Monitor Variable Costs

The monitoring process involves a line-by-line check of the individual components of the master control sheet for each payroll period. This provides a more timely monitoring of those costs than studying the monthly P&L. Each pay period—not every quarter—you should prepare a Labor/Billable Hours report and a Cost/Variance report showing projected costs, actual costs, and variance from control guidelines.

Reminder: *Whether you choose the hourly rate or the per-sale method of compensation for your services, billable hours are still the smallest and most effective units for measuring cost and revenue.*

FIXED/VARIABLE MASTER CONTROL SHEET

Average Rate – $27.60/HR.

Variable costs	$/HR.	%
Personnel Exp.	9.300	33.70
Salaries/Bonus	0.390	1.41
Empl. FICA	0.620	2.25
Unemp. Tax	0.380	1.38
Tele. Exp.	4.340	15.72
Wire Fees	0.110	0.04
Paper Supplies	0.350	1.26
Non-Paper Sup.	0.150	0.05
Oper. Supplies	0.070	0.03
Postage	0.080	0.03
Computer Services	0.380	1.38
Cmptr. Svcs (Rebilled)	0.080	0.03
Tot. Var. costs	**16.250**	
Total Var. %		**58.89%**
Gross Profit		**41.11%**

Fixed Costs	$/HR.	%
Personnel Expense	2.429	8.80
Salaries/Bonus	0.163	0.06
Employer FICA	0.183	0.07
Advertising-Help	0.132	0.05
Adv.-Marketing	0.007	0.00+
Auto/Truck Mileage	0.005	0.00+
Commissions	0.043	0.02
Contributions	0.003	0.00+
Conventions/Seminars	0.029	0.01
Depreciation	0.208	0.08
Amortization	0.012	0.00+
Dues/Subscriptions	0.006	0.00+
Entertain.& Travel	0.095	0.03
Employee Relations	0.047	0.02
Insurance	0.049	0.02
Employee Insurance	0.282	1.01
Prof. Fees	0.145	0.05
Misc. Expenses	0.006	0.00+
Office Expenses	0.140	0.05
Rent	0.551	2.00
Equipment Rental	0.183	0.07
Repair & Maint.	0.152	0.06
Taxes (Non-Income)	0.056	0.02
Unemploy. Taxes	0.099	0.00+
Telephone & Telegraph	0.775	2.81
Utilities	0.096	0.00+
Security	0.010	0.00+
Bad Debt	0.050	0.02
Total Fixed Costs	**5.956**	
Total Fixed %		**21.58%**
Total Var. & Fixed Exp.	**22.21**	**80.46%**

Divide the billable hours by the variable wage hours. That number is your efficiency rating.

If you are a manual shop and you come up with 62%, you know you have lost 3% efficiency. Go through the Cost/Variance report again to find where the 3% was lost. Analyzing those results for operational causes of the deviations from standards will help you isolate the areas that need attention and correction.

EXAMPLE 1: You check the Labor/Billable Hours report and find that your efficiency has dropped approximately 3%. When you look at the specific categories, you find that:

Labor/Billable Hours Control Report

Payroll Period: _____

Billable Hours: _____   **Avg. Rate:** _____   **Tot. Revenue:** _____

Variable

	Labor Hours	Payroll ($)	$ / Billable Hr.	% of Revenue
Biller				
CRT Operator				
Data Reporter				
Mailroom Clerk				
Materials				
Personnel				
Quality Assurance				
Receptionist				
Trans. Clerk				
Training				
Training Clerk				
TSR				
TSR Team Superv.				
Verifier-Phone				
Verifier-Tape				

Sub-totals

Fringe Estimates

Total Variable Cost/Hour

Fixed
Exempt
Non-exempt

Sub-total

Fringe Estimate

Total Fixed Cost/Hour

Total Fixed & Variable Cost/Hour

Billable Hours/Variable Labor Hours = _____ %

Labor/Billable Hours Control Report

Payroll Period: 10/16-31/87

Billable Hours: 6,880.13   **Avg. Rate:** $27.60   **Tot. Revenue:** $189,891.59

Variable

	Labor Hours	Payroll ($)	$ / Billable Hr.	% of Revenue
Biller	216.76	1,063.67	.15	.56%
CRT Operator	8.37	72.93	.01	.04%
Data Reporter	318.19	1,337.71	.19	.70%
Mailroom Clerk	78.17	375.66	.05	.20%
Materials	433.44	2,096.72	.30	1.10%
Personnel	337.30	1,845.12	.27	.97%
Quality Assurance	559.42	2,924.06	.43	1.54%
Receptionist	95.45	510.91	.07	.27%
Trans. Clerk	243.16	1,458.59	.21	.77%
Training	134.43	962.66	.14	.51%
Training Clerk	42.66	218.79	.03	.12%
TSR	6,426.04	41,453.47	6.03	21.83%
TSR Team Superv.	785.37	5,814.39	.85	3.06%
Verifier-Phone	31.51	172.07	.03	.09%
Verifier-Tape	417.96	1,750.99	.25	.92%
Sub-totals	10,128.23	62,057.74	9.02	32.68%
Fringe Estimates			1.08	3.91%
Total Variable Cost/Hour			10.10	36.59%

Fixed

	Labor Hours	Payroll ($)	$ / Billable Hr.	% of Revenue
Exempt		13,897.86	2.02	7.32%
Non-exempt	46.92	267.42	.04	.14%
Sub-total		14,165.28	2.06	7.46%
Fringe Estimate			.24	.87%
Total Fixed Cost/Hour			2.30	8.33%
Total Fixed & Variable Cost/Hour			12.40	44.92%

Billable Hours/Variable Labor Hours = 67.9%

COST/VARIANCE CONTROL REPORT

	Actual Feb.($/hr)	Budget Feb.($/hr)	Variance Feb.	Actual Y.T.D.($/hr)	Budget Y.T.D.($/hr)	Variance Y.T.D.
Billable Hours	13,860	13,750	+110	25,260	25,750	-490
Average Rate	27.45	27.60	-$0.15	27.53	27.60	-$0.07
Total Revenue	380,457	379,500	+$957	695,325	710,700	-$15,375
Variable costs			**$/hr**			**$/hr**
Personnel Exp.	128,819/9.294	127,875/9.300	-0.006	235,534/9.324	239,475/9.300	+0.024
Salaries/Bonus	5,388/0.389	5,363/0.390	-0.001	9,868/0.391	10,043/0.390	+0.001
Empl. FICA	8,605/0.621	8,525/0.620	+0.001	15,719/0.622	15,965/0.620	+0.002
Unemp. Tax	5,363/0.387	5,225/0.380	+0.007	9,718/0.385	9,785/0.380	+0.005
Tele. Exp.	60,001/4.329	59,675/4.340	-0.011	109,420/4.332	111,755/4.340	-0.008
Wire Fees	1,618/0.117	1,512/0.110	+0.007	2,895/0.115	2,832/0.110	+0.005
Paper Supplies	4,407/0.318	4,812/0.350	-0.032	8,488/0.336	9,012/0.350	-0.014
Non-Paper Sup.	2,269/0.164	2,063/0.150	+0.014	4,047/0.160	3,863/0.150	+0.010
Oper. Supplies	986/0.071	963/0.070	+0.001	1,841/0.073	1,803/0.070	+0.003
Postage	1,164/0.084	1,100/0.080	+0.004	2,110/0.084	2,060/0.080	+0.004
Computer Services	5,085/0.367	5,225/0.380	-0.013	9,497/0.378	9,875/0.380	-0.002
Cmptr. Svcs (Rebill)	1,092/0.079	1,100/0.080	-0.001	2,015/0.797	2,060/0.080	-0.003
Tot. Var. costs	224,797/16.22	223,437/16.25	-0.031	411,152/16.28	418,437/16.25	+0.027
Total Variable %	59.09%	58.89%		59.13%	58.89%	
Gross Profit	155,660/40.91%	155,857/41.11%	-0.20%	284,173/40.87%	292,057/41.11%	-0.24%
Fixed Costs						
Personnel Expense	31,500/2.272	31,500/2.291	-0.019	62,550/2.476	62,550/2.429	+0.047
Salaries/Bonus	2,300/0.166	2,300/0.167	-0.001	4,207/0.167	4,207/0.163	+0.004
Employer Fica	2,360/0.170	2,360/0.172	-0.002	4,722/0.187	4,722/0.183	+0.004
Advertising-Help	1,170/0.084	950/0.069	+0.015	3,620/0.132	3,400/0.132	0.000
Adv.-Marketing	100/0.007	100/0.007	0.000	200/0.008	200/0.007	+0.001
Auto/Truck Mileage	65/0.005	65/0.005	0.000	130/0.005	130/0.005	0.000
Commissions	600/0.043	600/0.044	-0.001	1,050/0.042	1,100/0.043	+0.001
Contributions	40/0.003	40/0.003	0.000	80/0.003	80/0.003	0.000
Conventions/Seminars	250/0.018	0/0.000	+0.018	1,000/0.040	750/0.029	+0.011
Depreciation	2,800/0.202	2,800/0.204	-0.002	5,350/0.212	5,350/0.208	+0.004
Amortization	150/0.011	150/0.011	0.000	300/0.012	300/0.012	0.000
Dues/Subscriptions	0/0.000	0/0.000	0.000	150/0.006	150/0.006	0.000
Entertain.& Travel	900/0.065	650/0.047	+0.018	2,700/0.107	2,450/0.095	+0.012
Employee Relations	600/0.043	600/0.044	-0.001	1,200/0.048	1,200/0.047	+0.001
Insurance	728/0.053	728/0.053	0.000	1,272/0.050	1,272/0.049	+0.001
Employee Insurance	4,250/0.307	4,250/0.309	-0.002	7,261/0.287	7,261/0.282	+0.005
Prof. Fees	1,275/0.092	1,275/0.093	-0.001	3,735/0.148	3,735/0.145	+0.003
Misc. Expenses	85/0.006	75/0.005	+0.001	160/0.006	150/0.006	0.000
Office Expenses	1,800/0.130	1,800/0.131	-0.001	3,600/0.143	3,600/0.140	+0.003
Rent	7,090/0.512	7,090/0.516	-0.004	14,180/0.561	14,180/0.551	+0.010
Equipment Rental	2,360/0.170	2,360/0.172	-0.002	4,720/0.187	4,720/0.183	+0.004
Repair & Maint.	1,875/0.135	1,875/0.136	-0.001	3,905/0.155	3,905/0.152	+0.003
Taxes (Non-Income)	715/0.052	715/0.052	0.000	1,430/0.057	1,430/0.056	+0.001
Unemploy. Taxes	815/0.059	815/0.059	0.000	2,542/0.101	2,542/0.099	+0.002
Telephone/Telegraph	10,185/0.735	9,975/0.725	+0.010	20,160/0.798	19,950/0.775	+0.003
Utilities	1,435/0.104	1,235/0.090	+0.014	2,670/0.106	2,470/0.096	+0.010
Security	140/0.010	140/0.010	0.000	260/0.010	260/0.010	0.000
Bad Debt	1,050/0.076	650/0.047	+0.029	1,593/0.063	1,300/0.050	+0.013
Total Fixed Costs	75,638/5.457	75,098/5.462	-0.015	154,747/6.126	153,364/5.956	+0.170
Total Fixed %	19.88%	19.79%		22.26%	21.58%	
Total Var. & Fixed Exp.	300,435/21.68	298,535/21.71	-0.036	565,899/22.40	571,801/22.21	+0.197
Total Var. & Fixed %	78.97%	78.67%		81.39%	80.46%	
Interest Expense	2,475/0.65	2,475/0.65		4,950/0.70	4,950/0.70	
Pre-Tax Income	77,547/20.38	78,490/20.68	-0.30%	124,476/17.90	133,949/18.85	-0.95%

COST/VARIANCE CONTROL REPORT

	Actual ($/hr)	Budget ($/hr)	Variance Feb.	Actual Y.T.D.($/hr)	Budget Y.T.D.($/hr)	Variance Y.T.D.
Billable Hours						
Average Rate						
Total Revenue						
Variable costs			$/hr			$/hr
Personnel Exp.						
Salaries/Bonus						
Empl. FICA						
Unemp. Tax						
Tele. Exp.						
Wire Fees						
Paper Supplies						
Non-Paper Sup.						
Oper. Supplies						
Postage						
Computer Services						
Cmptr. Svcs (Rebill)						
Tot. Var. costs						
Total Variable %						
Gross Profit						
Fixed Costs						
Personnel Expense						
Salaries/Bonus						
Employer Fica						
Advertising-Help						
Adv.-Marketing						
Auto/Truck Mileage						
Commissions						
Contributions						
Conventions/Seminars						
Depreciation						
Amortization						
Dues/Subscriptions						
Entertain.& Travel						
Employee Relations						
Insurance						
Employee Insurance						
Prof. Fees						
Misc. Expenses						
Office Expenses						
Rent						
Equipment Rental						
Repair & Maint.						
Taxes (Non-Income)						
Unemploy. Taxes						
Telephone/Telegraph						
Utilities						
Security						
Bad Debt						
Total Fixed Costs						
Total Fixed %						
Total Var. & Fixed Exp.						
Total Var. & Fixed %						
Interest Expense						
Pre-Tax Income						

- The training hours represent more than double the usual allowance for percentage of revenue;
- The sales supervisor percentage is quarter again what it should be, and
- The percentage of TSR hours is more than 2% too high.

You immediately look into the situation and find the reasons all center around a complex new program that the client has had severe problems with at their in-house telemarketing unit.

The service being offered is completely different than any your people have worked with before. Also, the marketing department agreed to use the same script the client had been using, and it is very different from the format your company normally uses. Finally, your operation has been directed to use the client's order form, which does not follow the company's usual format. The result has been as follows:

- Because of the complexity of the new program, the training for the new TSRs you have hired is taking two hours longer than normal.
- Again, because of the complexity of the program and the dramatic differences in the order form and script format, the crosstraining of veteran TSRs is taking approximately an hour longer than is usually budgeted.
- Even with the additional training, the TSRs are having difficulty making as many calls and closing as high a percentage of contact calls as expected. Because both the CPH and the Contact Conversion Percentage are lower than expected, the SPH is very low. As a result, the Account Manager asked the Facility Manager to temporarily change the normal Supervisor-to-TSR ratios from 1 : 16 to 1 : 10 to provide additional coaching and support on the program.

Behind those facts, what you find is not a single problem, but a set of interlocking problems that need to be resolved.

- Marketing has failed to educate the client about the differences between how your company works, why it works that way, and in what ways your creative and operational procedures might be able to bring *new* strength to the program.
- Because the trainers have become so frustrated with having to train a program that is so different from what they are accustomed to, they are communicating to the TSRs—none too subtly—that having to work on the program is a punishment worse than death.
- The account manager is feuding with the marketer who sold the account, rather than trying to enlist the marketer's help in persuading the client to listen to some suggestions for improving the program.
- The company's internal lines of communications are not working. All of the problems have been held at the operational and account management levels,

and none of the upper management team has been told about the severity of the problems or the variations from normal budgeted hours in the training and supervisory areas. Nor have they asked any of upper management for help.

You know you have a lot of work ahead of you, but at least you have found out about the problem, and it was the information in the Labor/Billable Hours control report that showed you where to look.

Not all of the problems that you discover will be on the control report. Still, the information that the report provides will help you eliminate some of the possibilities that you have to consider in searching for the cause of the problem.

EXAMPLE 2: Your model shows that 65% efficiency is needed to reach your objective of being 20% profitable, and you have been running at 65% efficiency and 20% profitability. Then the next month you are 67% efficient and 16% profitable. You have had a nice improvement in efficiency, yet your profitability has dropped. What's the reason? Either:

1. you have some increased fixed expenses that you have not accounted for by appropriately raising your rate,
2. you know you haven't yet raised your rate because you have added fixed expenses to accommodate growth that you know is on the way, or
3. your average hourly rate from clients has dropped.

In any of those cases, your margin has dropped in spite of increased efficiency. You have either made a preplanned move to structure ahead of growth, or your costs have gone up where they shouldn't without an appropriate rate increase.

Caution: *If that trend continues, you'll wind up with continually decreasing profits margins and continually increasing headaches.*

The monitoring and analysis of the data will point out the weak areas for you. You are making a mistake, however, if you rely solely on the data to do your monitoring. Effective monitoring of these areas comes first from the eyeball approach. When you *know* the operation, you will *see* many of the variations and be able to have them corrected before they show up in the data. Instead of finding serious problems to be fixed, you will be able to prevent them.

Tip: *There is no substitute for the eyeball approach, because nothing else is as fast or as personal in identifying the problems.*

It's not easy to hit those numbers, and it's easy to forget to check them. It's easy to forget to watch the sales floor for variations. It's easy to forget to make sure the new people being hired are sufficiently trained and committed to hitting those numbers. The larger you grow, the harder it is to reach those percentages. But when you see problems on the sales floor, or you see the overall efficiency number dropping from 65% to 63% or 62%, you have to step in and make the necessary corrections. It quickly shows you the overall picture and readily allows you to target any specific problem areas. The second the efficiencies are off, it raises virtually every other question you need to ask.

Quality management of the efficiencies hinges on personal management. You need to watch the floor and keep your eye on those numbers like your next meal depended on it.

It might!

Keep in Mind: *There's an old saying that fat cats don't hunt. You've got to make sure that your people stay* professionally *hungry.*

Regularly remind your people that the success the company has enjoyed can't be taken for granted. To continue and extend that success, they have to maintain the same dedicated and attentive style that got them there. You have to make sure your organization doesn't get fat as it grows, and you measure that in part by efficiency.

How to Deal with—and Budget for—Unusual Efficiency Deviations

There will also be deviations from the normal efficiencies for any given period that cannot be attributed to mistake or mismanagement. Allowances must be made in the budget planning for such things as paid holidays, unplanned down time, and specialized training. Discounting them for the purpose of analyzing the period is a statistical necessity, but they must be built into the overall budget if your operation is to be healthy.

Warning: *Discounting predictable cost deviations in constructing your budget is a financial irresponsibility that will destroy your view of the company's bottom-line performance.*

A part of budgeting for those kinds of situations is to project those months which you know will have unusually high variable-expense-to-billable-hour ratios. You can project, for example, that your February and December billings will be proportionately lower because of fewer work days. In addition, the December period may bring unusually high variable costs because of paid holidays. Perhaps you will be adding on additional supervisors in September as a part of your process of structuring ahead of growth. Once the projected month-to-month variations are made, you can determine a baseline which will provide the desired overall margin for the entire year. You then must make sure that your monthly margins for the months with fewer variations is high enough to compensate for those months when the margin will be lower.

Other deviations from the norm will occur that cannot be attributed to mistake or mismanagement. If the phones were down 3 days in a row and you lost 500 billable hours, you know that it was an operational problem that was not inherent to any part of the management system or procedures. If there is a paid holiday during the month, the figures will be skewed. Those costs must be discounted for the purposes of the efficiency analysis. Those are operational realities beyond the control of the floor management personnel.

The Ideal Management Ratios

You also have to maintain an overall budget on ratios that takes into account the varying requirements of different programs. An extremely effective and productive ratio is 1 : 8, done this way:

SAMPLE BUDGET

	Jan	Feb	Mar	Apr	May	Jun	Jul	Aug	Sep	Oct	Nov	Dec	Total
Billable hrs													
Avg.Rate													
Total Rev.													

Rate   Variable costs
Personnel exp.
Salaries/Bonus
Empl. FICA
Unemp. tax
Tele. exp.
Wire fees
Paper supplies
Non-paper sup.
Oper. supplies
Postage
Computer services
Cmptr Svcs.(Rebill)

Total Variable Costs
(Total @$_____ /hr. = _____ % of revenue; variable payroll=$_____)

Gross Profit (@ _____%)

Fixed costs	Jan	Feb	Mar	Apr	May	Jun	Jul	Aug	Sep	Oct	Nov	Dec	Total
Personnel exp.													
Salaries/Bonus													
Employer Fica													
Advertising-Help													
Adv.-Marketing													
Auto/Truck Mileage													
Commissions													
Contributions													
Conventions/Seminars													
Depreciation													
Amortization													
Dues/Subscriptions													
Entertain.& Travel													
Employee Relations													
Insurance													
Employee Insurance													
Prof. Fees													
Misc. Expenses													
Office Expenses													
Rent													
Equipment Rental													
Repair & Maint.													
Taxes (Non-Income)													
Unemploy. Taxes													
Telephone & Telegraph													
Utilities													
Security													
Bad Debt													

Total Fixed Costs

Total Var. & Fixed Exp.
Interest Expense

Pre-Tax Income (Loss)

	Jan	Feb	Mar	Apr	May	Jun	Jul	Aug	Sep	Oct	Nov	Dec	Total

SAMPLE BUDGET

	Jan	Feb	Mar	Apr	May	Jun	Jul	Aug	Sep	Oct	Nov	Dec	Total
Billable hrs	12,000	13,750	14,000	14,000	15,000	15,000	16,000	14,000	16,000	17,500	17,500	12,000	176,750
Avg.Rate	27.60	27.60	27.60	27.60	27.60	27.60	27.60	27.60	27.60	27.60	27.60	27.60	
Total Rev.	331,200	379,500	386,400	386,400	414,000	414,000	441,600	386,400	441,600	483,000	483,000	331,200	4,878,300

Rate	Variable costs	Jan	Feb	Mar	Apr	May	Jun	Jul	Aug	Sep	Oct	Nov	Dec	Total
9.30	Personnel exp.	111,600	127,875	130,200	130,200	139,500	139,500	148,800	130,200	148,800	162,750	162,750	111,600	1,643,775
.39	Salaries/Bonus	4,680	5,363	5,460	5,460	5,850	5,850	6,240	5,460	6,240	6,825	6,825	4,680	68,933
.62	Empl. FICA	7,440	8,525	8,680	8,680	9,300	9,300	9,920	8,525	9,920	10,850	10,850	7,440	109,585
.38	Unemp. tax	4,560	5,225	5,320	5,320	5,700	5,700	6,080	5,320	6,080	6,650	6,650	4,560	67,165
4.34	Tele. exp.	52,080	59,675	60,760	60,760	65,100	65,100	69,440	60,760	69,440	75,950	75,950	52,080	767,095
.11	Wire fees	1,320	1,512	1,540	1,540	1,650	1,650	1,760	1,540	1,760	1,925	1,925	1,320	19,637
.35	Paper supplies	4,200	4,812	4,900	4,900	5,250	5,250	5,600	4,900	5,600	6,125	6,125	4,200	61,862
.15	Non-paper sup.	1,800	2,063	2,100	2,100	2,250	2,250	2,400	2,100	2,400	2,625	2,625	1,800	26,513
.07	Oper. supplies	840	963	980	980	1,050	1,050	1,120	980ç	1,120	1,225	1,225	840	12,373
.08	Postage	960	1,100	1,120	1,120	1,200	1,200	1,280	1,120	1,280	1,400	1,400	960	14,140
.38	Computer services	4,560	5,225	5,320	5,320	5,700	5,700	6,080	5,320	6,080	6,650	6,650	4,560	67,165
.08	Cmptr Svcs.(Rebill)	960	1,100	1,120	1,120	1,200	1,200	1,280	960	1,280	1,400	1,400	960	14,140

Total Variable Costs   195,000   223,629   227,500   227,500   243,750   243,750   260,000   227,500   260,000   284,375   284,375   195,000   2,872,269

(Total @16.25/hr. = 58.9% of revenue; variable payroll=38.7%)

Gross Profit (@ 41.1%) 136,200   155,871   158,940   158,940   170,250   170,250   181,600   158,940   181,600   198,625   198,625   136,200   2,005,979

Fixed costs	Jan	Feb	Mar	Apr	May	Jun	Jul	Aug	Sep	Oct	Nov	Dec	Total
Personnel exp.	31,050	31,175	31,600	31,800	31,800	32,200	32,500	32,800	32,800	33,000	33,000	33,000	386,725
Salaries/Bonus	1,987	2,277	2,424	2,440	2,440	2,470	2,490	2,515	2,515	2,530	2,530	2,530	29,148
Employer Fica	2,362	2,392	2,392	2,424	2,424	2,389	2,301	2,286	2,147	2,039	1,918	1,862	26,936
Advertising-Help	2,450	950	1,250	1,250	3,450	1,050	950	1,250	2,450	1,100	650	1250	18,000
Adv.-Marketing	100	100	1,850	100	100	100	100	100	750	2,060	100	1,960	7,420
Auto/Truck Mileage	65	65	65	65	65	65	65	65	65	65	65	65	780
Commissions	500	600	600	600	600	600	600	600	650	650	650	350	7,000
Contributions	40	40	40	40	40	40	40	40	40	40	1,000	100	1,500
Conventions/Seminars	750	0	0	650	0	0	0	0	750	1,200	1,200	0	4,550
Depreciation	2,550	2,600	2,650	2,700	2,750	2,800	2,950	3,000	3,050	3,100	3,150	3,200	34,500
Amortization	150	150	150	150	150	150	150	150	150	150	150	150	1,800
Dues/Subscriptions	150	0	0	280	525	0	0	0	400	650	355	0	2,330
Entertain.& Travel	1,800	650	650	950	650	650	650	650	950	1,400	1,100	500	10,600
Employee Relations	600	600	600	600	600	600	600	600	600	600	600	600	7,200
Insurance	544	544	710	728	728	740	740	740	740	740	740	740	8,434
Employee Insurance	3,011	3,772	4,250	4,250	4,250	4,350	4,350	4,350	4,350	4,350	4,350	4,350	49,983
Prof. Fees	2,460	4,740	1,275	1,275	1,275	1,275	1,275	1,275	1,275	1,275	1,275	1,275	19,970
Misc. Expenses	75	75	75	75	75	75	75	75	75	100	100	100	975
Office Expenses	1,800	1,800	1,800	1,800	1,800	1,800	1,800	1,800	1,800	1,800	1,800	1,300	21,100
Rent	7,090	7,090	7,090	7,090	7,090	7,790	7,790	7,790	7,790	7,790	7,790	7,790	89,980
Equipment Rental	2,360	2,360	2,360	2,360	2,360	2,360	2,360	2,360	2,360	2,360	2,360	2,360	28,320
Repair & Maint.	2,030	1,975	1,870	1,885	1,875	1,875	1,875	1,875	1,875	1,895	1,910	1,975	22,915
Taxes (Non-Income)	715	715	715	715	715	715	715	715	715	715	715	715	8,580
Unemploy. Taxes	1,727	1,729	1,736	1,750	1,750	880	880	880	900	905	910	917	14,964
Telephone & Telegraph	9,975	9,975	9,975	9,975	9,975	9,975	10,650	10,650	10,650	10,650	10,650	10,650	123,750
Utilities	1,235	1,235	1,235	1,235	1,235	1,235	1,325	1,325	1,325	1,325	1,325	1,325	15,360
Security	120	120	120	120	140	140	140	140	160	160	225	225	1,810
Bad Debt	650	650	650	650	650	650	650	650	700	700	700	700	8,050

Total Fixed Costs	78,346	78,349	78,162	77,957	79,512	76,974	78,021	78,681	82,032	83,349	81,318	79,989	952,690
	23.7%	20.6%	20.2%	20.2%	19.2%	18.6%	17.7%	20.4%	18.6%	17.3%	16.8%	24.2%	19.5%

Total Var. & Fixed Exp. 273,346   301,786   305,662   305,457   323,262   320,724   338,021   306,181   342,032   367,724   365,693   274,989   3,825,069

Interest Expense	2,475	2,475	2,475	2,475	2,475	2,475	2,475	2,475	2,475	2,475	2,475	2,475	29,700

Pre-Tax Income (Loss)	55,379	75,239	80,738	78,468	88,263	90,801	101,104	77,744	97,093	112,801	114,832	53,736	1,026,001
	16.72%	19.8%	20.9%	20.3%	21.3%	21.9%	22.9%	20.1%	22.0%	23.4%	23.8%	16.2%	21.0%

	Jan	Feb	Mar	Apr	May	Jun	Jul	Aug	Sep	Oct	Nov	Dec	Total

- 1 Quality Assurance Representative for each 24 TSRs
- 1 Supervisor per 16 TSRs
- 1 Program Manager per 48 TSRs

For each 48 phones, that comes to:

- 2 QARs
- 3 Supervisors
- 1 PM

That's 6 : 48, or a 1 : 8 ratio.

The exception to the normal ratios comes during the training and development of new supervisors and new TSRs. Then you may go to a 1 : 6 or 1 : 7 ratio while they are going through their learning curve. You may assign a supervisor trainee to an established supervisor, or you may assign the supervisor trainee a team of only 5 TSRs. But you must realize that the additional cost above normal ratios should be assigned to the training and development budget. Supervisor training and development are the real causes for the additional supervision you have on the floor. That's a part of growth.

Red Flag: *Failure to make those allowances can cost you dearly in short-term productivity and in the long-term development of your people.*

But What if the Volume Levels Fall?

Whatever the market and the program calls for ultimately will determine what you can do. If you try to make your ratio 1 : 5 because you have fewer people calling on the phones and don't want to move supervisors or QA to the phones to reduce the ratios, you'll destroy your efficiency.

Important: *The entire team must know that the ratios are to be maintained and that any member of the team is subject to going on the phones on any given shift in order to maintain the mandated ratios.*

All supervisory and management personnel have to know how to do their part in the management of the financial health of their parts of the organization.

If the ratios change from 1 : 8 to 1 : 5, you are costing yourself money. When you lose ratios and go from 1 : 8 to 1 : 13, you lose quality and productivity for the client. That's why the supervision ratio balance is essential both to you and to your client.

Whichever route you take (variable or fixed) with the classification of supervisors, adjustments still have to be made if volume levels fall. The supervisors should work reduced time in supervision and increased time on the phones, in proportion to the amount of volume reduction. If your volume is cut in half, you can put half your supervisors on the phone all the time, all of your supervisors on the phone half of the time, or some combination thereof. That's one of the reasons it's so important to have regularly scheduled phone sales time be a part of the job description for all the supervisors.

Management sometimes makes the mistake with reduced volume of saying "Well, that's OK. We'll just have double the supervision for the next 4 months or until we pick up the volume." That's a big mistake to make on a cost/revenue basis.

When volume shrinks, profits shrink. That's the time to really manage efficiently. Not to cut corners on the client's programs, but to manage at optimum efficiency. It's a situation exactly opposite to managing growth. Instead of structuring ahead by adding management talent, you move into a lean mode and maximize your efficiency. Not undernourished; just a maintenance diet.

"THE BOTTOM LINE"

Growing a truly excellent telemarketing company and managing it for cost effectiveness and profitability is a constant balancing act. Achieving that balance comes from:

- your business acumen
- your level of understanding of telemarketing
- your instincts.

Core Strategy: *It sometimes is a strain on the budget, yet having real strength in all your management positions is the key to developing an outstanding organization.*

Ten Questions to Ask Yourself to Assess Your Financial Situation

The financial considerations are of prime importance. Money matters, and deep pockets do help. Ten important questions need to be asked honestly and answered realistically.

1. What is your business situation?
2. What is your cash position?
3. What are your credit opportunities?
4. What will your financing cost?
5. Are you prepared to pay the right opportunity costs . . . and to avoid paying the wrong ones?
6. Is your projected margin large enough to protect you during volume drops?
7. Are you properly prepared to stay ahead of growth?
8. Do you have the necessary understanding and systems to manage and monitor your costs?
9. Is your budget comprehensive, realistic, and accurate?
10. Is your overall financial plan as sound as you can make it?

Are you part of a large corporation that finances you easily and inexpensively? If you are, what is your mandate from the corporate level? Are they overly concerned about next month's profits? If they feel that the steps you are taking for growth are warranted, will they cover your financial needs and just ask that you make sure you are growing quickly and profitably?

As a good division manager of a cash-flush corporation, you might be able to go to corporate management and say: "We can buy a computer system for $500,000 that will dramatically improve our operation. We can depreciate it over 60 months, so it comes out to only 20¢ an hour. Let's do it." Cash flow, in that situation, is of no major concern.

Are you in your own business with a strong cash position and a good line of credit? Are you just starting out with a tighter cash position and personally mortgaged to the hilt? You have to be sure you can survive before you can grow effectively. If you're in your own business the reality of it is that—to get that same computer system—you first have to have the $500,000, or be able to borrow it. And even at 10% interest rates, that adds over $4,000 a month to your costs and increases the per hour cost from 20¢ to 31¢. Can you afford that?

If you can't get the half million, it doesn't matter. You've got to have the cash to pay the piper . . . or forget about hearing the tune!

A Final Reminder

In Chapter 2, we said that without a comprehensive business and financial plan, you would find that what you hoped would be the challenges of managing day-to-day growth becomes a much less enjoyable day-to-day struggle for survival, and that you would never have the opportunity to deal with the joys and the headaches of growth. The same can be said if you fail to give the financial matters of your business your full attention.

But it doesn't have to be. If you prepare the necessary systems and continue to manage your costs to maintain your margin, you can have a very enjoyable and profitable operation that grows in size and respect.

We will emphasize it once again: When the excitement of rapid growth is combined with a little fatigue and some "Fat Cat" complacency, it's easy to skip the steps that are necessary to stay on top of the efficiency and the financial health of your operation. You can skip those steps if you choose. In outbound telemarketing, they are required only if you want to survive.

27 KEYS TO MANAGING MONEY MATTERS

- The three greatest cost centers to evaluate and keep under control for effective financial management in outbound telemarketing are Variable Labor Cost, Fixed Labor Cost and Variable Phone Cost.
- Careful cost *optimization* is more important than deep cost reduction. Exceeding the budgeted amounts and percentages in either area quickly hurts the bottom line, but cutting costs too deeply opens the door to mediocrity.
- The effective management of the cost/revenue relationships is the key to keeping an outbound telemarketing business financially healthy.
- Calculating all revenues and costs on a "per billable hour" basis allows you to readily compare major cost centers to revenues.
- Profit margins must be high enough to allow you to stay ahead of your growth and low enough for you to remain competitive. A healthy outbound telemarketing

business needs margins of 15% to 25% to sustain it through the slower times caused by wide volume swings.

- A 20% margin gives a company the wherewithal to attract, train, and retain quality personnel; to spend some money on R&D; and to forge ahead with innovative, new ideas.
- You can base your rates on price per hour or on price per unit of production. Either way, your minute-to-minute cost of doing business decides what you have to charge the client.
- Total payroll costs usually represent 40–50% of total revenues, with 8–12% in fixed payroll, and 38–42% in variable wages.
- Total phone costs should fall into the range 15–20%.
- In determining which phone service to use, you should do a comparative analysis of the rates of different alternative carriers based on your own calling times and usage levels. Live testing of the service also should be done from your immediate location.
- Because telemarketing is extremely sensitive to the quality of its people and its phone service, cost should not be the only consideration in making decisions in these areas.
- There has to be a balance between keeping phone costs at a minimum and maintaining high-quality transmission and service.
- Scheduling a substantial part of your calling into the lower cost day parts can reduce your phone costs by several percent.
- To control cash flow, budget conservatively and manage aggressively. Budget all payables for Net 30 and all receivables for Net 60. Then convince your clients of the real need to be paid within 30 days—and your suppliers of the real need to give you terms of Net 60.
- You have to know the costs and charge for them, or be willing to walk away from the account. If it costs you "X," you have to sell it for "X" plus something.
- Don't believe that "economies of scale" will "cover it all." They will cover some of the cost differences between a 400-phone operation and a 40-phone shop. However they won't cover all the differences, because the economies of scale change as you grow.
- The rates you charge your clients and the effectiveness of your cost revenue relationships will determine the quality of people you can draw.
- You can't possibly raise your rates by the same amount as your increase in costs without dropping your profit margin . . . and your profit margin is important.
- Take the risk of paying small opportunity costs to stay ahead of growth, rather than paying the costs of lost opportunities.
- Before you take on the increased volume, make sure you know what the financial impact of the program will be. Do revised cash flow and profitability analyses for the company based on the impact of the cost/revenue relationships of the program.
- A major part of staying ahead of your growth is keeping somewhat more facility and

slightly more management talent than is needed for your existing volume requirements.

- It is essential to monitor and manage your operational efficiencies so you can control your costs as growth changes your economies of scale.

- Efficiency monitoring and analysis is a quick and effective tool which measures overall and individual component efficiencies. The deviations from target efficiencies will show where action is needed.

- When an outbound telemarketing shop is running under 65% efficiency, the operation has a problem.

- It is a mistake to rely solely on the data to do your monitoring. The front line of effective monitoring and management is personal observation of the daily operation. This allows for correction of problem situations before they appear as red flags on the reports.

- Identifiable deviations from normal costs for any given period must be built into the budget if your operation is to be healthy.

- Diligent management of reasonable costs—in both good times and bad—brings the optimum blend of reduced expenses and quality resources.

**The key to growth is quite simple: creative men with money.
(or with access to it)
The cause of stagnation is similarly clear: depriving creative
individuals of financial power.**

**—George Gilder
(Steve Idelman)**

He belongs to an organization that cares about him, challenges him, believes in him, and wants what's best for him, not just as an employee but as a total human being.
—*Michael LeBoeuf,* on why a person stays on a job.

How to Handle the People Issues

THE COMMITMENT AND THE CHALLENGE

The most important, long-term commitment you should make is not to the marketplace, because it will be there. The most important long-term commitment you should make is to your people.

You can't allow yourself to get frustrated and give up on the extended and complex process of building an organization. Yet, in today's fast-paced telemarketing marketplace, the challenges of managing and developing the labor force can be remarkably frustrating.

This is especially true when it comes to managing a quickly growing outbound telemarketing company. Keeping your existing work force happy and productive at all times can be an exacting project. It becomes a special challenge when you have to infuse massive amounts of new labor into the business and still have the newest people develop the same close feeling of involvement that your veterans have.

Key Point: *When telemarketing growth borders on being explosive, having enough talented and trained people to assure strong continuity and evolution can become an unrelenting battle.*

TELEMARKETING'S UNIQUE PERSONNEL CHALLENGES

In a traditional business environment, the labor force is generally comprised of "8 hours a day, 5 days a week" employees who accept the job as their primary source of income. In consumer telemarketing, that rarely is true. It frequently is not true in business-to-business telemarketing, which—while more like the traditional business environment—still has to deal with the unique "people problems" inherent in all fields of telemarketing.

The nature of consumer outbound telemarketing almost defines having a part-time labor force. In the Eastern time zone, you can productively start as early as 6:00 P.M. and have calls that run as late as midnight. In the Midwest zone, the most effective hours are from 5:00 P.M. to 11:00 P.M. West Coast operations are basically limited to operating from 3:00 P.M. to 9:00 P.M. To remain cost-effective, reduced-phone-cost weekend work is a necessity for most telemarketing companies.

None of those time frames are very appealing to the traditional labor market. In all of those situations, you have 6 good hours of work a night. On a 5-day week, you have a maximum of 30 hours a week. Even at 6 hours a day, a TSR must work 6 to 7 days a week to reach the traditional 40-hour standard of full time work.

While TSRs in business-to-business shops may be able to work 40 hours during a 5-day week, they have to deal with the burnout factor.

Remember: *The intense nature of telemarketing creates an urgent time line combined with an extremely high rejection factor.*

In either consumer or business operations, a 40-hour work week is really difficult for a TSR to handle. And the TSRs are just the beginning of the problem.

The same problem exists with the supervisors and managers. The hours and the work itself are extremely intense. Any service bureau—and many in-house operations—have to deal with inconsistent call loads. Volumes and work loads vary quickly, even when you manage them effectively, and supervisors and managers must be recruited and trained at levels sufficient to handle your current call load. When you're in a growth mode, you are building slightly beyond those levels. What happens when the work goes away or grows very quickly?

The Problems Caused by Lack of Educational Resources

All of the labor problems are complicated by the absence of centralized and formalized educational sources, and by the resulting lack of trained candidates from college campuses—as compared to the pool that most industries can tap. There is no formal educational system for the training and development of those key management people in telemarketing.

Effectively, the nation's education system acts as a "farm system" for the business community—from agriculture to medicine to high tech—for developing people. IBM can go to a campus and recruit the brightest young minds and talents who have been trained in the school system's electrical engineering programs. The graduates of the Harvard Law School are interviewed by firms in need of the students' demonstrated skills and specialized education. People develop a good basic knowledge of a type of business through the traditional educational process, and are then integrated in the appropriate companies. But, unlike all traditional industries, there is no formal conduit through which hands-on telemarketing knowledge and experience is passed.

While some specialized courses are available in a few schools, no 4-year degree programs in telemarketing exist anywhere in the nation. Seminars, trade show conferences, and courses offered by industry associations and organizations provide the best-available education. But those sessions barely go beyond the scope of a general introduction to the subject matter. As a result, the people who move into telemarketing management rarely have the specific and targeted background and education to properly prepare them to *run* the organization.

Education and development of telemarketing managers comes almost exclusively from on-the-job training, and that's bad for the industry. Even for the CEO who has the educational background and a dozen years in the industry, the most difficult part of managing growth is having to grow and develop talent from within. Does that mean you train, develop, and promote your TSRs into management? There is currently very little alternative, and that's what most of us have been doing.

Finding the problems is not difficult:

- The public perception of telemarketing as less than a career field;
- The youth of the industry;
- Shortages of trained talent;
- Finding time for quality training and development;
- Retention of personnel;
- Personnel compensation.

The people issues that all telemarketing organizations must deal with go on and on. Finding and implementing the solutions to those problems is considerably more challenging.

TWO DIFFERENT WAYS TO HANDLE COMPENSATION

From a growth standpoint, a very high price is paid for not drawing high-quality talent. On that issue, the guiding rule is this:

The #1 Growth Rule: *You can't do it without talented people.*

The corollary to that rule is:

Talented people cost more.

If you're not a large, in-house, business-to-business operation—where traditional business-trained people are working as TSRs and are being paid in the $25,000 to $40,000 range—you're probably paying an hourly wage. And the hourly wage you can offer will largely determine the kind of labor you can get.

You might try to get by with a $3.75 or $4.00 an hour wage if you underestimate the importance of getting bright, articulate, quick-learning people. And it might work over the short term. Low-level wages will look good on the financial statement . . . for a while.

Yellow Flag: *If you decide to build and grow your company that way, you've limited yourself in the quality of people you have available internally to promote.*

Why You Get What You Pay For

If you hire someone below the going rate in the labor market, you tend to get people who *can't* get jobs making more money. They rarely have the background, talent, or experience to get better jobs. They often lack the self image and confidence required to make much more, so they often are afraid to try for a higher base. They anticipate and are afraid of the additional pressure to sell and produce that go with the extra money. If they had the ambition, they would have gone for the higher-paying job in the first place.

Key Point: *Paying at the low—or even at the mid range—of the going marketplace pay range limits your ability to grow.*

When you need to promote from within, you'll find that the pool of employees you have attracted lacks the ambition and the ability needed to make the step up. You will find yourself with a pool of people who are already 99% Peter Principled. As a result, promoting from within will become an exercise in frustration and futility.

The sharper people in the labor market respond to the higher wages, and they are willing to take the challenge. They are a different breed entirely, and their work reflects it.

- The better candidates who come with higher wages will usually learn, produce, and earn more quickly
- You will draw a little older, more mature person who generally will have a little more work experience and life experience
- They are more likely to have experienced some of the basic frustrations and problems of being in the workplace
- They have greater tolerance for the challenges of the job
- They bring a stronger sense of commitment
- They tend to be more stable

If you are working consumer telemarketing programs or less than the traditional 40-hour work week, those people will often be working part-time for you to supplement their family's income. While they might not feel that it is worth the time spent away from their families at $4.00 an hour, they may very well justify that time at $6–10 an hour. Those people tend to have greater capability to deal with the juggling act of work and school or two jobs. They want a continuing source of income (either primary or supplemental) rather than a few quick bucks for temporary work at Christmas or other special occasions.

The extra money invested in the higher wages pays additional dividends. The incidence of aggravating problems is reduced, training (and retraining) costs are reduced, and productivity at the pure TSR level improves. Just as important—from a growth standpoint—you will have dramatically increased the ranks of the promotable talent you need.

As you continue to grow and promote from within, the quality of that original pool of talent will become even more important. These people are the ones who can contribute as they are promoted from supervisor to manager, to department head, and to director.

EXAMPLE: When Steve started his first telemarketing business in 1981, he started out with very little money and a small budget, and TSRs were paid $4.00 an hour. That was fine for attracting people who could do the calling on consumer-oriented, tightly controlled, and rigidly scripted programs. But they were *not* the people that were needed for more sophisticated consumer programs or for business-to-business work. Even worse, when management tried to promote from within, they found they had to go through 500 people to find 20 with the talent that was needed.

You have a similar set of challenges as you develop people for program development, fulfillment, training, and personnel. What originally appeared to be a question of simply filling the phones takes on an entirely new meaning and dimension.

Excellence vs. Cost Management: Catch 22

The concept of excellence is intangible and hard to define, but it becomes very tangible in terms of commitment and execution. The heart of the issue of excellence in telemarketing is this: How are you going to create an organization whose efforts will be defined as *excellent* by the *client?*

The Catch 22 of the situation is that to buy a whole crew of truly outstanding people with excellent track records in their given field of endeavor is very expensive. Suddenly, the relatively low rates that make it inexpensive to get into the industry at a modest budget level become almost impossible to achieve. The additional talent gives you a greater opportunity to achieve excellence, but you may no longer be rate-competitive.

Buyers may assume that one phone with a body is the same as any other phone with a body. They ask themselves, "Why should I pay $30 an hour when I can get the same thing over here for $22?" It's not the "same thing." But if they justify it *strictly* through hourly cost, without recognizing the benefits and value they lose in the tradeoff, that attitude can be hard to overcome.

If you staff all your key positions with excellent but expensive executives, you'll have to plan a pretty high hourly rate unless you reduce TSR wages. But doing that guarantees less than a quality effort, because that's the grass roots level.

It's worth repeating: the best companies pay *at* or even slightly *above* the going market rate so they can have their choice of the best people available. Yet they can't pay at a rate so high above going market wages that they become fat with wasted costs.

In 1989 you could hire TSRs at minimum wage. Or you could offer a "middle" of the labor market guaranteed wage per hour, plus *big* commissions, bonuses, and incentives. Or you could recruit at guaranteed wages that are at the "very top" of the labor market plus smaller incentives.

What's the difference in response, recruiting for the same kind of job, and equivalent work weeks (20 hours+) in a part-time labor market?

Frankly, you can wind up with good TSRs either way. But at the higher guaranteed wages you can have a *lot more* people. (Obviously, this is mandatory for a large and fast-growing operation.) And while it's true that a well-written script will factor out some of the difference in quality of candidate at a pure TSR level, there still will be a *significant* differential in TSR performance.

Perhaps of greater importance is that you will wind up with many more people who are ultimately *more promotable* to supervisory and management positions. In terms of promotion potential, the difference in the quality of talent you draw is astounding.

EXAMPLE: In 1984 we had an opportunity for tremendous growth. It meant adding many phones, hiring a large number of new TSRs, and promoting significant numbers of TSRs to supervisors and supervisors to managers.

Beyond the top level of promotable TSRs, we found that the layer of cream on the top was awfully thin; we simply were not deep enough in potential management talent.

We recognized that in order to grow the business, we *had* to have a better internal personnel pool to draw new supervisors from, and that we needed to increase the base wage for TSRs in order to attract the better talent. Partly to draw *better* people and partly to draw *more* people, we increased our pay structure for TSRs. We raised the rate enough to compete at the top of the market; in fact we *became* the top of the market.

What happened?

- The company had more calls than it could reasonably handle.
- Many more high-caliber people than the company was accustomed to attracting were interviewed, hired, and trained.
- As a group, those people were better on the phone than the company would normally have expected.
  - They picked up the essentials faster.
  - They were able to put the training into use on the phones better.
  - They were more resilient and better able to handle the pressures of the job.
- Many had the talent and the ambition to move into positions of responsibility in a very short time.

As the company upped entry-level TSR wages, management developed a *deep* pool of talent to draw on for promotions, with *all* the good supervisory talent that was needed even during periods of virtually explosive growth.

Growth Impact: *Higher guaranteed wages draw much better candidates, with an amazing difference in the talent that can be tapped for management.*

Importance of Incentives

Effective compensation goes beyond the initial base that is offered. Incentives should be added for most production positions. But it's important that you create incentives specifically for what you want. We recommend providing TSRs with a bonus incentive after working for the number of hours equivalent to six months of work (whether the TSR works part-time or full time), and again for the equivalent of one year . . . in addition to base increases at the same points.

- The increased productivity of the TSRs offsets the cost of the bonuses and base increases,
- The people will appreciate and look forward to the bonuses and base increases—and stay around to get them,
- The practice helps keep the better people on stall until they are needed for promotion,

When you are deciding how to compensate your people, you are making a mistake if you choose to hire and keep your entry-level talent at a cheap labor rate. When you're working to grow your business, you've got to allow for the kind of compensation that will draw and keep the talent you *will* need.

Good people don't come cheap, yet the general wages in the telemarketing industry haven't really been high for a long time. There is a lot of talk in the industry about how high wages are, but usually those high wages are reserved for management people at the top.

Tip: *If a company wants to have the people that will keep the organization competitive and growing, it is well served to share some of the wealth with its entry-level group.*

HOW TO RECRUIT PHONE PERSONNEL

Recruiting and hiring phone personnel is not a mysterious process. Yet it often causes problems for the growing company, especially during periods of particularly rapid growth. Hiring entry level positions is relatively simple, if not always easy.

Five Steps to Take Before You Start to Recruit

Several important initial actions must be taken to assure success in recruiting for the entry-level positions. In large part, the results of your search will be dependent upon the homework you have done before looking for the first person.

1. Determine the qualifications and basic profile for the positions you need to fill.
2. Make sure that your pay scales are competitive in the marketplace. If you can possibly do it, peg your pay level at the top of the labor market.
3. Establish incentives which will encourage good people who want to grow with you.
4. Determine where the people you need can be found and how best to contact them.
5. Make sure you have selected the right labor market.

The fifth point—selecting the right labor market—was discussed in the chapter on planning, and it is extremely important. If you can't recruit the phone personnel necessary for your expansion plans because they aren't available in your labor market, you can forget about growth. No matter how well you pay and no matter how well you define the candidates you hope to find, you are not going to find the people if they don't exist in the market where you are searching.

How to Find the Right Entry-Level People

Assuming you have taken those steps, finding the entry level people may be as simple as placing well-written ads in the community's most widely read newspaper. The best size, frequency, and placement of those ads is best determined through research and experimentation. Beyond researching the advertising policies of the newspapers where you might place ads, additional steps to take are:

- Research the public image and level of prestige that telemarketing has in the community. The perception of the industry in the public eye will influence your type of ads and your entire recruiting program.
- Ask the local Chamber of Commerce for suggestions on the best resources for attracting labor and their experience in how best to attract the labor in that specific market;
- Get feedback from Job Service about the availability of the skill levels you need and where to find the people;
- Determine which newspaper(s) will be the most appropriate to use in reaching your target candidates;
- Study the placement, types, sizes, and information provided in recruitment ads placed by the competition and/or by companies recruiting for similar skill positions; and
- Make certain your ad copy is thorough and descriptive enough to assure that those reading the ads can determine whether they are interested in and qualified for the position.

Once these issues have been addressed and the choices have been made about where to advertise, you should make sure you are getting the maximum results for your advertising dollar. That involves:

- tracking ad call results based on
  - placement (Part-Time Help Wanted, Sales, Inside Sales, Telephone Sales, Telemarketing, etc.)
  - ad size
  - ad copy
- determining optimum ad frequency
- establishing normal seasonal variations
- preventing/responding to ad burnout

By establishing performance tracking, you will be able to determine precisely where and what type of ads bring the greatest response. The most important factor is not whether a particular ad or ad placement is pleasing to the people creating and placing the ads. The critical factor is factually discovering how ad copy, size, layout, frequency, and placement affects the labor market's perception of the job and of the company, and the quality, number, and satisfaction of applicants who respond.

With a statistical baseline which includes separate information on seasonal variations, you will be able to discover:

- What types of ad layouts and copy communicates the message accurately and persuasively;
- What types of ad layouts and copy are most effective in different placement locations;
- How much the size of the ads affects the response;
- With what frequency (and on what days) the ads can be placed to achieve maximum return on your advertising dollar;
- How long a specific ad can be run before response dwindles significantly or drops below an acceptable level; and,
- How the effectiveness of new ads compares to tested and proven ads.

Those variables will change from market to market, within those markets at different times of the year, and as a given market's perception of the industry changes.

Note: *Unless you continue to track the ad results, you will be unable to make certain your ad budget is being most effectively spent.*

The following samples of ads run by Idelman Telemarketing, Inc. provide an idea of some of the different types of ads that may be effective. (See ads on pages 127 through 129.)

Supplementing Your Normal Sources

If you have a good labor market, hiring and training for the first 100 phones is a relatively easy trick. Yet it's not always that simple a matter.

A well-prepared profile may suggest additional special-interest publications which offer a high probability of success, such as:

- College newspapers
- Drama and entertainment publications
- Weekly newspapers specially targeted to senior citizens
- Technical publications related to your special applications.

Also, if your needs are primarily for part-time personnel, special arrangements may be made with local educational institutions to participate in their work/study or internship programs.

Ask yourself two simple questions: "Where are the kind of people I need?" and "How can I get their attention?" The ideal source is probably very close at hand; you just have to keep an open and creative mind and work until you find the sources that satisfy your needs. And don't rule out radio or television, dependent on the volume of people you need to recruit.

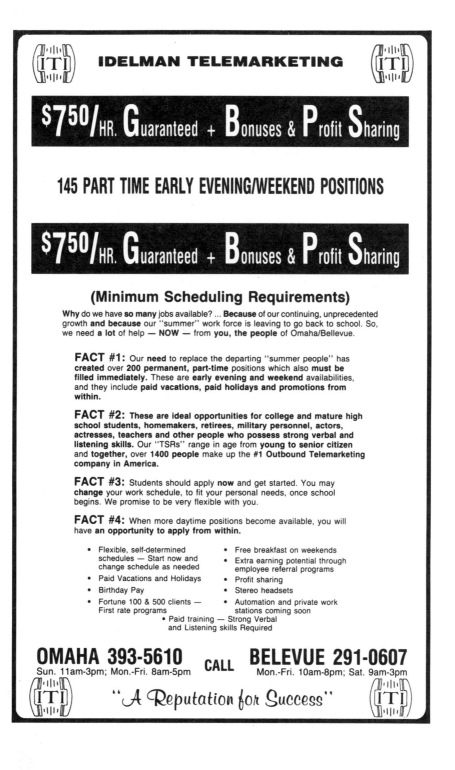

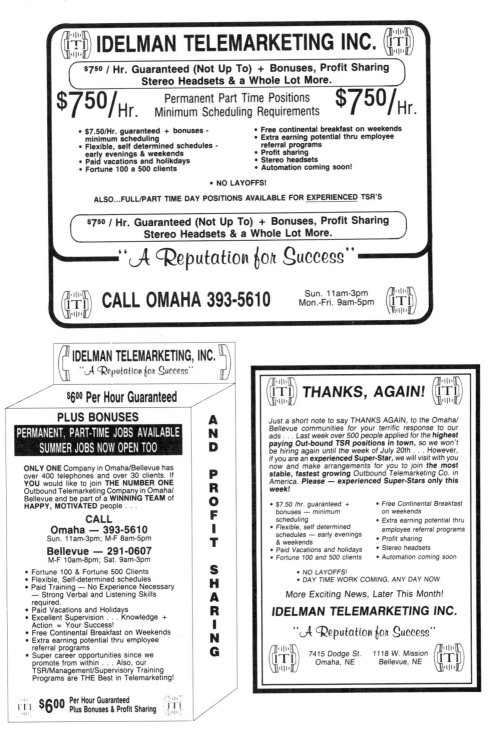

If your market is well defined but somewhat limited, or if you have particularly heavy needs, you may have to be considerably more creative.

You just have to know where the kind of people you want are and then figure out how to let them know that you have jobs for them. This is more difficult to do in a major metro area like New York or Chicago than in a smaller community like Omaha or Des Moines. But it can be done in either situation if you are creative and innovative.

> **EXAMPLE:** A telemarketing manager working a telemarketing agency in Chicago needed a bunch of people in such a hurry that he didn't have time to run an ad. He needed to fill 35 new positions in three days. He studied the profile of the TSRs who worked at the company to find out the areas where they lived; no helpful pattern was revealed.
>
> Next, he imagined he was one of the people he wanted to reach and where he might be during the course of a day or a week; that gave him the answer.
>
> He had a thick stack of flyers printed and gave them to his entire TSR staff to distribute in strategic locations:
>
> - Train and bus stations
> - Parks throughout the general area of the company
> - At the beaches on Lake Michigan
> - Outside nearby Wrigley Field (home of the Chicago Cubs).

Result: *The TSRs handed out more than 1,000 flyers, the company got more than 300 applicants overnight, and the demand for new TSRs was easily met.*

There are telemarketers who get some of their best people by keeping their eyes open for sharp people working in public contact positions, such as fast-food restaurants or supermarkets. When they see that the people work hard, do a good job of dealing with the customers, and show the kind of attitude they would like to have in their people, they invite them to call in for an interview.

Other companies have good success with internal recruiting bonuses. Their assumption is that the people who work for you associate with the people you would like to have work for you. The company offers a bonus to existing employees who bring friends and acquaintances into the company.

Tip: *Make the recruitment bonuses payable* after *the referred person has successfully completed a minimum period of time—such as 3 or 6 months—on the job.*

If the people you need exist in your labor market, there are ways to find them. Stay at it and you will find the methods that work for you.

How to Handle Large Volume Recruitment Response

When you are a large volume shop that is growing very quickly, it will cost too much time and money to interview one TSR candidate at a time. You have to be efficient. Yet you must be able to respond quickly to the needs of the business and the people. A major part of the solution is doing *group* interviews.

There is—justly—a lot of controversy and divided opinion on the subject of group interviews. When the entire hiring process consists of the group interview and the hiring is done *in mass,* it can be a demeaning, unprofessional, and unproductive experience for everyone involved.

More accurately, what we are suggesting is more like a group audition:

- The essential information—about the company, the job, and the requirements—is presented to the group (saving the time required to explain it repeatedly in individual interviews);
- General questions are taken from the group and answered;
- The audition process—including reading a scripted sample presentation—is explained;
- Those who are interested in the job and choose to audition are asked to stay;
- Those who choose not to audition are thanked for their interest in coming and are excused;
- Auditions are held, one after the other, with the other members of the group still in attendance;
- When all auditions are completed, the people who do not pass the audition are thanked and excused; and
- The people who pass the audition move on to the usual individual interview process.

The main benefits of this approach are twofold:

1. Large numbers of people can be screened very quickly;
2. You get a practical (although cursory) fix on each person's ability to perform before a group of peers, and within an environment similar to the one in which the successful applicant ultimately will be working.

This type of group interview can be very effective, *provided* the interviewer is excellent. No matter how well you build the organization internally and how fine-tuned it becomes with people who have learned and internalized the methods and concepts behind your operation, you're going to make some mistakes when you do mass recruiting.

Tip: *Although group interviews have been done with more than 100 people (with multiple interviewers for the individual follow-up interviews), they are generally most effective when the size of the initial group is around 10 people.*

HOW TO RECRUIT MANAGEMENT PERSONNEL

Recruiting and selecting the right supervisory and management personnel can be much more complex than recruiting for entry-level positions. The people who fill the management positions will determine how effectively the company's systems and procedures are implemented and executed. The right people in these positions will make a dramatic difference in the organization's effectiveness and productivity.

How To Determine the Management Candidate Profile

The basics of labor market, profile, and salary structure that are important for the entry-level positions apply to management candidates, as well. There are, however, four additional criteria that must be considered for management personnel.

1. They need value sets that are in harmony with the company's values. This builds chemistry whereas conflicting values lead to dissension.
2. They need more than basic skills and education to do the job.
3. They should have a clear desire to progress with the organization.
4. They need the talent and ability to support that desire.
5. They must be able to mesh with the personality and philosophy of the organization.
6. Their skills and attitudes should complement those of the existing management staff.

As we noted earlier, the last point does not mean simply to select people who share the skills of current management. Determining the qualities you need in the people who join the management team returns you to your vision for the company and the capabilities of existing management. In the same way that the initial structuring of a company should be done around the initial vision, primary contributions, and skills of the founders of the organization, new supervisory and management personnel selections should support the current vision and complement the existing management staff.

In defining the kind of person needed in a particular position, do some in-depth evaluation:

- Honestly appraise the amount of success you have had, and the factors that contributed to that success.
- Analyze the areas of knowledge and experience which have been gained during that process.
- Look very closely at the areas in which the existing management staff is weak or deficient.

Then ask yourself these key questions:

- What special talents and skills could help reinforce the strengths?
- What special talents and skills could help overcome the weaknesses?
- How can the addition of new management be accomplished in a manner that will capitalize on the opportunity to fortify the strong and diminish the weak points?

It is worthwhile to do a profile that will point you toward those candidates who can diminish some of the deficiencies of the operation or reinforce and maintain its strengths. They will have a value that is well beyond their qualifications and abilities to carry out the defined job function.

You may also find it worthwhile to contract with specialists to develop a tailored, professional skills and aptitude profile interview. Once you have established what traits are required of the people who can succeed in filling your positions, taking the time and making the investment to develop the profile can be of great benefit. When the profile interview has been developed, you can either continue to have the specialist conduct the interview or train internal personnel to conduct and score the interviews. It's an extra tool that can help save you from making costly mistakes.

Management Profiles: Areas to Evaluate

- General Information
  - Personal background
  - Education
  - Work history
  - Intelligence
  - Ability to focus and concentrate
  - Memory
  - Creativity
  - Energy level
  - Work ethic
  - Sense of values and personal philosophy
  - Leadership roles
- Job Knowledge/Skills
  - Performance in current and previous positions
  - Experience in and with the organization
  - Telemarketing knowledge and range of experience
  - Analytical skills
  - Verbal skills
  - Writing skills
  - Persuasiveness and sales ability
- People Skills and Interpersonal Relationships
  - Evaluations of co-workers and clients
  - Team play and interaction
  - Willingness to share credit and rewards
  - Ability to mesh with existing personnel
  - Responsiveness to superiors/subordinates
- Management and Leadership Capability
  - Organizational skills
  - Ability to plan, prioritize, and strategize

- – Accuracy in evaluation of the skills and talents of others
- – Development of subordinates
- – Ability to delegate
- – Team achievement
- – Leadership qualities
- – Management style
- – Willingness to accept different styles in others
- – Accuracy in judgment and decision making
- – Situational problem solving skills
- – Fairness
- Advancement Potential and Drive
  - – Ambition/Pro-Activeness
  - – Determination
  - – Competitiveness
  - – Initiative and Self-starter qualities
  - – Follow-through
  - – Individual achievement
  - – Special honors
  - – Promotability
- Stability
  - – Honesty and integrity
  - – Poise under pressure
  - – Ability to accept correction/criticism
  - – Personal financial management
  - – Personal and professional responsibility
  - – Attendance
  - – Consistency
  - – Dependability
  - – Loyalty

When you are clear on where the existing management personnel can best focus their energies, you will be much better prepared to look for people who have the talent and experience to balance the skills of your staff.

EXAMPLE: Many of the problems I experienced in my early days of telemarketing were *because* I was doing the recruiting. I didn't have a third party who could help with the evaluations, handle salary administration, and enable me to be more productive in my hiring.

I admitted my weakness and recognized that I either had to get better or hire someone else who already was better. I decided to hire someone else who was already good at salary administration, enabling me to focus on my strengths, instead of tripping over my own weaknesses.

The Importance of Promoting From Within

If you want to manage for growth, you must learn to develop your own people and promote from within. It is certainly the first avenue to consider whenever a position needs to be filled. Promoting from within brings a number of important benefits:

- The person promoted has a detailed knowledge of the company, its operations, its philosophy, its vision, and its style;
- The person is a known quantity; he or she fits with the company's style and is already committed to its philosophy and vision;
- The person is likely to be quickly accepted by others in organization; they see it as the advancement of one of their own;
- The promotion has a "trickle down effect," with the promotion "up the ladder" of people in positions below the first person promoted;
- The employees gain respect for and loyalty to the company for providing "first opportunity" to existing employees; and
- The promotion from within reinforces the hope of other employees that they have an opportunity for advancement.

Every position in the company should be promoted from within, whenever possible.

Yellow Flag: *If you consistently have to go outside to get the talent you need, it becomes demotivating to your internal people. They begin to feel that there is very little opportunity for them to advance.*

Making the Decision to Go Outside

As important as promoting from within is, sometimes it is not a realistic alternative. Some situations call for going outside the company for talent, but you shouldn't hire people from the outside unless you have carefully determined why. Some of the reasons for taking the step are:

- Internal problems that require new personnel to resolve;
- The need to infuse the company with new perspectives;
- Sudden, unexpected growth opportunities; and
- New, high-level positions created by growth in the company's level of maturity and sophistication.

It's unlikely that you will find a chief financial officer from within the entry-level ranks of your TSRs. And sometimes, new people are needed to avoid the company developing the "tunnel vision" that comes from being "so close to the forest that you can't see the trees." Fresh blood (if it's smart blood) can be a real plus to a growth organization.

Part of the problem is deciding the type of person you want. Generally, business people prefer to make one of two choices:

- The brightest mind they can find, just out of college with a little work experience; or
- Someone with a proven track record who's pretty happy where he or she is, and not even looking for a change.

It's pretty tough for a consumer telemarketing operation to get established people with traditional business backgrounds. Their self images make it hard for them to look at a job that starts at 2:00 in the afternoon and ends about 10:00 at night, with one—maybe two—days off a week, and not necessarily on the weekend.

In business-to-business telemarketing, you've got fewer problems than the consumer telemarketing operation. You're probably offering traditional business hours, daytime, Monday through Friday. The concept of business-to-business telemarketing is easier for people to accept and the image of it is better. It opens up more of the labor market to you.

Further, no matter how talented the person is, it is unlikely that he or she can ever become a *successful* telemarketing supervisor, manager, or executive until time has first been spent as a TSR. Until the people have experienced the work and its demands—including the patience required, the rejection, and the frustration—it's virtually impossible for them to bring real empathy to the job. And without that empathy, they just can't supervise properly. The exceptional supervisor might be able to learn it in a week, but usually it takes at *least* a month or more.

Finding the people you need to grow is really a mixed bag of tricks. It's an art, it involves luck, and it's a lot of hard work. If you know what kind of people you want or what you need, you can go out and look for them, as in any other industry.

How to Begin the Outside Search

When going outside, it's very important that you get clear on what you want by first asking yourself some probing questions. A good beginning question to ask is: "Why do we want the kind of person we've decided on?" Review the work you have done in determining your needs, then expand on that question by focusing specifically on the position and application you are working on.

To get a clearer image of what you want, start by examining the requirements for the position in comparison to the people you have internally who don't quite fit the profile. Ask yourself:

- What specific skills and characteristics do they have that made them worthy of consideration?

- What specific skills or characteristics do they lack that prevent you from choosing them?
- Would a person who has the skills or characteristics missing in the internal candidates have to have all of the traits that had made them worthy of consideration?
- In what type of industry, company, or job might a person develop the required traits and skills?

The questions can be quite varied, but an example may help clarify the concept and make it more specific.

EXAMPLE: You are going to be looking for a marketing person.

- Do you want a person with a strong telemarketing background?
- Would you rather have a good marketer without telemarketing experience who you can train in telemarketing?

You answer those questions and decide that what you want is one of the 10 best salespeople in the country—whether or not they are experienced in telemarketing.

- Do you want someone with broad-based experience or one who is expert in a narrow, vertical industry?
- Do you want that person to be a replacement for a top person who needs to concentrate on other areas of the business? Or,
- Are you looking for someone who can be a part of a larger team that you are building and will personally oversee?

Another important part of your identification process is determining if your budget for the position and the skills you are looking for bear any realistic relationship to each other. Many telemarketing heads have fooled themselves into believing that the person they chose was well suited for the job because they could be hired within the desired budget.

EXAMPLE: In 1983, our first operations manager was hired at $12,000, and what we got was a $12,000 guy who performed at a $12,000 level.

We weren't happy with the performance or with the choice we had made. We realized that, if we were to reach our goals, we had to have people who were more talented and could make a greater contribution to the company's growth. We also realized that getting a person of that caliber meant finding a way to increase the budget for the position.

By 1985, the equivalent position was budgeted at around $40,000. The skills and knowledge the $40,000 guy brought to the party were vastly greater. The job was being done in a much more productive way, and the company was growing ahead of projections.

You have to make sure you don't delude yourself about your needs or about what your budget will buy. Cost management is important, but playing "bargain basement" with people sets the foundations for mediocrity!

The Experience Quotient

Even more than in the recruitment of TSRs, the search for top management talent requires preparation, creativity, and persistence. Good management people are birds of a different feather. H. Ross Perot is well known for doing an exceptional job of hiring very good people. When asked his secret for finding so many talented management people, he replied: "Eagles don't flock. You have to find them one at a time."

But how do you go about finding them? Where do you go in your search to find the talented management people who can help you achieve your growth objectives?

How you conduct the search depends in part on your situation and your business plan. If you are just starting out, don't know where to get the people, and don't have good industry contacts who can help you find people, you probably will have to begin with a small, simple organizational structure. In that case, you have to start small and gradually build the organization while you find and develop the people you need.

As much as we might dislike admitting it, a person's age, experience, and contacts in the business are important. It is rarely written about or spoken out loud, because it sounds like age discrimination. But that's not what we're getting at. One person may be 30 years old, with eight years of solid and varied telemarketing experience. Another telemarketer might be 50 and have 25 years in the business, but only have one year of experience that has been repeated 25 times.

Yet the fact remains that the amount of life experience one has is important. It's almost like "the longer you take is equal to the more you make." What you can *bring* to the party is in great part a function of where you came from, *before* the party. Additional life experience teaches you certain things that you need to learn to manage and grow an organization of any kind, from a family unit to a business.

When the best people in the business first started out, they couldn't have hired some of the key players they hired later in their careers. In the early stages, they didn't know enough about the industry, didn't have the contacts, and hadn't been around long enough to have the kind of image to attract those kinds of people.

Their I.Q.'s are no higher at 40 or 50 than when they were 19 or when they were 30. But they each have much higher E.Q.'s: Experience Quotients. They are different people than they were 10 or 20 year ago. As they have gained greater experience, better contacts, and better positioning within the industry, they have found it much easier to attract excellent talent from the outside.

The reality is that it's important to know people in the industry and to be very sure of how you're going to tap those contacts when they are needed.

If you can find the right person—one with a track record and talent and stamina who can be productive and fit right into your business—be happy to hire that person and pay very well whether the lead came from a contact in the industry or from an ad in a journal. It's best to find people through good industry contacts, but the key is results.

Seven Tested Sources for Recruiting Management Personnel

If you need people and aren't sure where to find them:

- Contact other direct marketing companies (especially those where you have previously established contacts) to help you with recommendations.
- Look in specialized newspaper listings such as the *Wall Street Journal* Wednesday edition.
- The industry trade journals are good places to find people to interview. Look into industry publications such as:
  - the Direct Marketing Association Newsletter
  - the CADM Ad Marts
  - Direct Marketing Magazine
  - Telemarketing Magazine
  - Inbound/Outbound
  - Target Marketing magazine
- Call people within the industry who publish informational direct marketing and telemarketing magazines and newsletters.
- Organizations such as the DMA and the ATA often have information about people looking for a new opportunity.
- Consultants may be aware of good people in the industry who are looking for your opportunity.
- Industry headhunters can be helpful, especially if you know exactly what you need and precisely the kind of people you are looking for.

Why Raiding Your Competition Is a Risky Strategy

When some telemarketing companies need to expand, their first thought seems to be "Which company can we raid?" It's a rather limited perspective that reveals a lot about their understanding of telemarketing.

- First—looking at it as a practical matter—they reveal how small their thinking really is. If they are "stealing" from a truly excellent company, the people they will likely succeed in attracting will be those who the excellent company feels are expendable. Also if they have already determined that they don't mind "stealing" people, the industry is growing *so* fast that they can expect those who they steal to be stolen, in turn, from them (sooner or later)!
- Second, their attitude about the course of first choice to expand their company demonstrates how little confidence they have in their own abilities to develop people . . . and in the people they have developed.

Raiding to staff key positions with talent that has been developed by someone else really does show a lot of weakness on the part of the raider. First, it is not fair to the people who *have* developed the talent. Second, and more important, the attitude that leads to that approach prevents the company from developing its own people to levels of excellence and having them remain more loyal to the organization that has shown enough confidence to invest the time and money in them.

Remember, if you build a company by outbidding the competition and taking away their players, the odds are that the day will come when other competition will outbid you for those same people.

If you go to war, you want more than a few mercenaries in the trenches with you. You want trusted soldiers who are in the battle with you as a matter of dedication, commitment, and loyalty to your cause. You can get that kind of support much more often if you develop your *own* people and promote from *within*.

If you build that kind of loyalty and dedication, you won't need to raid other companies. Talented people who have heard about how you treat your people will be coming to you, looking for the opportunity to be treated in the same way.

Don't get us wrong, there are times when people are looking to make a change and you will be correct in hiring them. However, there is a big-time difference between recruiting such people and "raiding" a competitor.

BETTER LIVING THROUGH CHEMISTRY

Although the term "personality conflicts" is often overused in explaining the reasons for the failure of two or more people to work together, the values and styles of the people who will work together closely should be a major consideration in the selection process. Call it chemistry, or call it what you want; it *is* important.

> **EXAMPLE:** Andrew Carnegie was the father of the steel business in America. He completely restructured and reorganized the industry at the turn of the century. He was fanatical about finding and hiring the best people to work for him.
>
> When he wanted to develop a complicated new steel-making process, Carnegie charged his staff with finding the best chemist in the world. The search did, in fact, carry them around the world. When the search was complete, the man at the top of the list was a brilliant chemist from England. Although his salary demands were extreme, his credentials as a scientist were above question. The man was hired and brought to Pittsburgh to head the project.
>
> Within a matter of weeks, the entire project was in disarray. Chaos and contention were the rule. The man was indeed a brilliant chemist, but he could not fathom how to work cooperatively with other people.
>
> Carnegie ordered the man replaced with the best chemist on the list who could:
>
> 1. work with others and
> 2. fit into the organization.

The man who was subsequently hired was several places lower on the original list. But he was an excellent chemist, *and* he knew how to create an atmosphere of innovation and cooperation. The same group of people, with a new leader acting as the creative catalyst, developed the process ahead of schedule.

The group's chemistry was productive . . . on both counts.

Of all the personnel mistakes made in telemarketing, most come from very poor recruitment and selection. Sometimes they happen because of poor initial evaluations, ineffective questioning, or incomplete reference checking. Occasionally, the people selected simply lack the necessary talents. Mismatches do happen, to *everyone*.

Yet some of the people who don't work out have *more* than enough talent to do the job at hand. You do your best to select people who mesh with the other members of your organization. Then you teach them according to your vision, your values, your knowledge of the business and the way you work. But they aren't the right type of people for the organization that hires them. For whatever reasons, the person and the company just don't mesh or complement each other result in the advances that the talent would have indicated was possible.

Often, you cannot detect the chemistry in the job interview. It may take three months to get to know someone's real personality and chemistry and discover whether the basis for the necessary interactions is there or not. So you're still largely at the mercy of hiring from *apparent* talent, the resume, and reference checks.

Much of this problem is resolved only through trial and error. You have to take some changes on people with tons of raw capability. At a given position, you may try one person, guess right, and have that person with you for years. At another position, you may have to try several different people before you find the one who had not only the raw aptitude and capacity, but also the right approach and chemistry to fit into a compatible team.

It doesn't mean that the people all have to be the same type. You don't want a group of "yes men."

Remember: *When two people in a business agree all the time, one of them probably isn't necessary.*

But there *has* to be a common value set, and the people need to complement each other.

Ego and Chemistry

You should develop an organizational team with the "opposites attract" approach in mind. So long as the team members are not so totally opposite that they are unable to understand and relate to each other, each will bring different strengths and perspectives to the game. That type of team offers greater depth and versatility.

For a growing telemarketing unit, the development of more than one stand-alone leader is vital. Without multiple, independent leaders who can take control in their own distinct areas of the operation, the company will remain a "one-man shop"; it will simply have more people involved in the company. The number of personnel taking true leadership positions must be increased if the company is to grow beyond that stage.

Yet those key players must adapt to the reality that:

1. Growth in telemarketing requires cooperative, interactive, interdependent, teamwork;
2. There has to be a central figure who acts as the court of final authority for the company's management.

If two top people need the limelight of "top billing," the rivalry will cause confrontations and become counterproductive. Putting both of those people together in the same room won't work, because they will have a hard time coexisting; they will soon mutually self-destruct. The fact that both will be competing to be the center of attention will reduce the effectiveness of each of them . . . and hurt the company.

Important: *It doesn't mean that the needs of either person are wrong; it's just that their chemistry isn't right. When they are put into the same environment, their egos clash and productivity suffers.*

The top person—the one who sits behind the desk where the buck stops—must learn to give up the limelight somewhat . . . at least enough to *share* "center stage." That person *has* to be conscious of the need to manage the ego needs and balance the strengths of the other top people if strong, company-wide leadership is to be created and maintained.

Balancing the Leadership Strengths

If you look at the individual members of effective teams, there's usually a balance and a mixture of temperaments. There is a mixture of type A and type B personalities. If you look at their styles, you will find that within the group are people with totally different approaches. But their differing temperaments and approaches come together to complement each other. The team forms a camaraderie from common values: a shared vision and a shared commitment to excellence.

Every company needs a "Mr. Pitney/Mr. Bowes" type of balance; people with differing needs and differing strengths who combine to do more than either could do separately. When the different needs and strengths exist, the combination can bring tremendous productivity.

If you enjoy being in the background, recognize it and find someone who wants to be the up-front person. If you're in a promotion-driven business and you enjoy being in the background, getting the world's greatest promotional genius who is also a background person may be a fatal mistake. If you enjoy the limelight and need to do the up-front work, you'd better recognize it and get a person who doesn't have the same kind of needs and desires.

And it's not only a matter of job title or of the top position in the company. An immediately subordinate employee with the same kind of a personality as a superior may consistently defer to him/her *only* because of their positions in the company.

EXAMPLE: Terry is a new sales supervisor with a long track record of producing strong results as a TSR. The company is growing rapidly, and he sees his new promotion as the first in a series of steps that will eventually result in his assuming a position in top management. While he is pleased with the recognition of the promotion, Terry is very impatient to become a "real" manager.

Terry's immediate supervisor, Ken, has been a manger for only a few weeks, after being a supervisor for less than a year. He has been very effective in his position, yet he knows that his sales results were not as strong as Terry's, and he wasn't on the phone as long. Like Terry, Ken is very ambitious.

Both Ken and Terry have very strong people skills. Both have good analytical ability. Both have a good feel for telemarketing. And each sees the other as a competitor who could stand in the way of each other's career paths advancing as rapidly as they would like. The relationship between the two deteriorates in a very short time.

Although they agree on most courses of action, they frequently bicker over their areas of disagreements. Neither is willing to concede that the other might be right, and both want to gain recognition for their abilities in the same areas. In the end, most of their confrontations are resolved by Terry deferring to Ken because he is "the boss," yet he is continually seething underneath his deferential approach.

Which person could do the job better isn't the most important issue. As long as that confrontational situation exists, their productivity can't be as great as their individual talents could allow. Much of their talent is wasted in posturing and competing for recognition, rather than in combining their talents for maximum results for the company and for the rewards that would ultimately come for both.

Building a team that meshes is largely a matter of effort and patience. You either have to put in a lot of time and money, or have the opportunity to come out of the gate with a management team that you know and that already meshes. Given the talent, the key issue then becomes the chemistry. You have to have the right chemistry around you if you want to build a strong and cohesive organization.

No infallible guidelines exist to show you how to define the qualities of the people you will need on your management team. Yet, a core factor is consistent in the teams that mesh together smoothly and productively:

Cohesive organizations are held together by the bonds of shared vision, common values, and a deep commitment to the success of the group.

SIX ESSENTIAL POINTS ON TRAINING

Comprehensive training pays major day-to-day dividends in:

- employee confidence,
- work quality,
- productivity,
- employee satisfaction/retention.

While most telemarketing firms would agree with that concept, implementation of programs to achieve those results is less than universal.

The creation of training programs and the budgeting of time to conduct effective training of telemarketing personnel are often given low priority. Telemarketing training —especially beyond the TSR level—is frequently inconsistent and unstructured. Training for supervisory and management personnel is commonly relegated to a "when we can do it" status.

It is not surprising when the results of that approach are considerably less than satisfactory and the developed talent that is needed to expand is not available . . . and trained telemarketing talent is in extremely short supply.

Result: *If you want to grow in a controlled manner, a significant part of the commitment you make to your people must be the training programs you create and the work you do to develop your people and help them progress.*

Unless you "home-grow" your talent, the probability is high that you will not have the people required to support significant growth. Initial and ongoing training programs are essential parts of that commitment.

That holds true for each area of the company, from the TSR trainee to the outside marketing personnel and top management. If people are to be successful and grow in their jobs, they must be supported by the best educational programs that company can afford to devise. Those programs must go beyond the basic skills and techniques required in the performance of the job. The training should also include the development of the philosophies, values, and attitudes that are consistent with those of the company.

Key Point: *Nothing can replace the value of* quality training *in the development of* quality *people and the creation of a truly* knowledgeable *organization.*

Budgeting for Training

While employee education is a major requirement of properly managed growth, you must be careful when making projections for learning curves for your people and the resulting costs involved. Company founders and top managers too often make the business mistake of assuming that they, themselves, are just ordinary, everyday people with average intelligence, memory, and learning capacity.

Telemarketing is a high-energy, fast-paced environment, and most of the people who rise to the top have exceptionally quick minds and extremely good memories. Most of your line people won't have the same degree of ability.

Tip: *Allow extra time in your initial projections, then develop final time lines based on the actual learning curves of your people.*

If you base your projections on the learning curves of yourself and your key management personnel, you will usually be sadly disappointed and seriously over budget.

The First Building Block: TSR Training

It's not enough to give newly hired TSRs a script, have them listen in to other TSRs for a little while, and say "Go do the job." While results can be gotten in that way, the results will fall far short of the quality and the quantity that could have been produced. The TSR trainees must receive the thorough classroom and on-the-job training and support that will give them a strong foundation of knowledge and skills that will improve their initial productivity and their chances for ongoing success.

Included in the initial classroom training should be:

- *Orientation:*
  An overview of the industry and an introduction to the company, its history, its structure, its philosophy, and its goals.
- *Telemarketing theory and practice:*
  Core information about general telemarketing methods, the role of telemarketing in the business community, and the role of telemarketing in the company.
- *Universal telemarketing techniques:*
  What makes telemarketing work, vocal techniques, the elements of a telemarketing presentation (from making initial contact with the target party to call wrap-up and follow through), phone courtesy, callbacks, organizational procedures, call tracking for analysis of personal results, etc.
- *Specific program information, including:*
  - Product knowledge
  - Product features, advantages and benefits
- *Application-specific telemarketing techniques:*
  The telemarketing techniques involved in the specific program application: direct sales, lead generation, survey, etc.
- *Program-specific presentation techniques:*
  - Presentation format
  - Specific methods and techniques for the presentation of the program
  - How to handle the most frequent questions and objections
- *Practice sessions and role playing*
- *Explanation of company expectations for:*
  - Program goals
  - The new trainees' rates-of-skill progression
- *On the Job Training (OJT)*

Beyond the initial classroom training, the trainees should be provided during the OJT period with strong, direct coaching support and periodic reinforcement training in the classroom. After the TSRs have successfully moved beyond the trainee stage, they should be provided with ongoing skill enhancement training.

The Impact of Automation on TSR Training

It is often believed that the amount of training time required for new TSRs can be drastically reduced by having automation and CRTS. The concept is that you can train your people much more quickly when you put in tubes, because the tube does all of the work for them.

The best manual telemarketing operations (any many automated ones) have an initial classroom training programs of more than 20 hours for consumer work; for business-to-business work, the training may be much more extensive. That's before the trainee ever makes a live presentation. Following the classroom work, there is often an additional 40 hours of special on-the-job training and coaching.

It has been said that, with the CRT, a person will be ready to call in *four* hours. That is a gross generalization, and it is rarely—if ever—true. That kind of statement has *nothing* to do with the very real advantages of using CRTs and automated programs with branched scripting programs. It has *everything* to do with not understanding the dynamics of telemarketing.

Manual business-to-consumer telemarketers could train their people in four hours and have them just as prepared as the automated firm who gives four hours of training on the same program. That's not to say that either group will be adequately prepared to represent the client with a quality presentation.

The "four hours of training" statement simply means that the trainees know how to use the machinery. The TSRs may be ready to *place* calls more quickly, but that doesn't mean that they are able to do a good job of presenting what appears on the screen during that call. It doesn't mean that they are ready to be a *Telemarketing Sales* Representative. When the TSRs are assumed to be ready because they can get the right words to appear on the screen, the heart of telemarketing has been forgotten.

Good automated systems *will* do an effective job of bringing up the right portion of the script, but the TSR has to be able to *do* something with the little patterns of light that seem to appear magically on the screen. Those patterns form words, but the computer doesn't say them. The computer can't put *life* and *feeling* and *inflection* and *persuasion* into those words.

It's all too easy to allow the TSR to become an extension of the tube and give a very dry presentation. The tube has no emotion, but sales is an emotional game. The presentation shouldn't shrill or be melodramatic, but there *are* important ways to express positive emotion and feelings effectively in a conversation.

The ability to convey product knowledge, product belief and the proper tone for a presentation has to be internalized; that doesn't come *just* from looking at the tube. Today's computers aren't capable of that kind of training. Those skills come *only* from one human being training and coaching another human being.

Remember: *Effective telemarketing presentations have to be made from internal feelings prompted by the external stimulus of the script and the ability to apply strong listening skills. It's not an either/or matter. It has to be all.*

The best answer to the question is the combination of a good piece of branched scripting software *and* a thorough job of TSR training in the intangible concepts and techniques that bring that script to life. That's how telemarketing is changing, and that's how it will change for the better.

The Importance of Good Supervisory Training

Training plays a major role in developing and preparing your people for advancement. TSRs can have a great deal of natural talent, but they will lack the confidence and skills to use that talent productively if they are promoted to sales supervisory positions and immediately thrown onto the floor without adequate training.

Important: *The ability of the floor supervisors and managers will play a key role in determining whether or not the sales force develops and maintains a strong sense of involvement with, and belonging to, the company.*

The floor supervisors and managers must have the ability to empathize with the people and familiarize them with the organization. No matter what the natural abilities of an individual, that capacity to empathize with the TSR is *learned* rather than *instinctive*.

Most phone-room supervision is "home grown" and promoted from within the ranks of the phone reps. Yet the incentive for a good TSR to take the promotion often is simply "to get off the phone." Because the work force in telemarketing is young, the supervisors often don't have enough life experience to properly handle the new level of authority. If abused, that authority can turn a supervisor into an ugly power tripper.

Key Point: *Only an excellent supervisory training program—complete with follow-through and scheduled reinforcement after the initial training—can effectively manage the vicissitudes of the highly energetic, but sometimes immature, telemarketing supervisor.*

The Rewards of Crosstraining

The company's educational programs should also broaden the employees' perspectives of their positions and of the full operation of the company. They need to see the big picture. That calls for effective cross-training and exposure to the workings of the other positions in the department and those of other departments.

> **EXAMPLE:** All entry-level client services people—who rarely come from within because of the clerical nature of the positions—should be trained and educated in what goes on in the other departments. They need to understand each aspect of what the company does. They need a full understanding of and appreciation for the other job functions and requirements. They need a real appreciation for how everything fits together and why it fits together in the way it does.

Note: *Although crosstraining is often the last area of training developed by a company, the rewards of increased harmony and team spirit will pay valuable dividends.*

Comprehensive cross-training is extremely valuable in increasing the effectiveness of your internal staff. When there is a shared understanding between departments and between the positions within the departments:

- The team members enjoy their work more,
- Employees have a greater respect for the needs of others,

- They understand the impact on other departments of their performance,
- People work together better,
- Absenteeism is dramatically reduced.

Employees who have been cross-trained do their jobs better because they understand where they fit into the company and the importance of their being there. Their concept of "the team" is expanded, they want to be involved in the team's progress, and they don't want to let the rest of the team down.

All of the floor management staff, including the quality assurance personnel, need cross-training. It is the same for the cross-training of the various functions within a department, as well as for interdepartmental cross-training.

Key Point: *Each person needs greater understanding of the overall process of the company's functions and the demands of the other employees' duties. Such understanding can bring increased cohesiveness, cooperation, and results.*

The "grass is greener" syndrome is eliminated. Each person knows what is required of them to effectively and efficiently complete their role in the entire process. They know what is important to maintain, and they do a much better job of maintaining it.

The Value of Documentation and Manuals

We believe in committing the training programs and operational procedures to writing, and we strongly recommend that you create policy and procedure manuals for every department of your company. While this can be a major expenditure of time and money, it is one of the best investments you can make.

Important Benefit: *By having the manuals and documentation in place, the learning curve of your people will be improved, and the frequency of costly mistakes will be reduced.*

The value of operation manuals and other documentation frequently is not appreciated. In many cases, where they do exist, they are poorly thought out, hastily constructed and incomplete.

Operation manuals should be crated in such a manner that:

- the primary guidelines for the proper execution of the job are clearly and concisely stated;
- the various functions and duties of the positions are segmented into separate and distinct categories;
- the methods are given for completing all forms, tracking documents and internal reports;
- allow for quick and easy on-the-job reference to questions about policy, procedures and techniques;
- encourages thorough and repeated study; and
- they can be updated easily

When real care and attention are devoted to preparing documentation and manuals, that effort can provide both reinforcement material and day-to-day operating guidelines for your people.

If a company is to promote from within, good training and documentation are not luxuries; they are necessities. They are investments that are an integral part of the company's commitment to the future through the successful development of its people.

Note: *Documentation and manuals are not* substitutes *for classroom, on-the-job, or ongoing training. Ongoing training by experienced staff members is required to support and extend the value of the documentation and manuals.*

Keep in mind that it is a virtual impossibility to transfer instincts to documentation. Ideas and examples can be included in operations manuals, but the *feeling* of what to do in certain situations comes from the sharing of experiences, including "war stories" and discussion of mistakes that have been made and the lessons learned from those mistakes.

It's easy to put off creating manuals and ongoing training because developing and implementing them is so time consuming, but you need to find a way to take the step.

Key Point: *In a rapid growth situation, the combination of written manuals and proper training programs can make the difference between being able to accept a piece of business that will grow you or having to turn it down.*

This is a critical area, and one which is frequently a problem area in telemarketing. The common idea is that the frequency of problems in creating the documentation and scheduling training is explained by "Well, that's just telemarketing." That's just head-in-the-sand thinking.

The real problem is that as you're growing rapidly, your key people are getting busier and busier. While the lip service is given to the need to solve the problems, nobody has the time to do it. It is a step that telemarketing management must take if telemarketing is to be fully respected and accepted as an equal member of the direct marketing community.

How We Did It: We bit that bullet in 1984. At a point of growing even faster than we really would have liked to, we recognized it could no longer be put off. We knew that we had to make sure that our supervisors became better than they were at handling people issues. The challenge was to bring tremendous numbers of new employees into the company and still enable the newest people to have that same close feeling of caring and involvement that our first 60 people had.

We knew the key to that was the ability of our floor supervisors and management. They had to really know their jobs and the skills and techniques required to perform them. They had to have the ability to empathize with the people, to familiarize the new people with the organization, to integrate them into the existing culture, and to help them feel like they were an important part of the company.

We decided to contract with someone to help improve and standardize our management training and to create additional manuals. We identified the characteristics needed in that person:

- A strong telemarketing background;
- Excellent training and organizational credentials; and
- A specialist in people issues.

We knew from previous experience that the advisor we chose met those needs and could be trusted to handle the project properly while *we* were tied up constantly with the growth process.

Using an outside advisor to upgrade our training and develop manuals was expensive, but the results were *well* worth the cost.

SEVEN STEPS IN DEVELOPING TALENTED AND AGGRESSIVE PEOPLE

Beyond the scope of the formalized programs you implement, work must be done in the development of especially talented and ambitious personnel. This is required if you are to grow your management strength and depth. Yet those same people may challenge your methods of doing business, become overly aggressive, and appear to be a direct challenge to you.

> **EXAMPLE:** When Henry Ford's fitness to continue managing the Ford Motor Company was challenged in court, he was asked a number of simple questions about history and other common grammar school subjects. He could give correct answers to very few of the questions. He was asked how, in light of his ignorance of such basic factual information, he could possibly run the company.
>
> He answered that he didn't see why it was so important for him to be able to answer such simple factual questions; if he needed facts, he could push a button and have one of the bright people that he had hired and developed give him the information. That freed him from worrying about unimportant information, and it allowed him to focus his talents on the management of the company and the development of its people. He pointed out that the "very bright people" who had brought the suit—the executives who now thought he was "too ignorant" to run the company—were the very people *he* had personally hired, trained, and developed to create one of the world's most successful companies.
>
> Henry Ford won the case.

The Conflict: *Extremely talented people can be a problem if they insist on having more than the usual amounts of information, responsibility, and authority and want to do the job as if they were an owner. However, they can also be a major asset.*

When you're bringing people into the new company, you have to appreciate someone who is ambitious and aggressive. You also must exercise some caution. In light of that, how do you avoid losing the opportunity to promote and keep the bright, ambitious, and aggressive individual who could make a major contribution to your company? How do you walk the fine grey line between taking on wild and raw talent that can be tamed and shaped, and rejecting candidates who are unrealistic in their expectations and patience? How do you make sure you have those sharp and challenging people advance with you in your growth process?

A lot depends on their patience level. But a major part of that patience is the sense of timing for the right time to act. It's a part of playing the politics of advancement through cooperation. Not nasty politics, and not a "yes man" mentality. But there is a common-sense kind of politics that everyone who rises through an organization plays. Some people have a natural sense of it; other have to be taught.

It's difficult to teach people the process of patiently gaining information. You can more readily teach them what *not* to do. Yet there are some guidelines that incorporate both the do's and the don'ts.

1. Explain and demonstrate to them that being overly aggressive won't work.
2. Remind them that a rampaging bull is not welcome in a china shop, especially not in *your* china shop.
3. Show them that patience and good timing will pay bigger long-range dividends.
4. Look for (and point out) their qualities of patience and tact that allow them to recognize the right time to express their drives and ambitions.
5. Let them know that you will recognize, accept, and respect honest curiosity and well-reasoned persistence.
6. Show them how the best people, through their actions and achievement, win your confidence and will gain the information and advancement they desire without overtly demanding it.
7. Follow through with appropriate action based upon their actions and results.

If you have a positive but overly aggressive person, clear and rational communication and education is essential. Properly managed and directed, that person can be your greatest resource. Emotional and irrational communication, combined with over-protectiveness and refusal to allow the person to grow, will result in conflict and loss of opportunity.

Why You Have to Try to Develop Challenging People

Taking the emotional and irrational approach is a common problem—especially for the entrepreneurial person. Too many managers—entrepreneurs or not—stand in their own way by holding back the very people who can help them go far beyond what the managers can on their own. They want to have the talented personnel, yet resist giving subordinates the freedom to develop the very strengths they need for the company to grow.

The people who can do the things the manager does—and perhaps can do those things better—could create the opportunity for the manager to grow to increased levels of responsibility and productivity. But if a manager will not allow talented people to grow and develop, neither they nor the manager can possibly achieve the kind of success each would like.

Overcoming the Fears

If you can "do it all" in a small company, it is likely that you will *believe* that no one can do the things you do as well as you can. When you are actively running all aspects of a telemarketing company, it's common to *feel* that way and *work* that way. But when you move into large growth, you can't do it all; the company simply grows too large for you to effectively maintain hands-on management of everything.

At that stage in business, the tendency is very strong for many "hands-on, do-it-all" managers to kid themselves by saying "I'll simply do it all as long as possible, and then, when it is time to grow big, I'll just do it." That's the point where those people have to recognize and overcome their fears if the company is to grow and remain healthy.

It's not unusual for them—when they decide to build a management team—to find themselves choosing people who aren't capable of handling the increased demands of higher level positions. It's not because they really want sycophants; they simply haven't overcome the fear of giving up some of their power and their control. Often, they are afraid of people who might try to play politics and "big business games" or worry that if they have people who are *too* bright—or too *many* bright people—that they might lose control of the direction and growth of the company.

So the first people selected for promotion often are good workers, but don't seem to have much to say. They rarely are innovative or truly take charge of an area. They almost never question or challenge the boss's decisions.

Red Flag: *If you fail to promote good talent with the right intellect, you will discover you have to constantly bail those people out, continually be in the position of having to save the company, and find that the company is neither safe nor properly positioned for growth.*

Your fears might be aggravated if the first person you promote who *does* have the talent and the intellect:

- is overly aggressive;
- has unrealistic expectations for personal advancement;
- demands too much authority; and
- can't mesh with you effectively.

If your first experience is like that, it's easy to make a basic—if inaccurate—assumption. You may decide this is what will always happen and that it is best to steer clear of that kind of talent and intellect because it creates too many problems for you and makes your life miserable.

Growth managers have to get beyond those feelings, or they won't be able to develop strong organizations. Some people don't realize how wrong those assumptions are until they have the kind of serious growth problems that only deep and talented teams can resolve. The successful managers are the ones who realize that if they know how to treat those bright and aggressive people, and if they learned about structure and delegation and salary administration, they could develop their own roles well beyond motivating a small group of people and picking up a few pieces of business. They discover the need to commit to learning and becoming well-rounded and knowledgeable businesspeople. Successful growth managers learn the wisdom of the principle that hiring people who are *smarter* than you proves how smart *you* are.

Key Point: *At some point in the growth process, you must realize that you can't afford to be afraid of bright and talented people. They are the only ticket to your growth and greater success.*

Ten Additional Guidelines for Developing Talented People

If you want to develop those people, you must be able to recognize their levels of ability and understanding of how to use the subtle differences in timing and tact. Then help them recognize the same things.

- *Help them learn patience.*

  Teach them that common sense means they don't demand and insist on additional information or authority. Instead, they should work their tails off and watch for opportunities to gain the extra information or authority needed. Through their efforts, they wage a quiet campaign for what they want.

  - They should work through the periphery. But they should not sit quietly, waiting for additional information to be volunteered.
  - They should be assertive without being egotistical.
  - They should be inquisitive without being nosy.
  - They should be persistent without being annoying.

  What's the difference between those things? Timing and tact. They should know how to position themselves effectively to be able to receive the information and make productive use of it.

- *Help them learn tactfulness and timing.*

  Instead of immediately demanding to see the books and financial statements, those bright and ambitious people should work hard, demonstrate their capabilities, and develop management's confidence.

  Explain that successful people let management know how much they enjoy working for the company:

  - They point out that the more they can know about the company, how it works, and how to properly manage the costs, the better they could do the job and the more they could contribute.
  - They make it clear that the financial end of the business is something they are excited about learning.
  - As they gain that kind of information, they follow up with ideas and actions that encourage the "powers that be" to give them ever increasing information and authority.
  - They advance not through lip service, but through exceptional work that produces results for the company.

- *Help them understand the rewards.*

  - Set standards of performance and standards of excellence that, when achieved, can make them eligible for advancement.

- Teach them the realities of the need for both individual and company development before promotion is possible.
- Let the talented and ambitious person know that a smart, growing telemarketing company comes to value and respect people like that—and promotes them quickly!

- *Earn their respect.*

    Demonstrate your own honesty, integrity, and support.

    - Admit and correct the mistakes you make with them.
    - Care about them and show that you care.
    - Help them grow and help build their careers.
    - Help them realize their potential *through* the dedicated and excellent work that they do for the company.

- *Educate them well.*

    - Teach them, train them, coach them, advise them; share your information and experience.
    - Help them increase their knowledge level as they demonstrate their ability to integrate, internalize, and apply the education you have already given them.

- *Help them become stronger.*

    When you find those people, don't be afraid of losing your power base. Share some of it by helping them establish their own areas of power which will help the company's results.

    If you find charismatic people who develop the strong loyalties of their people, don't let your own ego be threatened by their success. Their ability to develop those loyalties is essential to your future growth.

    - Focus instead on developing *their* loyalties.
    - Show them how to make sure their people are also loyal to the company.
    - Reward their development of subordinates by recognizing their talent and by helping them advance.

    Your most talented people are more likely to hurt you if you treat them badly. And they'll do it in the way that hurts the most . . . by going to another company that will treat them right, or by starting their own company.

- *Provide personal support and attention.*

    Develop the talented people and give them the opportunity to help both you and the company grow.

    - Communicate to them clearly.
    - Treat them honestly and fairly.
    - Help them work on the areas where they are personally weak while you develop them in the business areas where they are strong.
    - Help them grow, realizing that in return, they will help you grow.

- *Give them opportunity to create at their capability level.*

    As they increase their knowledge and skills, help them to increase their ability for themselves and for your company.

- Help them to plan, to execute, and to remain flexible in their execution.
- As they show their capability, delegate small additional amounts of responsibility.
- Give them reasonable constraints and establish checks and balances.
- Let them make mistakes, teach them how to correct those mistakes, and give them the opportunity to do it right.
- Give them incentives that will reward their contributions.
- As they master an area, delegate again.

- *Increase their authority.*

   As those talented people gradually develop and help you grow your business, reestablish your own function and develop greater structure to capitalize on their talents.

   - Put them into increased positions of responsibility and give them commensurate authority.
   - Establish the executive councils and the checks and balances that maintain your overall control.
   - Give them the freedom to get the job done.

- *Continue to train, develop, delegate, and monitor.*

   It's a lot of work. It's not easy. But the rewards are very clear. Those bright, talented, ambitious people will carry you much higher up the ladder of growth than you can possibly climb by yourself.

TURNOVER AND RETENTION: HOW TO STOP THE REVOLVING DOOR

When a company is first starting, it's automatically exciting. There are many new things happening and many new things to learn. There are new developments every day, and the growth is very rapid. Everyone can see the opportunity, and the excitement increases. The energy of the founders spreads throughout the company. There is the very close feeling of a tight-knit family working together. The atmosphere of growth is pervasive and infectious.

A company will get a "bigger company" feeling as it grows and matures, even if it simply develops more programs and fills in a few new positions without adding a large number of phones. Unless you work hard at it, a lot of the original family feeling and closeness and camaraderie will be lost. As that feeling fades, it is all too easy to start turning over people that never would have been lost before.

Most people think that turnover is the name of the game in telemarketing. It is a *part* of the game, as it is in any business. During the classroom and initial on-the-job training, some TSR trainees will drop out as they experience the realities of the job. The high rejection factor, the production-intensive environment, the unusual hours, lack of self-esteem, and basic fear of the phone will take their toll on trainees in the early stages. The better the selection process, the less of a problem there will be. But turnover still will be a significant factor, as it is in any sales game.

As a result, there should be a give-and-take process with the candidates during the recruiting and hiring process. Let them know the realistic expectations they can have about the job, the company, and the industry. The candidates need to know that—as new trainees—they will be a part of a two-way evaluation:

1. the company evaluating the trainees' potential for success;
2. the trainees evaluating their satisfaction with the job and with the company.

They need to know that the hardest part comes in the early going, and that not making the grade—either by their decision or by the company's—is not a reflection on their value as individuals.

A Change in Thinking is Required

Still, the turnover rate in telemarketing—even after the initial training period—is *notoriously* high. Even the language used in and out of the industry reveals the attitude.

Outsiders refer to telemarketing companies as "meat markets," "body mills," and "human body shops." They talk about how the companies "chew people up and spit them out."

And the language of telemarketers shows that the whole industry popularly accepts turnover—in high numbers—as a part of the business.

- Many telemarketing personnel departments look at their job as "finding more replacements to send to the front."
- Some trainers consider the new training class as "more cannon fodder."
- Materials people may refer to their duties of keeping scripts and labels supplied to the sales floor as "feeding the animals."
- Some telemarketing supervisors and managers refer to the daily TSR attendance rosters as "body lists" or "body counts."
- Upper management talks about the "revolving door" in the sales department.

And we wonder why people in our labor markets don't think of telemarketing as a career!

The accepted idea and the current reality is that telemarketing *is* a high turnover business. Telemarketing has a serious problem with retention. That's a hard and cold fact. Yet, that is neither necessary nor cost effective.

Key Premise: *Telemarketing does not have to have the high levels of turnover that almost everyone in the industry accepts and, as a result, has come to expect.*

The industry needs dramatic improvement in its ability to deal with the retention of qualified people. Telemarketing people may not want to admit the problems to others, but—at least—we should be willing to admit it to ourselves.

If you are going to have dramatic growth, you need a lot of people, and the number of talented and knowledgeable people available today is very limited. You can't afford to alienate the people you have.

Red Flag: *The moment your people start to feel like faceless numbers in a faceless organization, they begin to lose the feelings of caring from the company.*

When that happens:

- Their feelings of excitement, commitment, and involvement fade;
- Their natural incentive to grow with the organization dies; and
- You are in serious danger of losing them.

Solutions to the problem of turnover are being offered in many areas: "Automation reduces the need for supervision . . ."; "Ergonomics keeps the people happier . . ."; "Money keeps them around . . . ." There is some truth in all of that, but none of these are lasting solutions.

Some companies say: "No problem, there are answers to that: ergonomics *and* benefits *and* phone rep salaries like $32,500 per year." Aside from the negative economic impact on the P & L statement, that approach *alone* all too frequently results in an environment that isn't very productive. There are exceptions to every rule, but usually *the rule* rules.

The Rule: *It requires a lot more than money and comfortable chairs to keep TSRs both happy and productive.*

What Keeps People at the Job

While money *is* an important factor, other factors consistently score higher than money. Most of these factors have to do with the person's feelings about their place in the company and the company's feeling about them. Management has to fulfill more than the money needs to sustain employee satisfaction and to reduce turnover.

Over the last 20 years, studies have consistently shown that money is much lower on the list than most employers would expect, and well below other factors of what satisfies and keeps people in a job. Issues such as "competitive salaries" and "pay that is directly tied to job performance" rank below "a sense of achievement," "recognition for a job well done" and a "sense of belonging" when employees explain why they stay with a company. Money may draw them initially, but it isn't the most important thing that keeps them.

The First Step in Reducing Turnover

Telemarketing's problems with turnover is caused—to a large degree—by managers' lack of understanding of how high retention can be, or their inability and unwillingness to take the steps to do the things that are required to reduce the problem.

Work on retention shouldn't start at the point problems actually begin to appear. It doesn't even start in the training or in the interview. Taking action at those points is important, but you have to start with the image you project to your labor market with your advertising. The ads need to be simple, classy, easy to follow, say what it is, and that's it. Using hyperbole or making impossible promises can actually set you up for retention problems.

EXAMPLE: A telemarketing ad for TSRs once appeared with a drawing of two people dreaming and the headline "Make Your Dreams Come True," followed in small print by "$5.00 an Hour Guaranteed." In larger bold type, it said "Earn Up to $10.00 an Hour."

Two years later, the same company ran an ad that said "$5.00 to $10.00 per Hour Guaranteed, and *That's* a Guarantee We're Living Up To."

However, the fact is that the company paid $3.50 per hour and *guaranteed* only an additional $1.50 per hour in bonuses. *Any* compensation above $5.00 was based *solely* on sales productivity.

Those ads were misleading, based on pure hyperbole, and created unrealistic expectations. People hired from the ad wouldn't expect to come in and work hard, sell a variety of new programs, and earn a little more than 6 bucks an hour; they *would* expect that they would be able to go to work, expect to earn $10 per hour, *and* to have their dreams come true. And who are they angry at when their dreams don't come true? The company—and the industry—that made the promise to them.

Using that kind of ad is a waste of money:

- It misleads and disappoints a lot of job applicants.
- It targets a labor market segment which doesn't respond well to "bait and switch" help wanted advertising.
- It results in adverse word of mouth in the labor market.
- It sets up the company *itself* to be disappointed with an extremely high turnover rate.
- It is irresponsible behavior which puts an unfavorable light on the telemarketing industry as a whole.

Telemarketers who take that approach to attracting their people simply haven't learned the importance of starting to work on retention even before their people walk in the door for the first time. They still have the outdated concept that you should get people in however you need to, whether it conveys the right message or the right image.

A Better Answer to Reducing the Turnover Problem

Grady was interviewed for a management position in the late seventies. He was asked: what his philosophy of management was. His answer had been formulated during many years of managing sales people and running his own companies:

> "If you want your people to perform for you and for your company, you must get them to think that you care about each one of them as a person. But if that caring is only pretended, they'll soon sense it and cut your legs out from under you.
> You have to honestly care about the people, who they are, what they want, what they need, and how you can help them achieve what's important to them.

Either you do that, or you stay our of management. *Really* care about them as *human beings* and show that you care, or *don't* make the mistake of *calling* yourself a manager."

Resolving telemarketing's retention problems comes down to a matter of caring—individual attention being given to each and every employee. The fact that so much of the solution to turnover *can* be so simple is not meant to imply that doing an effective job of giving that attention is *easy*. If it were easy, many more companies would be doing it—as opposed to concentrating on general or peripheral attention.

Peripheral attention comes from the supposed solutions which address the whole staff, such as ergonomics or group praise. That peripheral attention is important, but its benefits are overstated. Group issues need to be resolved so the *group* knows you care enough to take those steps. But greater benefit comes from recognizing that the group is composed of *individual people*. Unless individual and personalized attention is given consistently to each member of the group, the peripheral attention is soon taken for granted and loses the desired effects.

Caution: *Personalized communication is required on an individual level. Without it, all the peripheral attention is doomed to failure.*

How to Improve Retention Through Personal Attention

The rules for improving retention through personal attention are essentially rules of caring and common sense. The first is to know the people you are dealing with on a first- and last-name basis. Some people think that's basic, and they're right. But others take it lightly.

Even under the best circumstances, the economics of the business dictates that you have a fairly large span of control and a large workforce. Even if you have one supervisor for each 8 to 15 people, having a part-time work force means not having the same people working each shift of the week. Combine that with changing demands on your programs, and you may have to switch people from one supervisor's team to another. The teams may constantly be different. That means many more people whom each supervisor must get to know.

It's all too easy for the supervisor to say: "Those TSRs aren't on my team, so I don't have to get to know them." But you can't afford to let that happen, because it means giving up personal attention and motivation for those TSRs for that shift. That means a loss of productivity, and it encourages the attitude that the people are just bodies to be maneuvered and manipulated. The supervisors can easily cease to be effective members of the management team—and, instead, become expensive baby sitters.

The personal attention the supervisors provide begins with the way they greet the TSRs on their team. If a supervisor has 20 people to work with, it's easy to give the group an impersonal "Hi. How are you all doing?" for a greeting.

It is much more productive for the supervisors to spend the first five minutes giving special greetings to each individual, making pertinent personalized comments to those TSRs they know well enough to do so. The supervisors may make references to humorous situations they have been through with particular TSRs, or positive comments about their previous performances. With those people they don't know, the supervisors need to introduce themselves and begin developing supportive relationships.

That attention doesn't always have to be positive, but it has to be personal and individual. And it goes beyond the initial greeting of the day or the final farewell. It has to be extended to the management style on the sales floor.

On the upside, it includes:

- Acknowledgement of performance, whether it results in a sale or not.
- Recognizing when a TSR makes a good sales effort or an excellent and persistent presentation.
- Acknowledging when a TSR has done a good presentation, dealt with several tough objections, closed the right number of times, and still didn't get the sale.
- Praising a TSR who, rather than becoming pushy or hard sell, recognizes a definite "NO!" and politely ends a call.
- Encouraging a salesperson who responds to a long string of rejection by maintaining a good attitude.
- Congratulating someone who has made improvement in one area of the presentation, even though they still have a long way to go to become truly proficient in all areas of the presentation.

On the downside of that attention, you may have to reprimand someone who has gotten the sale in spite of not having made a good product presentation or responses to objections. While they should be congratulated for getting the order, they need to be reprimanded for improper techniques and redirected in the faulty or lazy areas. It requires both positive and negative attention:

- Give the praise for the order.
- Show them where they failed to do the *whole* job.
- Show them what to do instead in the future.

The coaching attention is not negative in the sense that it is abusive or demeaning; it is simply that the TSR's performance requires correction, in spite of the fact that a sale resulted.

The personal attention we give in doing follow-up on our sales people also needs to be improved. Almost everything we do in this industry is on the phone, and that includes special contact with our people.

- Most telemarketing managers call when they need extra people to fill in on programs. They send people home when the phone system crashes, and then call them back when the system's fixed.
- Good managers use the phone for regular daily contact with TSRs assigned to an important test, proactively calling all test people every day to make sure the roster is filled and the test results remain valid.

- Most managers call TSRs who don't show for a scheduled shift, either to try to get the TSRs in or to make sure they don't miss the next shift.

Why should we call people only when it involves problems or additional assistance that we require? If those are the only times supervisors and managers call the TSRs, it will soon give the sales crew the impression that the only people who are really important are those who are on the tests and those who are missing shifts. When the only reasons your people are getting special calls are for problem situations, it's not surprising that the people frequently are "not there" when you call.

Perhaps it would be wiser to call *all* the people—in an apparently random fashion— throughout the week. You could schedule a few minutes of every manager's day to contact every single TSR once each week, or at least every month. If you make a point of contacting everyone in that way, you can extend the TSRs' feeling that they are important and that you care about them as more than numbers.

How to Personalize Your Efforts

How the communication is handled is extremely important. Poor managers may make the calls to missing TSRs by berating the people and "beating them up" on the phone to prevent them from missing shifts again. Better managers call to say "The team misses you when you're not here. We really need you, and it's not the same without you." Those are important keys: *we missed you,* and *we need you.*

However, if you have developed—or want to develop—any kind of personal rapport with your people, you must personalize your communications with them. Say something that relates directly to them. Things like: "It's not as much fun without your smiling face around"; "I missed not getting to tease about how well you handle objections and turn them into sales"; or "It doesn't seem like it's a real day at work without having to get you to smile when you've gotten 11 'no answers' in a row."

Relate your comments directly to their personality, their particular work traits or past experiences, or your working relationship with them. Your comments don't have to be phrased in a positive way if you have the right relationship and use the right tone. You might say "I really missed having my little Butterball to kick around and stop from writing bad orders." But you only use that kind of nickname or that type of comment if they are inside jokes you share with them—and ones that you know *they* enjoy.

The communication needs to be made, to be personalized, and to be directed toward supporting attitudes for increased productivity. If a person gets praise, they can more readily accept criticism and correction. People need stroking, and strokes can be positive *or* negative. Positive strokes tends to reinforce behavior, but so do negative strokes. If people can't get positive strokes, they will do whatever is necessary to get negative strokes. If the only way to get personal attention from the "boss" is to cause problems, they will cause problems.

How the criticism and correction is handled is extremely important. Either too much positive reinforcement or too much negative reinforcement brings less than the desired results. The reinforcement needs to be blended, with a positive approach to what otherwise could be perceived as negative criticism. Too much positive reinforcement (especially if it is unrealistic praise that fails to address less-than-excellent performance) creates "fat cats." Too much negative reinforcement undermines the desire for, and the expectation of, excellence. It demotivates everyone. The key is not whether it is exclusively positive or negative, but that it is fair and individually personalized.

Combining Personal and Peripheral Attention

It is also possible to combine personal and peripheral attention in one package. Generally, the focus will be on the individual, but as a part of the group. There are many ways to do it. As long as the combined programs are not intended to replace the personal attention, they can be valuable additions.

You need to let your people—and individuals, as teams, and as a whole—know how they are doing on the program. Give them the feedback you get from the clients. Let them know that when the client compliments you on how well you are handling the program, that it's really a compliment on how well *they* are doing on the program. Get the client communication right down to TSR levels as frequently as possible. Remind the TSRs that *they* are the ones who are making it work. Acknowledge that it *is* a team effort, but that their individual efforts are where the rubber meets the road.

Posting sales results is a part of doing that. It focuses on the individuals within the context of the group.

Warning: *Posting sales results six weeks after the fact won't have the same impact as posting them on a daily or weekly basis.*

Giving your TSRs their sales results six weeks after the fact is no more effective than rubbing a puppy's nose in the mess it made on the rug three days earlier. Timely and immediate recognition—whether positive or negative—is essential.

This is an area where the automated shop has a definite advantage; it's hard to post results on a timely basis in a large-volume, manual shop. That means that a manual shop has to have supervisors and managers who have the people skills and sensitivity to make up for the lack of immediately posted results.

Reminder: *Make sure that that recognition goes beyond the TSRs. Pass the word to all other members of the team.*

The supervisors, quality control representatives, verifications personnel, even the material handlers, all need that kind of reinforcement. Some of these team members may not have the same kind of direct production involvement as the TSRs, but the efforts of the rest of the organization are worthless if materials personnel mess up the lists or scripts. They catch the flak for their mistakes, and they should be able to share in the successes.

How you handle your employee break rooms is peripheral attention that has definite impact on the individual. Aside from your local laws, having separate smoking and non-smoking break rooms is a good policy because the smoke irritates the non-smokers. The individual people appreciate that kind of peripheral attention. Still, while that might keep someone from leaving the job because of being uncomfortable on breaks, it won't keep them around if they feel no one knows their name.

Awards are another good example of combining both kinds of attention. Some people look at awards (certificates, plaques, trophies, etc.) as *the* way of giving personal recognition of achievement. The awards themselves are a *part* of the recognition, but certainly are not sufficient. In fact, they are the least important part of recognition. Those awards should be just the tangible expression of the personal recognition or congratulations they have already received.

Note: *The simple fact that attention is given tends to help improve the productivity of your people.*

There many other ways to offer combined personal and peripheral attention:

- Set up a company acting group to put on plays.
- Sponsor company sports teams, such as softball and bowling teams, or form company sports leagues.
- Hold company competitions such as backgammon tournaments, ping-pong matches, or racketball challenge ladders.
- Sponsor company events like summer picnics; Halloween; Thanksgiving, and Christmas/New Year's parties.

Those are just a few examples of what can be done. Anything supported by the company that gives its people an opportunity to play together and get to know each other in a relaxed setting is helpful.

The Benefits of Giving Improved Individual Attention

If you make the effort and focus on personal attention, you can make a powerful impact on attendance and retention. You *can* achieve 95% attendance, with people who will put out that extra effort *whenever* you need it. You *can* have people who will be happy to stay with you. And you can then afford to turn over the people you *need* to, instead of hanging on to people who perform below acceptable standards while wondering why a talented new group that had shown so much early promise has had an 80% attrition rate in a matter of a few weeks.

Does it happen automatically and without effort? Of course not. Not any more than it happens in a good marriage or in a close-knit family. As in any endeavor involving more than one person, quality results in telemarketing come through constant sensitivity and communication and dedication. But the rewards in increased employee satisfaction and productivity are enormous.

PERSONAL ATTENTION AND THE OPERATING ENVIRONMENT

When considering specific steps that can be taken to provide personal attention to the people, you should address some operating approaches. The nature of a company often shapes either the ability or the tendency of the company to give high degrees of personal attention.

The Change of Focus in Some Automated Environments

The difference in philosophies is particularly apparent between manual and automated operations. One of the sales points used by vendors of automated systems is that substantially less supervision is required to achieve the same levels of production in an automated operation. Most automated firms have followed that line of thinking.

Result: *There is a strong tendency—and often a policy—for the supervisors in automated operations to give reduced personal attention and coaching to the TSRs.*

In those situations, the supervisors are visible, and the TSRs get feedback about where they are falling short and what they are not doing right. But they often do not receive the additional attention provided by supervisors being out on the floor giving on-line attention, doing demonstration calls, and helping close sales.

> **EXAMPLE:** A Fortune 100 company developed and installed an excellent automation package for their in-house program. The management configuration was dramatically reduced: There was one supervisor for 25 TSRs. No other direct support system existed; no quality assurance monitoring personnel or additional floor management staff. No one was assigned to the floor to handle hour-to-hour motivation, coaching and direct personal support to the TSRs.
>
> One lone supervisor, seemingly chained to her desk, was *oblivious* to the sea of humanity about her. She was completely occupied with staring at the tube and taking down data. She was concerned with analyzing data, not with managing the people.

That may be *called* supervision. But that type of automated approach is managing *numbers* instead of *people*.

The Problem with Some Automated Approaches

Unfortunately, that is a normal situation for many companies that go to automation. When the telemarketing unit is automated, the hum and buzz of interactive excitement disappear and the loudest noise is often the hum of the tubes!

The automated management information system (MIS) is not the problem; it gives a different kind of support that is valuable and positive. The data base that can be achieved through the automated MIS can be more specific and timely, and provides information that is critical to the effective management of many programs. That information can help target specific problems more quickly and can help focus *what* supervision and coaching should be provided to the TSRs and *which* TSRs need immediate attention.

The problem comes when having the information results in dealing with the TSRs in a more peripheral manner. A labor-intensive environment such as outbound telemarketing requires not only accurate analysis of program data, but also direct and frequent motivation and inspiration of the TSRs. That second requirement goes unfulfilled when supervisors simply monitor the TSRs and spend the vast majority of time reading productivity reports.

Such a strategy focuses on the data management, while failing to adequately address the other side of the twofold drive that makes telemarketing work at the optimum level: the people-intensive operational demands.

Warning: *The perception that automation greatly reduces the need for the intensive supervision that good manual shops require ignores the requirement for the strong, interactive coaching and support of TSRs that are necessary for* any *effective telemarketing.*

It is a poor tradeoff if the levels of direct personal involvement are sacrificed in favor of the additional data. There is a cost—at the core of what effective telemarketing demands—that is not sufficiently recognized and compensated for. That situation needs to be changed if automation is to provide the full support that good telemarketing demands.

You still need people who can dedicate time to intensively monitoring and *assuring* quality presentations. You still need people who can *motivate* the people on those phones. Whether or not CRTs are in front of the TSRs, those salespeople still have the same tough task of getting and keeping the prospect's attention and handling rejection.

The need is especially acute in the consumer environment, where people often work full time at another demanding job. Usually, they are working at night not because they want the extra work, but because they need the money it provides. They may be tired and stressed from a full day's work, or they may be foregoing studying for a test they will be taking the next day. It's doubly important for the supervisors of those people to provide leadership, empathy, and individual motivation. That is essential to the full development and retention of the individual, and it is achieved through personal care and attention given to the individual.

The reduction of support for those people is neither good nor acceptable. Not for them, not for the client, and not for quality telemarketing.

The Flaw in the Staff Reduction Premise

Automation *will* bring a company the ability to reduce staffing levels. The problem is the failure to realize that most of the *effective* reduction in staff size is in the strict data manipulation areas. Automation *does* eliminate the need for most "number crunching" clerks, but it's a *fallacy* to say that automated shops should be able to dramatically cut the supervision on the floor.

Critical Factor: *Telemarketers have to realize that front-line supervision is not a clerical function.*

The function of the supervisors is to improve results through effective coaching and through gaining the willing cooperation of people. Supervision is a *people* function, not a *clerical* one.

A part of the supervisor's job in a manual shop *does* include doing a fair amount of clerical functions while he or she is supervising the shift. But that's generally limited just to taking TSR totals a few minutes of each hour.

Guideline: *The sales supervisor should spend at least 90% of each hour doing close monitoring, educational coaching, and inspirational motivation of* people.

The rewards of supervision come when the supervisor is directly helping the people improve their skills, making takeover and demonstration calls, and motivating the TSRs to do their jobs better. When TSRs become more skilled *and* have the enthusiasm for the work they are doing, the sales numbers improve. That's where 90% of a good supervisor's time is spent and where 95% of the positive results are achieved.

The automated shops that reduce levels of supervision either have failed to realize that fact, or have failed to do anything constructive about it. Their approach to managing people is: (1) to get the productivity reports, and *then* (2) to deal with the people.

What those shops are failing to realize is that the results of their automated productivity reports could be much better if people management expertise were to be applied *during* each hour, *before* those reports were analyzed. That's when the numbers *revealed* in those reports are being generated.

Key Point: *A too often repeated approach to automated supervision is to work on correcting problems after the reports discover them. Direct and active supervision prevents the problems and improves the results that the reports will reveal.*

The Automated Challenge

Today, too many automated shops are concentrating on *data management* and not giving enough attention to the *people*. The manual shops *can't* concentrate on the extensive data, so they rely *too much* on people management to reach the desired levels and quality of production. Neither *alone* is sufficient.

The growth of individual companies and the growth of the telemarketing industry will increasingly demand automation. Ultimately, automated shops need to find ways to financially justify depths of structure and supervisory attention similar to the levels that the best manual shops provide. Doing so will pay dividends in increased productivity, expanded market opportunities, and heightened employee satisfaction and loyalty.

When automated firms can put the same depths and degrees of management expertise and supervision on the floor, they can have an honest shot at giving the manual shops a real beating.

Tip: *Automated firms who achieve that may have a bit higher rates, but they will have a competitive cost per order. They will be able to do the whole job, with a cost effectiveness that will make the client glad to pay their rates.*

AVOIDING THE "IVORY TOWER" SYNDROME

Top executives usually are very good about networking with other businesspeople. They know that doing so can be an important part of building their companies and their careers. But those same executives often forget about the importance and value of networking within their own company—especially at the grassroots level.

The personal attention given to the TSRs by the supervisors and management starts with the example the CEO sets in giving personal care and attention to his or her staff and to the rest of the organization. Top management then needs to make sure that attention is extended to their staffs, and that the practice continues all the way down to the trainee level.

But that filtered extension of upper management's feelings and approach is not enough. Top management needs to get to know and remain involved with the people at all levels of the telemarketing organization.

Yellow Flag: *Top management that fails to take the time to keep in touch with their people at all levels—or who feel they are "above" that kind of contact—will soon lose touch with the heartbeat of the organization.*

The image people often have of top management in a large company is, "O.K., now the CEO can take it easy." But the larger you grow and the faster you continue to grow, the less "easy" the CEO can take it. Physically, the CEO does have less to do. But his or her perceptions have to become sharper and more incisive. A part of maintaining that personal and competitive edge is staying in touch with all of the people who make up the company.

Note: *Wal-Mart has been one of the fastest-growing companies in the world for the past few years. If Sam Walton can visit every one of his over 900 nationwide stores every year—and he* does—*top management of telemarketing companies has no excuse for not giving that kind of attention to the people in their facilities.*

The Right Idea . . . The Wrong Execution

Sometimes we start out with the right intentions and the right plan, but we lose track of what we intended to accomplish. In the stress and fast pace that comes with growing a telemarketing company, it's all too easy to do.

During the course of our careers, we all go through a few cycles of providing good and bad examples of personal and peripheral attention for our staffs and our people. But we need to learn from, and be reminded by, all of the examples. Perhaps the best lesson to learn is the importance of remaining in touch with what some top management refers to as the "little people."

> **EXAMPLE:** From the beginning of my career, I felt very strongly about keeping in touch with the grassroots people in the organization. I wanted to make sure to continue to keep in touch with them, and with the new people who followed, as the company grew.
>
> In the early days, keeping in touch was fairly easy. One of the most effective things we did was to have something special for the people who stayed with us. We had an awards party for employees who had celebrated an employment anniversary—one year, two years, etc. It was a fun time, with food and games and prizes.
>
> It was so well received by the people that we wanted to make the anniversary party a more frequent event. We formally decided that we would hold the celebration every month, acknowledge by name each person who reached an anniver-

sary date during the month, give out cash prizes and framed certificates of recognition, and list each person who had received the awards in the company newsletter.

Each person also was to get a personal letter from me. It was a form letter that I had originally written, but each one was individually typed. At first I knew everyone who received one of the letters. I always included a personal handwritten note on the letter and signed it "Steve." I dedicated time to each of the letters and wrote something special and personalized to each of the people who received them. If I had a nickname for them, I used it. If they had a nickname for me, I used it. I wanted to deliver a message to those people that let them know the company cared that they had chosen to stay.

It was very important to me to keep the bond between upper-level management and the rest of the organization so we didn't get into an "ivory tower" isolation. It was predictable that, as we got bigger, it would be harder, and ultimately impossible, for me to know everyone personally. So I figured that we should set up a system to make sure that I got to know everyone who had been with us for a full year.

I also felt it was important to meet with those people—that the longer they were with the company, the better I *should* get to know them. I could spend at least an hour or two a month getting to know them better. It was a chance for me to "let my hair down" and be one of the guys. I could make friends and let them know I legitimately cared about them.

The anniversary parties were great when they started. The company was small and the parties were very personal. I *always* went to them, and it was clear the people appreciated it. I got to know them better, and they got to know me in a less-businesslike environment. The parties were a highlight that helped bond a lot of good relationships.

Then, the company began to really grow and we got busier, either Sheri Idelman or I went. The company got even bigger, and the decision next was made that at least *one* of the people in upper management would attend. It was handled on a rotation basis. Then everyone began to make excuses why no one in top management could make it to the party.

At the time, I and the other top management people actually felt we were getting too busy to go. But we weren't being honest with ourselves. It was really a matter of being lazy, selfish, and short-sighted. We forgot how important that party and our involvement in it was to the people. The top management of the company had lost touch with how much their employees looked forward to it.

As the company got bigger and more successful, I got a little arrogant about it. I was always "too busy," and making excuses became all too easy. A client would be coming in the next day. Or there was a proposal that had to be gotten out. There was always something to prepare for.

Then the letters became a "pain." I started to feel that they took up too much of my "valuable" time. I would get 22 letters to sign for a month, but only knew three or four of the people. At first I would write personal notes to the ones I knew. But I thought that was negative to the rest of the people. I solved that. I stopped writing personal notes to any of them!

Finally, I stopped going, and soon the rest of upper management stopped

Idelman Telemarketing, Inc.

7415 Dodge Street • Omaha, NE 68114

(800) 642-0700

(402) 393-8000

October 17, 1988

IDELMAN TELEMARKETING, INC.
7415 Dodge Street
Omaha, NE 68114

Dear   :

Congratulations on completing your second 1,040 hours worked with Idelman Telemarketing, Inc. We all know that to complete this length of service takes a special person. It takes someone who can work through the "tough times"; someone who can handle those shifts where nothing seems to go right and where nobody seems to want to buy anything; someone who is patient and willing to complete the journey from Trainee to OJT to Veteran status; someone who can deal with the downsides and still keep that special smile glowing inside and out; someone who has spirit and enjoys being an important part of a winning team; someone who knows that there is no shortcut to success, just plain old fashioned hard work, dedication, commitment and loyalty. In a nutshell, we all know that you, Richard, are one of those special someones, without whom there would be no ITI success story to talk about.

Thanks very much for being with us as an ongoing member of OUTBOUND telemarketing's single most successful organization. As our way of saying thanks for your long-term commitment to ITI, you will be receiving a $75.00 "longevity bonus": We look forward to rewarding you with a higher amount when you complete your next 1,040 hours. In the meantime, keep on smiling and dialing and remember . . . "There's NO business like PHONE business"!

CONGRATULATIONS!!!

Sincerely,

Steven A. Idelman
Chief Executive Officer

SAI:sjh

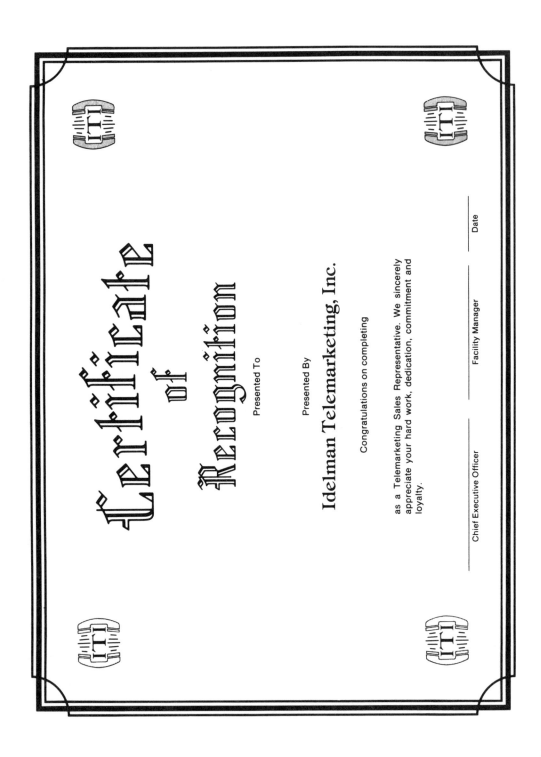

Certificate
of
Recognition

Presented To

Presented By

Idelman Telemarketing, Inc.

Congratulations on completing

as a Telemarketing Sales Representative. We sincerely appreciate your hard work, dedication, commitment and loyalty.

_____   _____   _____
Chief Executive Officer   Facility Manager   Date

going. I had actually forgotten the reason I had wanted to start the program in the first place.

The parties became a function run by the personnel department.

Later, by accident, I learned how badly I had messed up. I got a bunch of letters that had been prepared on two different word processors. The form letter and the address block didn't match. The alignment was off and the type faces were different. I was out of town, so my secretary signed and initialed them for me.

The appearance of the letters clearly said that the president didn't care. And the people actually *received* those miserable letters!

When I found out about it, I went nuts. My secretary and the personnel department caught hell. I told them that the letters should have been held up and the party delayed for a week so they could have been done right. I insisted that the quality of the letters be corrected.

The next batch matched OK. But instead of starting "Dear Don" or "Dear Denise," they started "Dear Don Prohaska" or "Dear Denise Robertson." It was absurd. It was worse than a poor direct-mail piece.

The letters were fixed. A few months went by, and one of the few employees I *did* know asked when she would get her two-year anniversary letter. I explained that personnel was probably a little behind. Over the next couple of months she asked about the letter again. I finally decided to find out where the letter was.

I called personnel and found out they had decided that the letters were such a nuisance, that they were so much in arrears, and that personnel was so busy—all of which was true—that the program would be discontinued. And they had done so. No parties. No letters. It was the first I had heard about it.

The "ivory tower" was in place. And I knew it was my own mistake.

- I had circumvented the mechanism I had put in place to avoid *exactly* what had happened.
- I had stopped doing the very things that I had known it would be so important to do.
- When I turned the function over to personnel, I had failed to explain to them the original intent and the importance of the parties.

I had lost a wonderful opportunity to solidify the people who had demonstrated loyalty to me and to the company. It was the failure to keep in perspective the importance of the people who had been with the organization for at least a year. I lost touch with the people, and they knew it.

I had gotten too far from the well. What had started as an excellent program that would help assure that people felt the attention and involvement of top management had become meaningless—and then negative—peripheral attention.

What did I learn from the experience?

- If the original intent and concept is good enough to start, it's worth finding a way to keep doing it . . . even if it has to be modified.

- Before modifying or eliminating a policy, make sure you know why it was originally put in place.
- If you are to be able to remember why you implemented a policy, you are going to have to document what it was intended to do.
- Don't keep the reasons to yourself; make sure each member of the management team knows the purpose of each policy. (Then someone is *sure* to remember it!)
- No matter how good your plans and intentions are, it's too easy to get away from them in the hectic pace of growth.
- You are never really "too busy" to keep in touch with the people who make your organization successful.
- Don't let it happen. Never get too far from the well.

Top Management's Biggest Challenge

It's no secret that upper-level management in a successful telemarketing company is well-paid, but they need to be very low-key about it. They can't afford to lose touch; they have to go out and relate to the people. All upper-level managers—including the CEO—should maintain hands-on involvement with the people. You never want to create a "we/they" relationship between upper management and the rest of the company.

One of the most important responsibilities of management is to occasionally go out and have fun with the phone people. It is hard for top management to do it as frequently in a 500-phone operation as in a 50-phone shop, because they have other duties and responsibilities to the organization. But they should never stop doing it. When they make the time, everyone goes home feeling better after sharing the warm smiles and laughter. Sometimes it's even worth killing productivity for a few minutes to remind everyone that we're all human.

Many CEOs and top management people feel they are above taking personal time and a light approach with the grass-roots of their company. But that's the kind of special attention that people need beyond the routine attention that is usually given.

Other top managers simply don't understand how to do it.

EXAMPLE: A telemarketing COO had four branch operations, all in the same city. The COO held an "open house" in his private office once a month, with different employees invited to attend each meeting to represent the work force at large. The idea was to motivate his people and to get to know them in a relaxed setting.

The COO had the basic idea, but he missed the point of individual attention. He failed to understand that an open house in his office was intimidating, as much as it was motivational. That type of attention is best given on the employee's turf, or at a neutral location.

If he had taken a few minutes to think, he would have realized that it was worth taking a little bit of time to solidify his relationship with them in better setting.

You can't be the COO or the coordinator for branch offices and not visit them. When you visit those facilities, you can't just stand in the front of the room with your arms crossed watching the operation run and expect to do anything *but* intimidate the people. It is much better to make your presence known, be at ease with the people, and let them enjoy the attention. Any problems can still be handled discretely behind closed doors.

Remember: *Our people are our only real asset in telemarketing, and they are certainly the only asset that can help us sustain effective growth over the long run.*

Those of us in top management need to make the effort to relate to our people and to give them the chance to relate to us as something other than detached, isolated, and unapproachable "Brass." The investment in that kind of extra effort returns big dividends.

People are what make you successful in any business, but it is particularly true in telemarketing. Upper management people need to keep their egos in check. You can't forget the people who brought you to where you are. These things all sound simple, but they're among the most important issues in managing growth in an outbound telemarketing shop. The bigger the shop and the larger the work force, the more you need leadership, and the better and more responsible that leadership needs to be.

Key Point: *The management and development of your people is your biggest challenge. It also brings your greatest opportunity.*

Making the commitments and taking the actions will bring about a conducive environment, well-developed and loyal people, knowledgeable and effective supervision and management, and reduced personnel turnover. If you really care about your people, it will become second nature to:

- Put the development of quality training programs and operation manuals high on your priority list.
- Find things to praise about people and their work. The feelings behind your words will be felt.
- Demonstrate—through your everyday actions—the respect and recognition that is so important to everyone.
- Make sure that the honors and awards you give to your people are public confirmations of the caring you have already shown your people.

When those kinds of actions are part of your daily life, the real expectations that you have for your people will soon be achieved. And the relationships you develop with them will enrich your life and theirs.

The growth and development of your business is shaped by the growth and development of your people. Growing and nurturing a telemarketing business means growing and nurturing people relationships. When it is done well and done with care, nothing is more thrilling.

34 KEYS TO MANAGING THE PEOPLE ISSUES

- The faster your rate of growth, the more difficult—and more important—it is to have a sufficient number of talented and trained people to assure the continuity health of your telemarketing unit as it grows; you can't grow without talented people.

- Because there is very little formal telemarketing training in the educational process, learning to develop your own people and promoting from within are essential to growth.

- Unless you pay entry wages that are high enough to attract quality people, you will have a very limited pool of internal people of the quality you need to promote.

- The best companies pay at, or even slightly above, the going market rate for comparable positions so they can have their choice of the best people available in the labor market.

- Beyond the first stages of growth, finding enough good people involves learning where the kind of people you want are and figuring out creative and innovative ways to let them know that you have jobs for them.

- Group interviews or auditions can be a major part of the solution to the problem of hiring enough TSRs to support rapid growth in a large volume operation.

- Qualifications for new supervisory and management personnel should include their ability to support the current company vision and to complement existing staff.

- There are situations that call for going outside the company for talent, but you shouldn't hire people from the outside unless you have carefully determined the reason why you need to do so.

- No matter how talented the person is, it is unlikely that he or she can ever become a successful telemarketing supervisor, manager, or executive until time has first been spent as a TSR.

- If you want strong growth, you need to build your staff with the kind of people who deliver real talent and job-satisfying capability.

- It is important to determine if your budget for the position is realistic for the skills you expect to get; if you try to "get by on the cheap," you are likely to be disappointed with the results.

- Sources for finding outside talent include personal industry contacts, specialized industry publications, direct marketing and telemarketing associations, and referrals from telemarketing consultants.

- Once you have established that a candidate for a management position has the required talent, the key issue is whether the chemistry is right between the person and the company.

- Cohesive organizations are held together by the bonds of shared vision, common values, and a deep commitment to the success of the group.

- A significant part of growing in a controlled manner is the training programs you create; nothing can replace the value of quality training in the development of knowledgeable people.

- You have to work to create the training programs that will develop the people you need to help you grow, yet not have the cost of that training be prohibitive.

- If you base your training budget projections on the learning curves of your key management personnel, you will usually be sadly disappointed and seriously over budget.

- TSR trainees must be given the thorough classroom and on-the-job training and support that will give them a strong foundation of knowledge and skills.

- The best telemarketing operations have initial classroom training programs of 20 or more hours for consumer work; for business-to-business work, the training may be much more extensive.

- Effective training cannot be dramatically reduced with automation; good automated systems will do an effective job of bringing up the right portion of the script, but the TSR has to be able to do something with the script when it appears on the screen.

- The ability of the floor supervisors and managers play a vital role in the development, maintenance and success of the TSRs.

- An excellent supervisory training program—complete with follow-through and scheduled reinforcement after the initial training is completed—is required in the development of quality telemarketing supervisors.

- The company's educational programs should include cross-training which will broaden the employees' perspectives of their positions and of the full operation of the company.

- In a rapid-growth situation, the combination of written operations manuals and proper training programs can make the difference between being able to accept a significant piece of business or having to turn it down.

- Extremely talented and aggressive people can be a problem; they can also be one of your most important growth assets.

- If you fail to promote good talent with the right intellect, you will soon discover that the company is neither safe nor positioned for growth.

- At some point in the growth process, you must learn to accept and develop bright and talented people; they are critical to your growth and greater success.

- Telemarketing does not have to have the high levels of turnover that almost everyone in the industry believes are normal and, as a result, have come to accept and expect.

- Money and ergonomics aren't enough to keep TSRs and other staff members both happy and productive; they require personal attention and a sense of belonging.

- The perception that automation greatly reduces the need for the intensive supervision that good manual shops require ignores the requirement for the strong, interactive coaching and support of TSRs that are necessary for effective telemarketing.

- Telemarketing sales supervisors should spend at least 90% of each hour in close monitoring, educational coaching, and inspirational motivation of people.

- Top management that fails to take the time to keep in touch with their people at all levels soon loses touch with the heartbeat of the organization.

- Our people are our only real asset in telemarketing, and they are certainly the only asset that can help us sustain effective growth over the long run.

- The management and development of your people is your biggest challenge. It also brings your greatest opportunity.

It is one of the most beautiful compensations of this life
that no man can sincerely try to help another
without helping himself.
—Ralph Waldo Emerson

He who believes is strong, he who doubts is weak.
Strong convictions precede great actions.

—*J. Clarke*

Chapter 6

How to Create and Maintain A Growth Atmosphere

An essential part of effective telemarketing growth management is creating an atmosphere of growth throughout the company. Creating that attitude and feeling involves many issues: the establishment and maintenance of quality communications, the realistic communication of goals, the creation of career paths, the handling of resistance to change, and the encouragement of personal growth. Each plays an important part in cultivating and maintaining a growth environment.

When a scientist causes all of the energy in a beam of light to move in a single, focused manner, the light is said to be *coherent*. That coherent light forms a powerful laser bream with amazing potential. Like the laser, the power which is created by your organization can be awesome. Like the scientist, your task is to bring coherency to your company.

ASSURING QUALITY INTERNAL COMMUNICATIONS

Because telemarketing is such a people-intensive business, it is a communications-intensive business, as well. It demands clear communication throughout the entire structure. But maintaining consistency and quality is a demanding process. It is not enough just to develop that level of communication. It also must be nourished to be maintained.

Part of that communications process is to convey that the company has to remain flexible enough to respond to changing market conditions and developments. Those changes and their implications need to be communicated to your organization. You know the game plane has changed. But without full dedication to communication, you may find that the rest of your organization may not be aware of what the changes are or why the modifications have been made. You will be working on one plan while they are working on another.

The Need for Constant Communication

The need for quality communication is pervasive. Internal communication of plans and objectives is essential to the well being of any venture. The impact of improper or insufficient communications is greatly magnified within the more complex and fast-paced activity of a growing telemarketing company. Yet the consequences can be the same: inefficient operation, unnecessary mistakes, increased costs, and lost opportunity.

One of the big mistakes most telemarketing entrepreneurs make is that, for much too long a time, the top couple of people in the company are the only ones in the know. They are so busy that they simply feel they don't have time for consistent and thorough communication sessions. They plan the operations, know the TSRs, and just fill the rest of the people in as they can. Unfortunately, the communications get to some people, but not to others. They don't have operations meeting or staff meetings, because they believe they don't have time and that frequently scheduled meetings are a sign of weakness.

At some point in the growth process, these telemarketing entrepreneurs need to recognize the problems caused by the lack of communication and make the changes required.

We believe in keeping meeting time to a minimum, but some meetings are necessary on a regular and frequent basis. The nature of the telemarketing business is such that programs change daily, and something is learned about a program every day. That's particularly true in the testing and development stage, but it happens on a regular and ongoing basis with all existing programs.

Programs change with:

- market condition changes;
- competitive requirements;
- realignment of competition in the marketplace; and
- TSR population changes caused by restaffing, new training, and reassignment of TSRs to other programs.

The daily list make-up changes, by definition, every day:

- the inventory of callable names on a list is reduced with each day's work; and
- there is a lesser inventory on any given list every time you put it back on the floor.

Additionally, departmental situations affect the running of the programs. If, for example, the verifications department gets behind on a program, you may have to cut some of the volume until they can get caught up, so you don't produce more than you can fulfill.

The need to keep up with these constant changes may cause you to decide it is wise to have a daily operations meeting. The need for communication is so strong that it can be worth the time spent sharing the information about changes in the program, the lessons learned, and the perceptions gained in the previous day's execution.

Those telemarketers who have established these meetings have found that they:

- gained new and better insights into the marketplace;
- enhanced their understanding of managing lists;
- more quickly and effectively developed script refinements; and
- improved their understanding of what was happening in the operation.

EXAMPLE: When we started the operations meetings, we found that our management ratio needed to be modified on some programs. The normal supervision ratio of 1 to 8 might be effective on most programs, but other programs were more effectively run with modified ratios. A 1-to-8 ratio might be overkill for a one-dimensional program that was easily learned and quickly internalized by the TSRs, while a more complicated program might require a 1-to-6 ratio.

We found we were cost-ineffective in some areas and were charging the client more than we had to. You often can't discover that kind of thing before the fact. That's one of the reasons for thorough testing and program development *prior* to rolling out. But we discovered that unless we communicated daily about what is happening on the floor, we couldn't gain the full benefit of the lessons being learned.

While those kind of communications can be very valuable during the normal course of telemarketing management, it is essential to assure that you have effective two-way communications during growth periods.

How to Establish Two-way Communication

If you limit communication only to a downward process, you have a big problem. Trying to force communication down to lower levels of the structure just isn't effective. You also have to encourage the information to flow up through the organization to the top management. Quality analysis can be done at all levels, and refined by top management when the information arrives from below.

It's also a matter of educating your people on the fact that you want them to be an active *part* of the creative management process, rather than just automatons who follow directives. That requires more than simply passing along the "what to dos"; it also requires communicating the "why to do its" and the "how to do its." You have to communicate the full information to your management and supervision staff if you want to develop them, their understanding of the business, and their thinking processes.

If you want to be able to grow effectively, you need to have your people understand the whys and the hows. Without that, they will never be able to free you to manage the broader company growth and development issues.

EXAMPLE: Your people need (and want) to understand *why* certain programs are assigned a supervisor-to-TSR ratio of 1 : 6 and others 1 : 12. They need to understand *why* you make exceptions to the ratios in the training process. They need to understand *why* the supervisors of the newest TSRs have slightly smaller groups to handle than those who are supervising teams composed of proven TSRs who have a great deal of experience on the program.

Unless they understand the *reasons* for the variations, they will begin to assume that it's OK to play with the ratios *any* time, for *any* reason. Once that happens, your variable expenses will soon be out of sight.

Warning: *If the top management of a telemarketing company must constantly deal with problems of employee mismanagement that are the result of communicating only the "whats" without the "whys" and "hows," then top management will never find the time to be more than glorified (and overburdened) operations managers.*

That communication process has to be an ongoing and a two-way activity. The correct information, problems, and suggested solutions can be passed up from the grassroots levels. The appropriate praise, corrections, answers, and refined solutions then must be passed back down to the people in the trenches. The communication comes up and goes back down. Properly executed, it provides a conducive environment for growth.

There's nothing mysterious about the need to communicate, but it is often over-looked in operating a telemarketing business. As long as there are other people involved with your job, so much depends on good communications.

Key Point: *You've got to communicate well, thoroughly, and often if you want to create an atmosphere and attitude of growth.*

COMMUNICATE THE VISION AND THE REALITY

With quality communications established, the most important communication for the development of an environment conducive to growth is the communication of your vision. From that vision is developed a sound business plan, realistic goals, and expectations, and the proper organizational structure to implement the plan.

But you can't keep your vision, goals, and plans secret. If you fail to share those things with your organization, you won't create the kind of environment that will nurture and inspire your people to do the work that will result in the growth you envision.

Communicate Solid Information, Not Empty Promises

A meaningful sharing of your plans and vision are critical to growth. You can't afford to create the growth atmosphere by making empty promises. Otherwise, you may soon find yourself—in the attempt to fulfill those promises—caught in the trap of growth for growth's sake. The only way out of that trap may be by breaking the promises you made. Neither of those situations is conducive to an environment that will support healthy growth.

Yet, your people still have to be sold on growth through a thorough communication process. That starts with the statement of philosophy that you provide to your people. You may want to include:

- honest statements about providing growth for the key people over a period of time;
- a statement about your honest commitment to excellence; and
- an honest explanation of opportunities that can be created through individual and team commitments.

The key is *honesty*. If your statements just give lip service to growth—if they are not real plans and objectives that you intend to work for and accomplish—sooner or later, you'll be seen either as a liar *or* as an incompetent who can't follow through and accomplish announced goals. Neither reputation is one you want to develop.

Identify the Situation at Hand

Being honest in your communications doesn't mean you should communicate every aspect of your planning and marketing process. Nor is it either necessary or wise to announce every specific detail of your dream when you communicate your overall vision.

General MacArthur was a hero because he simply said "I shall return" and did so. Had he said "I shall return next week," he would have looked like a jerk when he finally got back years later. Joe Namath said "I *guarantee* we'll beat the Colts in Super Bowl III." When the Jets won, it shook up the football world and made Namath a folk hero. If, instead, he had he said "we'll win 36 to 3" and then proceeded to win 16 to 13, there would have been a lot of people who would have felt that Broadway Joe was a big-mouth who couldn't deliver on his promises.

Whatever the plans of the company and the people who run it, the events of the marketplace may change those plans. Plans are only that: plans. They are not "etched in stone" guarantees to be followed without change or exception on a day-to-day basis.

You have to identify the situation at hand at the time you are going to communicate. Before talking to people about a firmly time-dated growth plan, you have to get over the hump of establishing a reputation for success in the marketplace.

> **EXAMPLE:** If you're planning for growth and have signed seven contracts that will give you a total of "X" amount of guaranteed business with stipulated start dates over a two-year period, you can reasonably announce more specific time parameters.

If you don't have the established contacts or reputation, all you can do is talk about the vision and the monomaniacal commitment to excellence. Then you must go out and *earn* a position of respect in the marketplace!

How to Reduce the Problems Caused by Marketplace Changes

You *can* talk to people about how you will take steps toward growing when the company has accomplished the desired image and performance. You can even say: "As soon as we have 'X' amount of retained earnings, we can embark on additional structuring and development to prepare for future growth." Remember that *you* are not in control of the ultimate marketing plans; your clients are!

Warning: *The moment you commit to a time schedule without regard for performance factors and the vicissitudes of the marketplace and the maturation of the company, you expose yourself to misunderstandings and conflict.*

EXAMPLE: ABC Telemarketing Service, Inc. receives initial letters of intent from a client for 70,000 hours of work. It isn't a signed contract, but it indicates what the client plans to do if there are no major changes in their overall plans. So the top management of ABC makes a major announcement to its people based on the initial letters of intent. They announce the full 70,000-hour opportunity, and promise that major growth and advancement opportunities will be made available to the employees within four months. A specific time line for additional training, promotions, and new responsibilities is given to certain people.

Then the unforeseen happens. Economic changes in the marketplace put the client's entire industry into a major tailspin. Cash flow and profits fall dramatically. The outlook indicates that a quick turnaround is extremely unlikely. Action is taken to shore up the companies. Budgets are cut across the board. Layoffs occur. The client company, which had provided the letter of intent, is caught in the slump and has to make severe cutbacks. The budget cuts directly affect the client's marketing plans and reduce the number of hours which can be farmed out on the program by 40%, with a 90-day delay from the originally planned start dates.

Additionally, the client's upper management decides to split the hours between two vendors in hopes of reducing their risk and of enhancing the opportunity for early success. As hard as ABC's top management tries to convince the client that it is better to leave all of the project with one vendor, the client remains determined. The original 70,000-hour letter of intent results in a 21,000-hour contract to ABC.

Note: *Cutbacks and realignment of projected volumes to be placed with a given telemarketing unit is a reality for* both *in-house shops and service agencies!*

ABC's lack of control of the greater marketplace has put the company in a very difficult position. Since the company's top management had not yet taken on additional fixed costs or additional variable wages, there is very little direct *financial* loss. Yet top management has a direct loss of *credibility* within the organization. What ABC's top management must do is clear and logical:

- announce the lesser contract received;
- address the reduction in plans required, as compared to previous announcements; and
- indefinitely delay the scheduled training and promotions for most of the people targeted for advancement.

Those are the *logical* steps to take, but the *emotional* response of the company's employees will be one of severe disappointment.

- Everyone feels that the company has had a severe setback.
- Some of the people who were targeted for advancement feel betrayed.

Although it was made with the best of intentions, the premature announcement of volumes and timelines has backfired.

Who created the problem?

Was it the client and the marketplace that had to deal with changing conditions? Not at all; they did what they had to do to keep business moving with the realities of life.

Then is it the fault of ABC's top management? You bet it is!

A simpler and more productive initial announcement could have been made by ABC's management. It could have created a more realistic expectation—one that would have been much less vulnerable to changing market conditions—if it had announced instead that:

- the company had "secured a commitment of intent from the client"; and
- that more details would be given "as the client finalizes them, and as the company is in a position to begin planning implementation of the program."

That announcement, made without indicating either the volume or the time line for additional growth structuring, would have left the company looking great—and the environment of positive expectation intact—when the starting dates of a contract for an additional 21,000 hours of work for ABC was announced! That action would have:

- maintained and furthered the atmosphere of growth; and
- resulted in people being *excited* at the *increase* instead of being *disappointed* by the *perceived setback*.

Tip: *When working with people, your communication should always take into account that for every action, there's an equal and opposite reaction.*

How Much of the Plan to Share

Deciding how to share your vision and your overall plans is a critical matter. The questions that come up are:

- How much of the vision do you share?
- How much of the plan for achieving the vision do you share?
- With whom, and down to what level of the organization do you share information about each?

Where you are talking about the vision for company growth, you should emphasize communicating it *all* the way—from the upper echelons down to the entry-level trainees. Every person needs to understand the company's aspirations for growth and the role of individual positions in relation to it. What are the primary reasons for that belief?

1. *Everyone* tends to feel more important and more involved.

2. You avoid rumors and misinformation that otherwise winds up being communicated "accidentally."

Remember: *When more than one person knows something, it's not going to be a secret very long!*

If you have 100 employees and 78 of them are on the phone, it's not sufficient to have 61 of them know what their role is, because that leaves 17 of them who don't. Those 17 who don't know their role are the ones who will be most inclined to:

- give lazy and less-than-quality efforts;
- do things that will automatically stunt your growth;
- make it harder for everyone to excel; and
- rack you with dissension,

Their actions in those areas, while not acceptable, are understandable and predictable. They tend to do those destructive things because no one has effectively *communicated* with them. They don't perform effectively because they don't *understand* the importance of *their* roles. They make the company's growth harder because you have failed to make sure they feel they are a part of the growth environment.

That doesn't mean that you need to make broad, sweeping, hyperbolic statements about their potential or promises about their individual opportunities for advancement.

You need to communicate information to all of your people honestly and accurately. If you fail to do so, you may have potential superstars who become frustrated and hurt you by either performing seriously below their levels of capability, or by exceeding your expectations . . . but with another company.

How to Communicate Your Plans

Some telemarketing companies attempt to build their expansion plans around production milestones. But trying to build implementation plans and schedules based strictly on volume levels is risky. You may find that:

- the costs of reaching those production points are much higher than you have anticipated and budgeted for;
- you cannot afford to grow on the planned schedule; and
- time projections, money, and key players will have to be extended for a period of readjustment and retrenching.

Instead, you should give the broad outline of the process and the sequence, with no chronological commitment for the plan. That outline should include:

1. the overall concept;
2. the general sequence of steps that can be anticipated; and
3. your plan to accomplish each of the steps in that sequence.

Make sure they internalize the underlying values of dedicated work habits and quality performance required to achieve the objectives. Explain how the structure of the organization will change as you meet objectives of:

- competitive performance superiority;
- billable hours;
- profit margins; and
- retained earnings.

Then you can suggest the general timeline *desires* you have, so long as it is with the clear understanding that actual timelines will be determined by a combination of actual performance and market events.

HOW TO OVERCOME RESISTANCE TO CHANGE

One of the words used most frequently in this chapter is "change." That's not a coincidence. It is impossible to deal with growth and not face change, yet it is important to keep in perspective that change makes people uncomfortable. People resist it because it represents the unknown. No matter how unpleasant or unfulfilling their current situation, it is known. At worst, they know how to tolerate it. They fear the unknown precisely because they don't know how it will affect their lives. The only solution is to keep them "in the know" and to make sure that they perceive the change as a natural evolutionary process, rather than one of revolutionary upheaval.

Three Approaches to Managing Change

The way you approach change with your people is extremely important. There are three primary choices:

1. *Mandate:* There are times when you will have no choice but to mandate change, but it is best to save it for the major issues when something has to happen immediately.
2. *Internal Marketing and Involvement:* This sometimes leads to debate, but selling people on new ideas and approaches is often the best way to go. It certainly is a better choice if mandate would create massive resentment.
3. *Test It In Small Areas:* This can work very well in many situations, and it provides the added bonus of getting good suggestions from the people involved on how to improve the new systems before they are fully implemented.

While caution and compromise on people issues sometimes seems the hard way to go, its long-range effects on attitude, receptivity to change, and maintaining an atmosphere of discussion and innovation are extremely valuable. If people understand that change is a part of your philosophy, they will be much more apt to look at planning for growth and change as a sign of past achievement and an opportunity for future success. The fear of the change that comes with growth is—at least partly—negated.

Test and Compromise

The choices aren't always easy when you embark on managing telemarketing growth. The answers to some problems come with trial and error. But you will experience change. And when the changes begin, you have to be willing to look at new ways of doing things organizationally that you personally have done in other ways.

> **EXAMPLE:** When you are running a small telemarketing company, it's possible to have the head guy be the only trainer. Up to about 50 phones, those people can really be "his" people; he can know them all and know them well. But when growing the scope of operations from 45 to 200 to 600 phones, then to more than 1,200 phones, there is no way the top person can recognize all 2,000-plus people—let alone know them well.
>
> When we faced that situation, we had to establish systems and structures that could compensate for that lack of direct contact. So we went to the process of gradually moving to another trainer, then to other trainers, to a full training department, and eventually to a full human resources department.
>
> As we grew in size, we began to see absenteeism and turnover increasing. We found that much of the early sense of personal involvement had been lost. So we decided to provide an orientation session in which the recruits met selected TSRs to observe the work and discuss the job and the company. It was the old buddy system, in a updated framework.
>
> But there was a problem. The TSRs, the supervisors, and the managers didn't like the idea. The managers and supervisors felt that:
>
> • it would be an intrusion;
> • it would be an added complication to their management duties;
> • it would distract the TSRs.
>
> The veteran TSRs didn't like the idea any better. They felt it would:
>
> • take away from their productivity time;
> • be distracting;
> • cost them bonus and incentive money.

Rather than risk the goodwill of the entire group, we proposed a short test of the system with only a small portion of the recruits and the TSRs. They compromised with us and gave it a try.

After the first night of the test, it was so well received that all the TSRs were *clammoring* to be selected for the orientation program. Suddenly we had a new and very effective incentive program. The selected TSRs were chosen not just for their sales performance, but for being model TSRs in work habits, dress, and attitude. Before long, it wasn't necessary to choose selected TSRs for the orientation. We could pick them at random because of the overall improvement.

Key Point: *If your ideas for change are good, they will stand the test. Compromise may be* *the key that will convince your people to give your ideas a fair test and discover how good the idea is.*

Exercise Your Patience

Exercising patience is not often a great virtue of telemarketers. With the fast pace, rapid change, and urgency placed on being responsive to the client, the closest many of us come is when we say "God grant me patience . . . right now!"

Still, in managing people during periods of change, patience can be a virtue that pays large rewards.

> **EXAMPLE:** We started out as a tight-knit, family-feeling organization with *fast* promotion of people. We continued to grow, and since we didn't know all the people, we sometimes had problems telling the managers and supervisors apart from the TSRs. One night I asked a question of a supervisor who was standing by a TSR and monitoring his call. I asked the supervisor a question about the management of the program. All I got was a blank stare.
>
> It turned out that the "supervisor" was the TSR, and the "TSR" was actually the supervisor making a demonstration call. When I found out I wasn't the only member of upper management who had experienced the problem, we discussed instituting a dress code for the supervisors and managers. All of the upper management agreed it was a good idea. The supervisors and managers didn't. Rather than force the issue, we let it slide and bided our time.
>
> When the managers, supervisors, and TSRs started complaining about not being able to keep track of who was who, *they* raised the idea of a dress code! This time it was the floor personnel and the TSRs who had the problem, and they convinced the rest that it was a good idea. After being duly persuaded, we quietly agreed, and a dress code was implemented.

Key Point: *Managing growth means managing change, and sometimes the best way to manage change is to just let it evolve naturally.*

Recognizing the Need for Change

One of the greatest challenges in managing the change that comes with growth is being able to recognize when it is needed. Upper management is normally as set in their ways as the rest of the organization. Even after you make some decisions about what kind of people are needed, you have to come back and look at those decisions as the company grows and your needs change.

There are very few exceptions. Even the position of secretary to the CEO changes and needs to be understood. A "Gal Friday" who may not be the best in terms of typing and those kinds of functions, but who can act as a general assistant, may be the ideal person for that position in a smaller company. In a larger company, a truly excellent executive secretary or full service administrative assistant is needed.

The concept is very logical, but recognizing when the change is needed isn't always easy.

Key Point: *As a company grows, your needs may change before you recognize that the change has taken place. You must remain aware if you are to recognize the new needs and be open to making the changes that will better suit them.*

CAREER PATHING: PERCEPTION AND REALITY

How you approach the subject of career pathing depends on what you want to achieve. The smaller an organization and the smaller its plans for growth, the less of a need there is to formally address the career pathing issue. As a company becomes larger—and to the degree that significant growth is expected to be a part of its future—career pathing becomes more important. As more distinct and specialized positions are needed and created and better people are required to fill those positions, the issue will become more important, to both the company and the employees.

Employee Expectations of Career Pathing

As your company begins to grow—no matter how cautiously you approach the announcement of growth plans—you will have to deal with the issues of promotional opportunity and career pathing. Somebody is going to ask: "What kind of career path do I have?" When your people begin to ask about career pathing, you can't afford to ignore the questions, whether or not you are prepared to address them

Caution: *Growth stirs expectations of individual promotion and advancement, especially in those employees who are ambitious and aggressive.*

Those expectations and that ambition can work in your favor if you handle them properly, or they can backfire if you simply ignore them. The problem is that when the issue of career pathing is raised, it carries the connotation that a person's career is going to move only *upward.*

> **EXAMPLE:** Career pathing can mean that someone, who has risen to a supervisory position, may never be promoted to more than a supervisor—in that department or in another—for the rest of his career. If—during the process of previous career pathing—he has demonstrated that a supervisory position is the highest level at which he can make a meaningful contribution, it means that all he really can expect in the future is pay raises and the possibility of supervisory positions in other areas of the company.

Yet, to most people, career pathing usually means promotion and growth. They assume that there's never a Peter Principle, at least not for *them.* And, to an extent, that's good. They don't want to consider that their career path may be lateral or stagnant or, even worse, downward. But that might not really be "worse"; not if they are in a job that is beyond their ability to handle it.

The Problems Created by Poor Career Pathing

If you have employees who are at the maximum level of their capabilities, then your challenge is to recognize that you still have a responsibility to maintain the satisfaction of those who do outstanding work but have reached their optimum level of advancement—at least as they are currently evaluated within your organization.

The employees can see the company is growing rapidly, and they just naturally assume that getting a promotion means they are away and running along an unlimited, predestined career path. But, it doesn't always work that way.

Of course there will be people who don't understand. Unfortunately, some of those people want to progress and—under the pressure of growth—the company may give them the chance, rather than disillusion them. But the results will be constant problems that require extensive and repeated troubleshooting just to keep performance up to a barely tolerable level.

If you make the mistake of taking that overaggressive approach, you will find that it will take a *lot* of extra stress and diverted energy to finally fix a situation that could have been avoided in the first place.

Yellow Flag: *Under the pressure of rapid growth, many telemarketers make the mistake of making the wrong kind of promises for promotions and growth to the wrong people.*

The Costs of Moving Too Fast

In many ways, for all the difficulties caused by promoting the wrong talent, bringing along the more talented people is even more of a problem. There's always the temptation to try to move them along too quickly, especially when you are growing fast and need more management personnel.

Again, it's a mistake you shouldn't make. We know. We made it more times than we would like to remember. And it cost a lot—it cost some of the people, it cost the company future talent, and it cost us personally.

> **EXAMPLE:** For a number of years, we did too many things purely instinctively. We went through a lot of people trying to find the ones who could do the job. In our rush to grow, we moved some of them along too quickly and assured their failure.
>
> Once we had done that, it was hard to recapture or salvage them. We watched a number of them walk out the door knowing in our hearts that they eventually *could* have done the job, if we had only been more patient in training, developing, and promoting them.
>
> With the real survivors, we were lucky. A few of the people got promoted and demoted two, three, and even four times. They hung in there and believed in themselves. They were willing to take the step back, learn, and mature, and come back at it again. Some of them eventually made it, and we were ecstatic for those people.

Unfortunately, many of the people who are lost in that kind of situation never return to the company. Either they become so disenchanted and frustrated that they leave the industry, or they are so embarrassed by not having made it that they feel they can't stay with the company. When that happens, all you have done is create opportunity for your competition.

Career Pathing Starts with Your Own Commitment

Unless you make career pathing one of your a real goals, you'll never achieve it. While the lip service you give may be serious, in the back of your mind you'll be saying "Of course, if I can't pull it off, I'll come up with a rap at that time to take care of it." That does no one any good.

Unless you have made a clear commitment to real career pathing and career growth for the top talent, you are likely to lose the best people in the organization and have the remaining, less-talented ones become quite disenchanted with the company. You'll also find that life isn't what you like and that quality growth is almost impossible to achieve.

But a commitment to career pathing is not one that can be taken lightly. Career pathing and the development of people is not an overnight process in any business, but it's especially true in telemarketing today. Home-grown talent is the rule, and the crop of potential talent with strong roots in telemarketing is very limited.

Most successful telemarketers have learned, over the years, that commitment requires them to be:

- more accurate and realistic in their appraisals of employee capabilities;
- more thorough and patient in their development of the people;
- less impetuous in their advancement of people; and
- more complete in the planning, creation and execution of career pathing methods.

As those telemarketers successfully developed more of the people that were needed, the job became easier for them. Eventually, the best people they have developed take over the bulk of the development of the first couple of levels of management. That frees up top management to concentrate on the development of upper management personnel and on the continued growth of the company.

So, if you are going to grow, you need to develop the people you've got and address the issue of career pathing. To provide effective career pathing for the growth of the individual and for the growth of the telemarketing organization, you first have to make a commitment to creating an organized career path management approach.

Instead of promoting people into the wrong spots or beyond their capabilities, you have to figure out how to:

1. keep those employees who have little opportunity of advancement happy and productive; and
2. develop the employees who have the capability for progressing to higher positions, and have them be patient while they are being developed;

In each case, that requires:

- Honest evaluation of the people's skills and performance;
- Clear communication of that evaluation;
- Recognition for the positive values they bring to their jobs;
- Well-packaged explanations of their weaknesses and negative areas of performance; and
- Providing variety in their work experience without advancing them beyond their levels of capability.

In addition, the employees who show promise of development need:

- Cautious and patient development of their skills; and
- Gradual increases in their levels of responsibilities so they are not "set up to fail" by moving them too fast.

A More Realistic Approach

It is a very limited perception that career pathing simply means promotion and growth. On a larger scale, it represents:

- a course of developing greater depth and breadth of experience in the company and the industry;
- a variety of possible patterns for assuming duties or positions which will increase an employees understanding of and worth to the company; and
- an opportunity for the company and the employee to discover the areas and the levels of involvement in which the employee is happiest and most productive.

To provide real career pathing for your employees, you need organized plans for development, promotions, and growth—with a careful system for announcing those plans.

A part of that system is being clear and straightforward with your people in creating the growth environment.

- The concept of controlled management of growth should be explained.
- The reality that movement in career paths may include both vertical and lateral movement must be clearly understood.
- The need for careful development and the reality of changing market conditions and client plans should be honestly addressed.

When your talented people understand both the challenges and the responsibilities of growth, they will have much more realistic perspectives of the opportunities. Without that full understanding, they may become frustrated when—in spite of the value of their contributions—their immediate promotions do not fit into the growth plan.

Talk to your people about their present individual roles. Discuss what it means to grow and progress in their current positions. Let each person know what the next position or alternative positions normally would be *if* they were to progress far enough to be considered for further development. Clearly explain both the realistic opportunities and the minimum performance required to earn consideration for further development.

You should also let them know that the discussion should not be taken as a promise that their position will change, or even that a developmental change would necessarily be a promotion. A promotion is only one of the options. Another might be a higher classification of their current position, with increased responsibility. It could also be a lateral move with exposure to another area of the company's operations.

The people should be encouraged to communicate their desires and expectations for growth within the teamwork frame. Solicit their reactions and their hopes. An encouraging professional discussion can be the first step in the development of a person who may play a primary role in the future achievement of your goals.

Key Point: *It is a vital that all members of the team understand the company's goals at the level of their own roles.*

Create and Communicate the Alternative Paths

You need good communication, but you also have to have a structure to support and give credibility to the concepts that you deliver. You can't start up with 20 or 100 phones, tell the people that you're planning to grow, and not tell them what jobs are logical to grow into from the TSR position. You'll find that the people are making up their own competitive rules if you don't tell them what they can work toward and what to do to get promoted. That leads to dissension and vicious infighting that can tear a telemarketing company apart.

Instead, make use of the organizational charts you have created for your company and for its future growth. Show people what the most likely alternatives for their career path might be. Show that the straight sequence of progression in the operations area might be: TSR, sales supervisor, product manager, facility manager, operations supervisor, operations manager, etc. Then show the person how lateral movements in the structure, that might not appear to be positive moves, will actually round their knowledge and expertise and make them more valuable to the company over time.

> **EXAMPLE:** Ellen is a TSR who is interested in advancement and has shown skills and talents that cause the company to share her interest. However, she expects to move up to the sales supervisor position (with an increase in pay), while the company is in greater need of a quality assurance representative (at a similar rate of pay). Ellen is hesitant to take a position that will move her out of the "direct line of advancement" in Operations.
>
> The facility manager explains that what might appear to be a "side track" of moving from TSR to quality assurance representative actually has the potential of resulting in greater future value. An employee who gains the additional knowledge of a key part of the company may, if they have the talent, become a prime candidate to move into the sales supervisor position they had originally hoped to gain, or to become the quality assurance supervisor.

The facility manager explains further that a career path from TSR to QAR to QAS does not prevent an employee from being able to move into the sales supervisor position if it comes open. And—with the additional experience and broader understanding of the company's systems and operations—that employee who has successfully mastered the TSR, QA, QAS, and sales supervisor positions would have some very real advantages in eventually being considered for the product manager position.

Ellen sees the logic behind the progression and, with a better insight into a career path that she finds more attractive than the one she had considered, accepts the lateral move to QAR.

The ability to explain the alternatives in progression is a valuable tool to have in the management arsenal. Developing that tool for every department requires some serious analysis and consideration, but it is a step worth taking. The time that is required for department heads to put together alternative career paths within their departments, and then to work together to develop interdepartmental career paths is time well invested.

Career Path Options
(Operations)

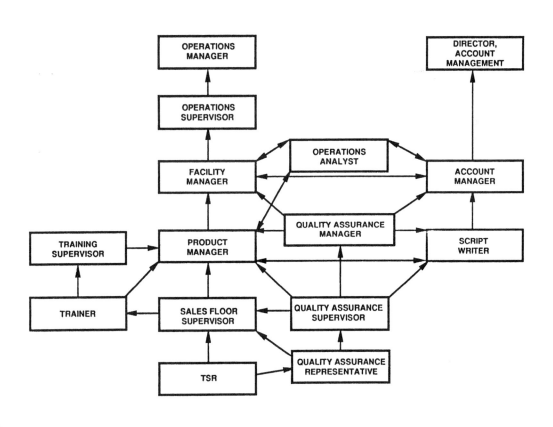

The net result will be a well-developed set of career pathing options which can:

- help employees understand the different paths that might be followed and the advantages of lateral moves; and
- help management personnel recognize options for developing their people and their departments in ways they otherwise would not have considered.

Combined with a system of quality communication and the careful training and development of people, the basis for meaningful career pathing will be in place.

WHY (AND HOW) TO MANAGE PERSONAL GROWTH

Remember that, as a manager, you are in the business of shaping and guiding other people. You have a responsibility to educate, to train, and to share your values with the people who look to you for guidance. The training and the education are relatively easy to do, and they bring the most immediately observable and measurable results. The sharing of values is the most difficult of those responsibilities.

Disraeli said that the most successful person on the face of the Earth is the person that has the best information and values. It would follow that the person who possesses and can transmit that information and those values is more likely to be successful than the person who lacks the information and values, or who is unable to transmit them.

Those values include the concept you have of your business and your industry, but they go well beyond those professional values. Your personal values—your perception of life—is equally important in the development of your people. Your personal values include how you see the individual fitting into the company, into the community, into their family, and into their own sense of purpose and contribution.

It is always more difficult to help and to change yourself than it is to help others. We can make suggestions and teach others all day long; we consistently show them how to do their jobs as well as possible and to make their lives the best they can possibly be. But when it comes to applying that to our own lives, it becomes significantly more difficult. Application is always harder than education, and we can see that most clearly in our own lives.

We determine the level of accomplishment that our people can achieve under our direction and development. Through our own capacities and qualities, we will either assist them in going forward or hold them back from progress. Through our own examples, we will demonstrate the value we place on personal growth.

The Speed of the Leader Determines the Rate of the Pack

If you're going to be the driving force behind the organization—if you're going to be *the* leader—you have to know that the tone you set will be the one that the rest of the organization is going to follow. It will be your vision they will follow . . . good, bad, or indifferent.

There is no story so common as an entrepreneur who can build the organization only to a certain size before someone else has to take over its management so the company can continue its growth. Often, the entrepreneur has taken the organization to a size and structure that no longer suits his or her style and capabilities. He or she is no longer happy or no longer effective in the environment that has been created to support the success that has been achieved. Steven Jobs and Steve Wozniak needed different kinds of challenges to be content after Apple Computer, the company they founded in a garage, became a major corporate entity.

That's not necessarily bad. It's just a part of the maturation process.

Were their choices right or wrong? That isn't the right question. The question is: "Did their choices further the development of their companies and of their personal satisfaction?"

Ultimately, that is a question each of us must answer for ourselves.

Maintaining Personal Satisfaction

Growth doesn't automatically mean the loss of the personal satisfaction that inspired you in the beginning. If you maintain the personal involvement and the boutique environment, you can have a large organization and maintain your satisfaction. You can be a Famous Amos with thousands of bakers doing what you originally did, yet maintain the grassroots connection that keeps you in touch with a part of you that needs the satisfaction of making a quality cookie. But if an executive is to maintain the pace of the company's growth, commitment to personal growth and change is required.

If Famous Amos had not been content to get out of the kitchen and let others do the baking, he could never have achieved the kind of organization he created. Bill Hewlett possessed the skills, temperament, and desire to remain successful at the helm as his company grew into a computer giant. Both of them experienced change. They had to decide what their focus was to be and what provided them with the personal satisfaction that would keep them motivated, productive, and happy. And they had to be willing to grow beyond their old skills and comfort levels to manage their *own* personal and professional growth, as well as that of their companies.

Admit What You Don't Know

Let's say you have the desire to be a businessperson . . . but that you are afraid. That's something Steve used to level about with all his friends—that he was afraid.

He used to think about "How do you do this, and how would I do that?" in different business situations. He would sit through business meetings and wonder about terms he had never heard before, such as "ROI," "Contribution to Margin," and "Blue Sky." At first, he was afraid to ask and show his ignorance, but he quickly learned a lesson that all managers need to learn.

Wisely nodding your head and pretending to know something—when you don't really understand—will kill you. If you want to grow, you have to admit what you don't know, and ask others to teach you.

An important part of the essence of being an entrepreneur or an aggressive businessperson is deciding to take the gamble and say "The things I don't know, I'll learn when I get there. I'll cross that bridge when I come to it." That's fine, but when you find things you don't know, don't cheat yourself by failing to take the opportunity to learn by asking for the help of others.

Learn From Your Failures

It is often said that most successful people fail in business a few times and go broke once or twice. Learning from those experiences is important. But you can avoid some of that pain and be much better equipped for success with dedicated application to personal growth and the development of greater degrees of experience.

> **EXAMPLE:** When I was a brash young man of 26, I borrowed money to get started in my first business. (It was about $8,000, and it seemed like a fortune to me.) But I didn't have the foggiest idea of how to use it properly. And since ignorance and misery love company, I selected a partner who I kidded myself into believing could handle the things I couldn't. But my partner was as inadequate to the task as I was.
>
> Still, the product became the hottest design item in the country for about ten years. We only needed to spend about a thousand or two on samples, and the same on T & E with wise budgeting of costs for a sales trip to New York. We could have stayed with friends while getting commitments for consignments.
>
> Instead, first we argued about who was going to get to go on a sales trip to sunny California. Then, we both went there and wound up vacationing a lot and selling a little. Neither of us ever went to New York!
>
> Were we in on the success of the product? No way! In a business that could have been successful with $5,000 capitalization, we went through that $8,000 without accomplishing anything. We blew it because we didn't have the life experience to know what to do to take advantage of the opportunity.

Part of Paying Your Dues Is Learning Your Industry

Knowledge and experience are two of the things most desired by telemarketing businesses today. Experience can be gained only through your own efforts. But you can learn from the vast amounts of information about the experiences and wisdom gained by others. A dedication to continuing education—including consistent and disciplined study of books, tapes, and professional seminars—should be a part of the life of any good manager.

If we want to achieve anything beyond mediocrity in our chosen field, we also have to put in the time learning it better by doing the job. Trying to perform for our clients before we pay enough dues to learn how to give them a quality product at a reasonable price is a sure way to set ourselves up for failure.

> **EXAMPLE:** When I first started to work for a telemarketing company in Chicago, I decided to go prospecting as soon as I got the opportunity. But when I got the opportunity, I didn't even know how to *begin*! So I picked up the *Yellow Pages* and started looking for businesses to call. I didn't know where to find the right sources, the right lists, or the right people. I didn't know that places like the

Catalogue Council had already done much of the research work that I needed. I was 30 years old and had already been involved in running a national telephone shop, but I just didn't know *anything* about sophisticated telemarketing. I had so little experience in the overall telemarketing field that, out of ignorance, I was trying to reinvent the wheel.

If I had started a business then, it would have had to be in one very specialized area of telephone sales, because that was all I knew. If I had tried to start a service agency, I would have drowned in my own ignorance.

Fortunately, my instinct told me that I wanted more than I was ready for. And that same instinct told me that there was much more I could do if I would just go out and learn the things I didn't understand. So I studied and worked at the business a while longer.

Then I got the opportunity to start a small operation with someone peripherally involved in the business. That person was experienced in handling the financial end, so I figured that I didn't have to know anything about raising money. I stepped in before I was really ready, and I learned a great deal . . . including how to get involved in a wrong partnership!

It was because I still wasn't a very good businessman. I just made the mistake of trying to take on the challenge before I had gained the knowledge and life experience required to make it work.

Strive to Be as Good as You Can Be

The greatest success that we can achieve comes after we have gained the knowledge and experience necessary to make a business successful. That is when we really concentrate on going beyond the immediate demands of learning our trades and work on learning how good we can be.

No matter how much any of us achieve, we need to maintain the drive to set and achieve new goals. Among other things, that keeps us challenged and learning. When we set new and different goals for ourselves, we soon find that we have no idea how to do some of the things that we will want to be able to do five years from now.

We can keep ourselves fresh and growing by setting our sights on doing things that we know we can't do today. We may have no idea how we will do it. We may have neither the knowledge nor the staff required. If we seriously considered trying to do it today, we know we would be foolhardy to try. But that doesn't mean that we shouldn't make it a part of our business plans or our personal goals. What it does mean is that we need to recognize that, in order to reach those goals, we will have to attract the necessary people and take the time to 'go back to school'.

The drive to set and achieve goals keeps us fresh. It keeps us challenged. It keeps us alive. It keeps us growing. And that's a big part of working on being as good as we can be.

Remember to Lead the Way

How often have we heard young people say things like "Gee, if only I had the money, I know I could make it." Or, "Why haven't I had the opportunity?" Why is it that as we get older we learn how to make the money and create our own opportunity? Part of it is that as we get older, we get wiser and more experienced and we learn how to make money!

But that comes—for *anyone* at *any* level of management—from a combination of life experience, a lot of study, a commitment to personal growth . . . and the help of others. You need to set the standards for that commitment to personal growth, and you need to encourage that commitment in your people. That's a mandatory if you want to *lead* the growth of an organization. Unless you are willing to try something beyond what you have already mastered, you're not going to grow. And unless we set that example for our people and work to help them grow, we are failing to create an atmosphere that supports the growth of the company and its people.

Key Point: *We need to manage our personal growth if we are to be as effective as possible in the management of the growth of our people, our companies, and our industry.*

It's really true: the speed of the leader *does* determine the rate of the pack!

HOW TO MAINTAIN THE GROWTH ATMOSPHERE

In telemarketing, creating a growth environment isn't enough. You have to make sure that the atmosphere is maintained. If it is lost, your gains may soon be lost as well. Yet maintaining the atmosphere that has been created can be as difficult as creating it.

Are You Satisfied?

In the 1985 NFL season, the Chicago Bears dominated the league. They capped the season by winning the Super Bowl, and there was a great deal of speculation that it was the start of a new dynasty. The Bears were young, talented, and aggressive. And the public fell in love with them. Their "Super Bowl Shuffle" became a top selling video. Commercial endorsement and speaking opportunities poured in. Two books—by Jim McMahon and Mike Ditka—became bestsellers. No less than seven members of the team were given radio shows. They had worked hard and had hit "the big time".

But they were in a new situation. They were no longer playing strictly to get on top. After having the best two-year record in football, they were in a defensive position: they had to fight if they were to keep their dominant position—and the perks that went with it.

At the beginning of the 1986 training camp, Coach Mike Ditka realized that the team lacked the drive and the intensity they had had the year before. He challenged the team, saying "Are you satisfied? If you are, then you don't belong here. If you want to stay #1, you have to *keep* growing . . . you can't be satisfied!"

In spite of their talent and their youth, the "new dynasty" lost some of their aggressiveness and intensity. They were still very good, but they lost some of their competitive edge . . . and their World Championship.

If you want to stay at a high competitive level—whether in sports or business—you can't lose the drive and the desire that got you there. You have to keep growing. You can't be satisfied. If you are, it will cost you in ways that won't be satisfying at all.

EXAMPLE: Shortly after the Bears won the Super Bowl, Idelman Telemarketing Inc. was formed. The team was young, talented, and aggressive. In the first nine months, ITI grew very rapidly, going from a new startup with 100 phones to a major force in the industry with 400 active phones. ITI brought in $4.5 million in billings, with over $300,000 in pre-tax profits, in its first nine months of existence. The business was growing very rapidly and getting lots of great press clippings and client kudos.

Then we made the mistake of believing our press. It wasn't that the praise hadn't been earned. Our people had done a great job. After the first three months, the company had grown so quickly that a lot of people were putting in 60- to 75-hour work weeks and sometimes pulling success off with mirrors. But we had so much success that we lost sight of a part of what had gotten us there. We forgot to "dance with the lady what brung us." We got too far from the well. We became a little too self-assured about our talent, and we lost some of our front-end intensity.

One of our clients was a large insurance firm that was a low SPH, back-end type of program that is hard to get going. But our management team had started with the client five years before, paid our dues, and proved ourselves—on both the front end and the back end—to the client's satisfaction. Unfortunately, there is a basic axiom of telemarketing:

You can't make a living off of your reputation.

You have to continue to produce, and—although we kept a strong back end—we failed to balance it with superior front end production.

We *should* have seen the signs, and *would* have if we were just looking a little harder. The production was down almost 50% *and* the normal and projected cancellation rate for that program had dropped from 15% to 10%. We didn't have the sharp edge, and we didn't put two and two together fast enough to realize that we had to put more concentration into our sales intensity.

By the time we realized it, the client had forgotten our past victories. They pulled the plug . . . and it was our fault. We were really angry, but we had nowhere to look but in the mirror.

When You Seem to Be Satisfied, Go Back to the Basics

The entire top management team got off its collective inflated egos and went back to giving the extra effort that it takes to maintain excellence. We instituted special reinforcement and review training for all the management staff and, as the "head coach," Steve did much of the training. We went back to basics like it was the first day of training camp—and we started by letting everyone know that we could not afford to believe the press clippings and be satisfied any longer.

It took a lot of extra effort, as it always does to achieve excellence. But everyone was willing to pay the price. We regained our commitment to doing whatever it takes to get the job done, and we straightened out the problem. We regained our reputation for success.

You can't be satisfied and grow beyond the status quo. There's always someone coming up who is hungry and not satisfied yet, so you can't be satisfied—whatever your talent—and maintain your ranking. And, like a professional athlete, a telemarketing firm is only as good as its last performance. Both fans and clients can be very unforgiving.

Innovate to Keep the Air Fresh

It's all too easy to lose your edge. If you see it happening, how do you maintain the atmosphere of growth? You start doing new things—you innovate. That doesn't have to mean innovation out in the marketplace. You can do certain things internally to put a new wrinkle in an old idea or a new face on a tired routine. That may mean:

- varying the responsibilities of your people;
- giving them chances at new programs to keep them fresh and challenged; and
- making lateral transfers with people who are doing as well as they can in their jobs, but can't make the step up to the next position.

> **EXAMPLE:** On one occasion when we were growing too fast to handle it properly, we brought in a consultant to work with our program development people. On another occasion, Grady was brought in to assist with the development and implementation of new structure, expanded educational programs and operations manuals. Each brought a fresh approach and some new views.
>
> When you do that kind of thing and make that type of commitment, people start to see things happening. They see and sense a changing environment. If you package those changes properly—so they are both perceived and real opportunities—you can soon be ready to go again.

Suggestion: *If a person has given their best and wants to stay with the company, but can't be as productive as necessary in their current position, you should give them a chance to enjoy the opportunity for a change of duties.*

If you want people to keep the feelings that create growth opportunity, you can put together a better piece of internal packaging. For example:

- Change a system.
- Introduce a new education quotient that wasn't there before.
- Train people above and beyond the job function they have today, whether you do it formally or informally.
- Take a few TSRs off the phone and get them involved in a couple of preshifts, even though you're not promoting them.

Why do those things? So you can give people a little more exposure to the operation, a sense of their importance to the organization, and a hint that they might be considered for future growth. That's a type of lip service, but it's *meaningful* lip service.

You have to keep challenging yourself and your people.

32 KEYS TO A GROWTH ATMOSPHERE

- Creating a growth atmosphere involves many issues: the establishment and maintenance of quality communications, the realistic communication of goals, the creation of career paths, the handling of resistance to change, and the encouragement of personal growth.

- Because telemarketing is such a people-intensive business, it is a communications-intensive business, as well. It demands the development and maintenance of clear, two-way communication throughout the entire structure.

- Regular operational staff meetings are a valuable part of developing and maintaining quality, consistent, thorough two-way communication.

- If you want to be able to grow effectively, top management needs to communicate to the employees both the "whats" and the "whys." Without that, the support staff will never be able to free upper management to manage the broader company growth and development issues.

- You can't keep your vision, goals, and plans secret. If you fail to share those things with your organization, you won't create the kind of environment that will nurture and inspire your people to do the work that will result in the growth you envision.

- While honest communication of your vision and goals is required, announcing every specific of unconfirmed plans is not wise. Whatever the plans of the company and the people who run it, the events of the marketplace may change those plans.

- Committing to a time schedule without regard for performance factors, marketplace changes, and the maturation of the company exposes you to misunderstandings and conflict.

- Cutbacks and realignment in placement of projected volumes to be placed with a given telemarketing unit is a reality that must be considered in making growth announcements by *both* in-house shops and service agencies.

- It's not sufficient to have only a part of your employees know what their role is in the company's growth, because those who don't know their role are the ones who will be most inclined to do things that will automatically stunt your growth.

- Trying to build implementation plans and schedules based strictly on volume levels is risky, because the costs of reaching those production points may be higher than you have anticipated.

- Make sure your people internalize the underlying values of dedicated work habits and quality performance required to achieve the objective. Then suggest your general timeline *desires,* along with the clear understanding that actual timelines will be determined by performance and market events.

- To deal with the natural resistance to change, keep your employees "in the know" and to make sure that they perceive the change as a natural evolutionary process, rather than one of revolutionary upheaval.

- There are three primary approaches to managing change: mandate, internal marketing and involvement, and testing in small areas.

- While caution and compromise on people issues sometimes seems the hard way to go, its long-range effects on attitude, receptivity to change, and maintaining an atmosphere of discussion and innovation are extremely valuable.

- If your ideas for change are good, they will stand the test. Compromise may be the key that will convince your people to give your ideas a fair test and discover how good the idea is.

- Managing growth means managing change, and sometimes the best way to manage change is to just let it evolve naturally.

- One of the greatest challenges in managing growth is being able to recognize when change is needed. After decisions have been made about filling needs, re-evaluating those decisions should be done regularly. Then you need to remain open to making the changes that will better suit current needs.

- How you approach the subject of career pathing depends on what you want to achieve. The smaller an organization, the less you will need to formally address the career pathing issue. As a company becomes larger, career pathing becomes more critical.

- Giving "lip service" to career pathing, without it being a real commitment, will result in disillusioned employees who are upset because you misled them.

- Career pathing and the development of people is not an overnight process, especially in telemarketing. It requires organized plans for development, promotions, and growth—and a careful system for announcing those plans.

- When the issue of "career pathing" is raised, it carries the connotation that a person's career is going to path only *upward,* not laterally or downward.

- Without your careful selection and thorough development, many employees will "hit the wall" and not be able to handle their promotions.

- When employees are at the maximum level of the capabilities, your challenge is to maintain the satisfaction of those who do outstanding work but have reached their optimum level of advancement.

- One of the hardest temptations to avoid is moving the more talented people along too quickly, especially when you are growing fast and need more management personnel.

- Employees must understand the company's goals at the level of their own roles, and how their roles might change with excellent performance on their part and the company's.

- As a manager, you have a responsibility to educate, to train, and to share your values with the people who look to you for guidance. The sharing of values is the most difficult of those responsibilities.

- You must manage your personal growth if you are to be as effective as possible in the management of the growth of your people, your companies, and your industry.

- A dedication to continuing education—including consistent and disciplined study of books, tapes, and professional seminars—should be a part of the life of any good manager.

- The greatest success that you can achieve comes in learning how good you can be. It's also your biggest and longest-term challenge.

- If you want to stay successful in telemarketing, you have to *keep* improving . . . you can't be satisfied. You can't be satisfied and grow beyond the status quo.

- If you want people to keep the feelings that create growth opportunity, start doing innovative things internally to put a new wrinkle in an old idea or a new face on a tired routine.

- If you continue to challenge yourself and your organization to be as good as you can be, you'll grow. And your people will grow with you.

He who ceases to grow greater becomes smaller.

—Amiel

Small opportunities are often the beginning of
large enterprises.

—*Demosthenes*

---

Chapter 7

*How to Develop
and Direct
the Marketing Effort*

One of the major problems in telemarketing has been that only a handful of firms have really had any meaningful plans for *how* they were going to grow. It has just been "The industry is hot. Let's grow." The main goal of too many marketing departments in the telemarketing industry has been "to pick up more business as quickly as possible," without enough regard for the company's plans or strengths. To make it worse, in some cases those goals were set without any significant telemarketing background and expertise.

When Vince Lombardi took over as head coach of the Green Bay Packers, he knew that the team wasn't performing up to its potential because it wasn't executing on the basics. In his first meeting with the players, he held up a football and said: "This is a football. The object of the game is to take this ball as far in that direction as is necessary to cross the goal line, and to prevent the other team from bringing the ball back far enough to cross the other one."

From the back of the room came the reply: "Slow down coach . . . you're going too fast!

Sometimes the fundamentals seem too simple, but the core strategies of every winning team are built upon them.

THE IN-HOUSE MARKETING EFFORT

The marketing effort for an in-house shop is somewhat different than for a service bureau. The in-house unit:

204

- has a clearly identified market;
- has a client that is predetermined;
- does not have to be concerned about commission-earning marketing salespeople doing the prospecting, sales, and qualifying of prospective clients;
- does not need to be as concerned about classic marketing strategies.

Yet the in-house unit has many of the same concerns as the Service Agency, particularly at the consultative level of dealing with the product managers.

The goals of the company's product managers are:

- to hit the sale volume goal that has been targeted; and
- to meet the budgeted cost per order.

To provide true consultative assistance to the product managers, the in-house head of telemarketing must know everything possible about the company and its products.

Strategic Marketing Decisions

Any telemarketing service has to make strategic decisions about the marketing effort. Even with only 25 phones, either:

1. your security is dependent upon a variety of programs and clients; or
2. you have one very large client and your exposure is extremely high, because any problem that causes that big client to withdraw can be deadly.

Telemarketing Reality: *Internal problems or conflicts in the client's organization may cause them to pull the plug, even though you're doing a fine job. If the plug that is pulled is the one to your sole life support, the loss may be fatal!*

The in-house telemarketer is especially vulnerable to (and has to be particularly sensitive to) that situation. The greatest safety and security comes from the development of a close and consultative partnership relationship with the product division, which is—for all practical purposes—the telemarketing unit's client.

Additionally, although the in-house unit has an inside track, there are many service agencies that would love to compete for that business—and will market aggressively to get it. As a result, the in-house telemarketing unit is well served to consider how to apply and modify the same concepts of marketing to maintain quality internal company relationships.

Key Point: *The relationship between the in-house operation and the product divisions is still a partnership in progress, and it is absolutely essential for the telemarketing arm to be able to advise the product divisions of the realities of the situation.*

IS IT MARKETING . . . OR IS IT SALES?

The relationship between the provider of the telemarketing service (whether in-house or service agency) is critical to survival. It follows very naturally that it is vital to determine the role of the marketing and sales functions of the telemarketing organization.

The Role of Sales

There are a couple of schools of thought in the industry about the marketing/sales role:

1. One group says that it is simply the marketer/salesperson's responsibility to:
   * do a very good job of lead qualifying, and
   * bring the account to the door and involve upper level Account Executives in closing the sale.
2. The other group says that the marketing/sales role is to:
   * qualify leads correctly, and
   * close the sale effectively and *then* turn it over to upper level Account Executives.

Either approach will work, but if you follow the first of those two approaches, you will have a better chance of closing the sale and of closing it in perfect harmony with the operation's real capability levels. In either case, a support system will have to include:

* Excellent script writers who can do more in program development than create the presentations;
* An internal team which can provide the full interface, education, consultation, design, and development of the programs;
* Top management that is more active in each account than simply discussing the account and program needs with the client as the program is working;
* An extended company support system in which everyone is prepared to work through the problems that can be expected to be caused by the uneducated salesperson's hype and misinformation

The salesperson has a specific role, and it is:

* to identify and qualify the right kinds of business,
* to sell the right service . . .
  - at the right price,
  - at the right time,
  - to the right people,
  - in the right way.

Too often, *salespeople* try to go beyond the essence of their role. They need to stay within their limits and to work with the design specialists and the rest of the team to get the *whole* job done *right*.

Once the marketing strategy is developed, the salesperson's role is to sell according to the guidelines of that strategy. The business needs to be sold with honest promises that are consistent with the company's overall image, and that are based on the company's capability to fulfill the promises. Sales is part of the marketing function, and it remains the #1 function of the people out on the street who are charged with bringing in business.

What Drives Telemarketing Growth?

One popular belief is that telemarketing is both a marketing-driven *and* a product-driven business. That's really not that unusual; most industries have that situation to some extent. Industrial manufacturing organizations, for example, fit into that model. Ford and GM and BMW market constantly. But when any one of those car makers has thousands of cars recalled for defects, it quickly becomes apparent that they are still performance-oriented—even after the fact.

Those recalls and how they are handled are as much marketing-oriented as production-oriented. Some of the biggest multinational corporations probably could fight the recalls and delay, if not prevent, having to resolve those product problems. But they can't afford to take that approach, because of the damage it would ultimately bring to their marketing efforts.

In service businesses, it is extremely difficult to determine where the production drive ends and the marketing drive starts. It's hard to discern where you move out of marketing into execution, or where you move out of execution into marketing. It is more than an overlap; the two are integrated.

Marketing's basic function *is* bringing in business. In fact, John Freund has said that "Marketing is simply sales with a college education." Still, the term "marketing" implies more than the basic ability to sell. It includes the ability to function with expertise in areas such as:

- planning strategy,
- plotting course,
- coordinating all promotions and sales thrusts,
- selecting and intermixing multiple media, including telemarketing,
- creating and placing ads,
- handling targeted direct mail and more.

It is the *organization's* responsibility to develop and implement an overall marketing plan. It is the marketing function to decide and execute the best approach to fulfill the plan.

Tip: *The keys are what kind of business to bring in and how best to do it.*

If the growth of the telemarketing company is to be good for its long-term health, the new business that comes from that shared focus should:

- be consistent with the company's expertise;
- offer a high probability for success; and
- have the potential to develop into a long-term relationship for the company.

In developing the plans to accomplish those objectives, you should recognize that—in telemarketing—the operation truly drives what the sales and marketing department can offer to the market. Costly ad campaigns and flashy multimedia presentations can create an *initial* image in the marketplace. But how the *clients* feel about the *quality* of the service will define the company's long-term image.

Note: *It is the telemarketing operation that is the product, and it is always the product the client refers to in a positive, mediocre, or negative light.*

That remains a core axiom of telemarketing. It should not be forgotten while the marketing strategy is being developed.

The Role of Marketing

The proper role of marketing starts with the company developing a focus, goals, strategies, and tactics. It requires:

- the company's dedication to finding the right people;
- an understanding that the marketing role is more than just to bring in business;
- a commitment from the company to thorough training of the sales and marketing force;
- that the company help the salespeople sell in a way that is consistent with the overall image of the company, and in a manner that reflects the company's real capabilities.

Result: *The company should ensure that its salespeople first become truly knowledgeable about the entire process of telemarketing, the company they represent, the market being developed, and the companies within that market.*

The proper role of marketing also includes correctly educating the prospect about the industry. That means:

- carrying the torch to clean up existing misinformation and misperceptions about outbound telemarketing;
- educating the client in the realities of the extent to which professional telemarketing can *and* can't be a productive addition to their marketing mix;
- analyzing the client project and its needs;
- advising the client about how best to meet those needs;
- providing expert program design and development;

- assisting in the implementation and problem-solving stages of the program;
- participating in the follow-through and analysis of the backend performance for the client; and
- maintaining client contact to suggest improvements and assist in the development of new alternatives and additional programs.

Key Point: *Quality marketing means developing quality client relationships. This is done by giving an honest marketing story, followed by the creation of quality programs that generate excellent, cost-effective production.*

A Rarity: The Professional Telemarketing Marketer

The above points *should* reflect the role of marketing in the telemarketing industry. Yet, today many of the people "marketing" telemarketing services are simply salespeople who are working to close accounts and bring in business even if they have no expertise in that market. Then they learn at the client's expense.

Note: *That's why some programs that haven't worked suddenly perform very well when they get in the hands of the right firm or firms.*

Challenge: *Companies in telemarketing should commit themselves to do what it takes to create the type of quality marketing that will clean up those problems. When we can do that, we will have a cleaner marketplace with better-educated, better-served, and happier clientele.*

The problem has not been created because the companies out there are inherently or intentionally unethical; that's not the case in the vast majority of the companies. It has happened because the industry is booming. Everyone is growing and striving to capitalize on the growth opportunity. More marketing and sales people have been needed to handle the increasing needs of the company and the marketplace. The companies have gotten the best people they can find quickly, then have moved those people into the field as rapidly as possible. The salespeople learned how to sell the basic concepts, the brochures, the image, the positioning, the capacity, and the systems . . . and ready or not—they're off and running.

Result: *Many of the salespeople in telemarketing rarely get to learn the telemarketing business; they don't learn how to consultatively educate and how to design and develop programs.*

How to Improve Marketing Efforts

The essence of marketing is bringing a product to market, keeping it in the market, and hopefully widening market share on a controlled-growth basis. The end goal or desired result comes down to selling the right service at the right price, at the right time, to the right people, in the right way, on a profitable and ongoing basis. Selling is a part of that marketing process, but—in the vast majority of cases today—it's unfair to call the telemarketing salesperson a "marketer." Such usage is nothing more than packaging, because that one person can't be singularly responsible for the marketing effort.

> **EXAMPLE:** At McDonalds, the total marketing effort involves the uniforms that the kids wear behind the counters, their smiles and cheerfulness, and the tone of voice they're all supposed to have. If that part of the total effort hadn't existed at the level of delivery of service—when the customer came in to test the marketing promise—then proclaiming "You deserve a break today" would have had no real meaning and no significant long-term payoff.

Marketing consultants Tony Alessandra and Phil Wexler say that "Marketing is not a department; it is a philosophy." In a service business, marketing *is* an organization-wide process. The *whole* product you deliver is a part of the marketing effort. It really is a team effort, from the very bottom to the very top of the organization. It's that complete team that leaves the ultimate image and impression in the mind's eye, and establishes a reputation that transcends the marketing effort.

You can't sell telemarketing in a vacuum. Sooner or later, the client has to come into your operation and talk with the people. They want to talk to your people—at all levels of the organization—and see them in action. Therefore, you can't afford to think in terms of a "one-man marketing team." One person can only be a *member* of that team.

When the client is listening to a TSR on remote monitoring, what the TSR says and how the TSR does the job has just as much—and maybe more—impact on the client's decision to use your service as the salesperson who contacted the client. And the supervisors and managers and department directors are equally a part of the marketing chain. How they conduct themselves plays an important role in the functioning of the overall marketing team. They have specific roles within that process and the appropriate titles for their roles.

The clients are smart enough not to believe that the marketing of a telemarketing service business of any size relies only on the efforts of any one person. They want telemarketing organizations with depth.

Key Point: *The marketplace knows that "The Marketer" exists only as the whole company, its make-up, its levels of knowledge and productivity, and the image it leaves with the client. Clients can not be "fooled," in the long run.*

HOW TO DEVELOP YOUR MARKETING STRATEGY

The essence of marketing strategy is universal. Whether the company is IBM or ABC Telemarketing has very little to do with the basic principles. The marketing effort needs a central focus. All of the marketing elements should come together into a central marketing strategy, rather than "shotgunning" in a variety of directions. A company's brochures, ads and marketing materials need to match and complement the overall concept of the organization.

If you try to play with several separate pieces of the plan without bringing together the focused whole first, you confuse the marketplace's perception of who you are. Each element of your strategy may stand alone, but you are likely to discover that you have unintentionally created conflicting marketing efforts.

Result: *The dilution of each separate marketing effort, and considerably less bang for your marketing buck.*

The Four Key Marketing Elements

There are four core parts to the marketing effort:

1. *Marketing Analysis:* A study of current situations and trends to find existing problems, emerging marketplaces, and new opportunities to fill special needs. It starts with the analysis of your own client trends, current industry trends, and projected future trends. It includes focus on types of businesses, rates, receptivity, etc.
2. *Marketing Goals:* Objectives are determined based upon the findings of the analysis. These goals may include overcoming existing problems, capitalizing on profitable opportunities, and targeting new market segments.
3. *Strategies and Tactics:* Overall approaches are developed to achieve the goals that have been established. Specific methods of carrying out the overall strategy are identified, including the marketing mix of advertising, promotion, direct mail, telemarketing, field sales, etc.
4. *Controls:* Measurement of results are maintained for periodic analysis.

The initial analysis determines the focus or specific marketing niche; the market segment that is not currently being filled in the marketplace, that you can service well, and that can provide the returns you desire. You identify the companies that fit the niche and develop strategies and tactics that will complement your existing resources, structure, and client relationships. In doing this, you balance the company values, production capabilities, and expertise against the impact of the marketing efforts and the administrative capabilities to execute effectively.

Three Primary Marketing Thrusts

Once the elements are in place, the methods of execution come into play. Each of the three most commonly used thrusts has its own advantages:

1. *Insertion:* A gradual development of small segments of a market to develop the company's understanding of the market and its visibility in that marketplace. This is sometimes called the "introduction" or the "slow but sure" approach.
   Advantages:
   a. You can build gradually with lower initial marketing costs.
   b. You can develop greater expertise in a market segment before stepping up your marketing efforts.

    c. You can discover whether the market segment is done which lends itself to your marketing philosophy and margin requirements before committing a great deal of resources to it.

2. *Extension:* Building upon the market segment or related market segments that you are already servicing. (This follows Booker T. Washington's advice of "Let down your buckets where you are.")

Advantages:

    a. You can develop greater volume in a market segment where you already have expertise.

    b. Your established clients can provide very powerful references for you.

    c. It helps you maintain market share in the areas of your existing strength.

    d. It is almost always easier, less expensive, and more profitable to build new volume with existing clients than it is to add new clients and new markets.

3. *Attack:* Blitzing a market with information, ads, promotion, and sales efforts.

Advantages:

    a. You gain marketplace awareness very quickly.

    b. If your market is well selected, you can establish a number of new accounts very quickly.

    c. You may be able to establish market dominance, especially if it is a new niche in the marketplace.

To grow under control, it is much more important to make changes in your marketing thrusts than in your overall marketing plan. You will be much more efficient and more effective in maintaining the momentum of your past success.

Keep Your Focus

Establishing your niche is extremely important, and you have to be very careful about abandoning it once it is successful. Otherwise there is a very strong tendency to try to be all things to all people. When that focus is lost, strategic drift sets in.

It happens all too easily and frequently in all kinds of industries, including telemarketing.

The development of new market segments, the establishment of new services, and rapid expansion is tempting. But abandoning the core of your marketing strategy and the marketing niche you have established often fails to bring the joys and rewards that had been anticipated.

Avoid Tunnel Vision

When you are working on a telemarketing strategy that particularly affects a specific competitor, you have to be careful not to get tunnel vision. For example, it may be extremely important to focus your attention on that given competitor in the early stages of your work. Yet, if you are too successful in beating that one competitor and you continue to target them, you may soon find other competitors beating you to the business in both your existing and new markets.

No matter what the situation, it is not the only competitor with which you should concern yourself. Even if it is currently the *only* competition, the more you succeed, the greater the likelihood that new competitors will appear. They may come from the ranks of currently existing companies, or they may be new companies created to jump into the niche you have entered. If you are spending all your time worrying about how to handle one competitor, you may not be aware of the others that are focusing on you.

Tunnel vision may cause you to miss opportunities to develop other areas of business that your targeted competitor is not in and is not likely to get into in the near future. Yet your sole focus on that competitor may blind you to 10 other excellent opportunities. Don't be blinded by tunnel vision.

Key Point: *Keep focused on how you can best manage and grow your own telemarketing business and you will have much greater success.*

Plan How You Will Sustain Your Growth

One of the things that can happen after you grow very large is that you can't win by beating your competition, because your enemy doesn't remain the competition. A General Motors or an AT&T, with the majority of the market share, stands to lose by winning more share from the competition. At that level, the competition becomes the SEC, Congress, and other government agencies which feel the need to control a company's success levels and market dominance. But what also happens is that you have a responsibility to your stockholders everyday. And if you can't reasonably enlarge your slice of the pie, you have to grow the pie.

Note: *Significant growth presents a lot of positive challenges above and beyond just how to manage it.*

If you decide that you're going to grow very large, you'd better know that you're capable of offensively widening the marketplace to defensively sustain your growth against the competition. Capturing 60% of the entire marketplace probably doesn't apply to telemarketing, but as you do grow, you can—effectively—build a 60% market share. That happens when you carve out a portion of the market and then capture that kind of control over that segment. You can serve out certain segments of the market and say: "That's where I want to be a dominant force."

When you plan your marketing strategy in order to grow, you need to be more focused than just deciding to go out and pick up a ton of new business. The *kind* of telemarketing business you pick up is important. There's always a temptation just to pick up any business that promises to bring cash in the door. But you have to be careful to determine what your real production expertise and capacities are. It's more than a question of what you can or what you want to grow into. You have to know the true production capacity you can achieve while maintaining your commitment to quality.

Whether you want to grow from 5 phones to 10, from 50 phones to 100, or from 500 to 1,000 phones, the basic principles are the same. What many telemarketers have done is say "What I want to do is start to price-compete for the large-volume, $22-per-hour accounts, because I know they're out there." But what if your long-range plan calls for going after Fortune 500 accounts and becoming a first-class service bureau? You have a problem.

If you grow based on lower hourly rate accounts, it's hard to justify why you should get a higher rate from someone else. Without the necessary developed internal organization and existing production capacity to extend and accommodate the additional phones needed for the larger accounts, you may have serious problems. Something's got to come at the expense of something else.

Warning: *If you overload your phones with cheap business and inadequate staff and equipment capacity to cover the accounts, you're going to get some bad references. The clients who are hurt while you grow your facility will pass the word.*

You can't afford to give in to the temptations and pressures to get away from your basic philosophy and plans. You need to make sure you have enough resources. You have to map out a plan that you can stick with. It requires having the strength and finding the wherewithal, in both capital and talent, to continue on with the marketing plans in the markets that you really believe you can impact. This is not to imply that there's anything wrong with the $22 markets. If those are your goal, then you'd be crazy to go after the $35 markets at the same time.

Key Point: *Whatever your overall strategy and target market, remember to not put a lot of energy and money into going after the market segments that aren't the meat and potatoes of your business.*

DEVELOPING NEW IMAGES AND APPROACHES

There are good reasons that the bigger and older companies such as American Airlines or Dun & Bradstreet or AT&T entered the outbound telemarketing service business. Whatever their ultimate success in the industry, the early success of those large firms in their entry to telemarketing service was not just because they were automated. Automation *was* one of their key sales features with obvious benefits attached to it, but automation was only part of their overall ammunition in their marketing arsenal.

Nor did their early success come solely because they did or didn't have a given level of entrepreneurial telemarketing expertise. Rather, in large part, they succeeded because of what they *were,* that most of the entrepreneurial firms *were not.*

- The real guns in their arsenal were their marketers.
- They were deep in experience in the development of the overall organizational and marketing business plans.
- They were very effective in the execution and management of that plan.
- Their parent companies had the ability to commit heavy resources to support the plans.

Most telemarketers don't have budgets that are even comparable. The big companies have the resources to buy—in the most positive sense of the word—market share.

That doesn't mean that they are doing anything that is illegal, unethical, or immoral. It simply means that they have the capability and the capital required to go to market with a sound business plan.

American Airlines Telemarketing advertised in the American Airlines inflight magazine. Someone without much understanding of real life might have said: "Of course they're in the inflight magazine. That's not because they're spending money. It's because they get it free!" But that would have been a very narrow and naive view. They didn't get it free. That advertising space could have been sold to someone else. Whether it's a paper transfer or the telemarketing unit takes it out of their books, there is still a cost associated with it. But they had the resources to incur those costs.

We're not trying to single out American Airlines Telemarketing. The same thing can be said of other firms. AT&T American Transtech's first ad was a full four-color glossy production. And the other large firms have made the same kinds of quality efforts as they have moved into the telemarketing industry. When they move into a new industry, those kinds of large corporations *can* and *should* capitalize on the positions they have spent many years, a lot of energy, and tremendous amounts of money to achieve.

They would not have achieved those positions if all they had been doing was *marketing* their services under their corporate logos. They had been *delivering* quality services that made those logos means something to the general public and to the business community.

Those types of companies have had a long history of executing and delivering. Their strengths and profits have made it possible for them to support telemarketing operations in developing the people, the facilities, and the accounts needed to establish their place in the new market. Then the ultimate reputation and success of the telemarketing ventures depends on their capability to deliver quality services. That's a reality of the free enterprise system.

Few entrepreneurs have that kind of earned name recognition or national reputation to draw upon. They don't have that kind of advance planning experience and capability. They don't have the experiences or the resources to develop the same kinds of full-fledged, traditional marketing plans. And they don't have anything close to those kinds of financial resources. Most of them can't wait five years to become profitable; their money and their company will be gone well before that.

In spite of the advancement and development of the industry in the past couple of decades, many telemarketers still think of themselves as phone sales managers. They are the old breed, and their days are numbered. Those telemarketers who can truly identify themselves as marketers, as opposed to salespeople who utilize the phone, are moving far beyond the stereotypes of the past.

Prediction: *The telemarketers who are true marketing professionals—and those who can join them in this larger perception—will be the leaders in the development of a new and more profitable markets.*

How to Develop a Quality Image and Reputation

We've worked hard over the last dozen years to develop a good reputation for success in the telemarketing and direct marketing world. If we didn't value that reputation and if we were interested only in increasing total volume, we could just go out and market with abandon. We could bring in new accounts that could generate over 20 million calls a year . . . *if* we went out and sold at $21 an hour and promised all the service and quality that we were able to deliver in 1986 for $30 an hour. But it would be dishonest, and a dishonest sell can't be acceptable. It might work short term, but we couldn't grow and build a healthy company that we could be proud of based on that tactic.

If we did that, we *couldn't* deliver the same levels of tiered structuring, depth, and overall management expertise at that price. If a company's costs are $21.01 an hour, it can't charge $21 and survive. Either it would have lied to the client and the quality would suffer because it can't afford to deliver that quality at those rates, or it would wind up going broke trying to meet its promises. Neither of those choices will build an acceptable future.

You can spend tons of money for advertising, elaborate brochures, and the highest-class advertising agencies to represent you. But much more is made of the need to do heavy-duty marketing for outbound telemarketing than is necessary.

Fact: *We grew dramatically from 1981 to 1986—from less than $500,000 a year to almost $16 million a year—while spending less than $50,000, total, on advertising. From 1986 through 1989, Idelman Telemarketing grew from $4 million to $40 million and spent about $150,000 total, on advertising.*

If you know what markets you want to go after, and if you have the kind of people who can do the prospecting and make the contacts, the real question is whether or not you have the kind of service you can sell.

Key Point: *Advertising doesn't create long-range image in this business.* On the other hand, advertising does hlep create awareness and perception. It helps deliver increased numbers of opportunity. It is what a company does with its opportunities that determines long-term image and reputation. Performance is still the bottom line.

It doesn't take long for the marketplace to find out if you're a pretender or a contender. Good word of mouth travels fast, and the only thing that travels faster is bad word of mouth.

Making a Smart Marketing Proposal

A part of a good marketing effort is being clear and educational in your marketing approach. That includes what you say in your ads, your brochures, your direct mail pieces, and all the rest of your marketing effort. But if this is to remain a healthy industry, some of the industry's marketers need to stop confusing the marketplace with a lot of hyperbolic promises. Instead, they need to do more *smart marketing* proposals.

> **EXAMPLE:** ABC Telemarketing receives an RFP (Request For Proposal; see sample in Appendix) from a client who has never done telemarketing and is very nervous about the project. The RFP calls for 70,000 names per month at the test level. It also indicates that the contract would be for a 1-year period with a 90-day notification provision to terminate, with the right of the client to reduce volumes at any time to any level desired. While that provision is to be based on the productivity

and cost effectiveness of the program, it effectively means that the client has a 24-hour termination clause.

ABC's top management knows that most companies would immediately propose a 70,000 call a month program. But they realize that's probably a bad marketing move and that it would display very poor business logic. Choosing to propose the full program would create the immediate need to staff up for 70,000 additional calls a month. Clearly, that would mean having to do extensive new hiring and training for many more TSRs and for more supervisory and management personnel.

But exactly how many?

- Assuming that the 70,000 figure means names with phone numbers and that reaching 80% of that list is a reasonable expectation, then 56,000 completed phone calls can be projected.

- Since it is a consumer program, the company managers could budget the calling at 10 completed calls per hour per TSR. That's a 5,600 hours-per-month requirement.
- There are 26 consumer calling shifts per month, so they would need 215.4 hours per shift.
- With an average shift length of 5 hours, they would need to fill 43 phones a shift. As a safety margin, they round that to 45.
- With a 1:8 management ratio, they would need to increase operations management by:
  - 1 program manager
  - 3 sales supervisors
  - 2 quality assurance representatives
- Using a part-time sales force, they would need 1.4 TSRs to cover each phone for the full week, for a total of 63 new TSRs.

Some companies might then be tempted to go for a major commitment to pick up 56,000 calls a month. But ABC's management recognizes that the program has yet to be tested, and nobody has any idea what the productivity will be or how long it's going to last. Worst of all, it would be a heavy commitment of their resources. They would have 45 phones that couldn't immediately be sold to someone new or used to expand an existing program. They would have to hire and train the new people, bring up the additional management staff, and create a new account management team.

Consider the Consequences

The client is brand new to telemarketing and they have reserved the right, based on productivity and cost effectiveness, to essentially pull out of the deal on a moment's notice. Why would management want to create that kind of exposure? What happens if the productivity isn't there?

If that volume for those 45 phones goes away tomorrow, what will the company have to do? It's unlikely that those open phones will be able to be covered immediately. The company will have to lay off or permanently terminate some people who have just been hired and trained. That will lose the company credibility with its labor market. What about the additional floor management personnel and the new account management team? What happens to all the people whose hopes and expectations the company would have so foolishly raised? What would ABC's management say to those talented employees as they watched them walk out the door?

With marketing assuming the appropriate role in a consultative and educative approach, the decision is made: the program needs to be tested carefully before expanding the volumes to the maximum level. ABC makes a proposal, saying to the client: "Unless it is absolutely mandatory that you get those 56,000 calls out this month, we don't think you are best served by rushing the program to get them out. Let's go in to our ankles first, and then to our knees. Once we have tested the waters, we can dive into it head first. Let's make sure we do it right by making the first test stage 2000 calls."

The Right Decision for The Right Reasons

ABC's management has made a smart marketing proposal for the client and a smart business decision for itself.

- By taking the more conservative approach, they can solve the whole program development puzzle before the company *or* the client commits major resources to the test phase of the program.
- ABC can run a more readily controllable 7-phone test instead of having to gear up for 45 phones.

A key part of your test parameters should always be that you keep the test units in controllable 5- to 10-phone groups. That way, you can test in a smaller and better controlled environment. You can identify problems before you waste a substantial portion of the list.

Key Point: *You need to go slowly and surely, not just because it's safer for your company, but because it's better for the client.*

Don't be greedy, and don't feel you have to take the 56,000 calls today if you haven't done any testing. The downside risks of rushing in is not fair for either you *or* the client. If you don't, you may blow away 40,000 of the 56,000 calls before you resolve the problems. You shouldn't do that kind of learning on the client's dime. Through careful testing, you are more likely to resolve the problems with the program early enough in the game to make the program workable and cost-effective for the client.

It's a matter of considering good direct marketing axioms and principles. If you were in direct mail and had a universe of a million names a month you wanted to drop, you wouldn't start out in your first month's test dropping a million names. You probably would start with 50,000 to 100,000 spread between two test packages. You get the winner out of that test situation, get a control, and continue on a limited basis until you come up with the final shelf-piece mail offer. Only then do you start rolling out big numbers. Otherwise, committing all that printing and postage expense on an offer that may not work is an amateurish crap shoot.

In the same way, it doesn't make good business sense to commit all of the people resources, telecommunication resources, energy, effort, and expense to 56,000 calls that may or not work. Especially not if you can accomplish the same thing on 2000 calls. Then you can roll it out with what is needed to make the program work.

Remember: *Smart marketing concerns itself with more than just "bringing in business." The positioning you establish in the marketplace is very important, and it should* never *be abused.*

HOW TO TRAIN THE SELLERS OF TELEMARKETING

Since most salespeople are commission-oriented salespeople, their natural inclination is to want to sell as many calls as possible *now*. You have to get them to understand the long-range benefit of doing the whole job, even if it takes a little longer to close the business. Show them the benefits of doing the job right, of doing a thorough job at a reasonable expense to the client, and of looking at the future relationship with the client rather than worrying about the size of next month's paycheck. If they really learn the lesson, the results of doing the whole job will keep them from having to worry about whether or not their commissions will be big enough.

Complete Organizational Knowledge is Critical

The first role of the organization in developing its marketing team is to provide them the answers to some key questions:

- "What is the role of our marketing team?"
- "Why is that its role?"
- "How do we create that as a reality?"

And the final critical question is:

- "What is the role of the company in working with its sales and marketing staff to insure that these things are done properly?"

Establishing a quality marketing team requires that you communicate thorough information about the company's methods and performance standards. As a result, the organization's first step in training its marketing organization is to provide the salespeople with extensive organizational knowledge and understanding. If your marketing and sales people do not understand your entire organization, from the organizational philosophy to how you recruit and hire to how you execute in fulfillment, they can't do an accurate and effective job of selling your organization. The salespeople also need to know how the company wants to be represented while selling in the marketplace, as well as how their performance will be measured and what the expectations for results will be.

Theory is not sufficient to communicate a deep level of understanding about what the telemarketing company does and how it does it. The salespeople need to live through each phase of the whole process, observing and experiencing the hands-on reality of how the company functions. Without that, they can't possibly have the complete information that will allow them to advise the clientele in a thorough consultative manner.

Furthermore, if you don't continue to communicate with your sales personnel on an ongoing basis about the lessons being learned on the programs they have brought in, then you're not giving them a fair shake in expanding their knowledge base. And that's not just on their individual programs. They need to be given the opportunity to learn about the experiences gained and the lessons learned on *all* of the company's programs. Without that, they cannot sell properly. The ability to sell creatively is important, but it can cause serious problems if the "creative selling" has nothing to do with the reality of what the company can successfully execute.

There is also an alternative problem. Salespeople who are not sufficiently grounded in the company's operational expertise may simply sell the basic features the company offers; phones, people, facility, quality assurance, fulfillment. As importance as those features are, salespeople who lack in-depth knowledge of your organization will make sterile, shelf-piece presentations that will make your company sound like everyone else. If you have these type of people, get them into a team-selling situation with your real "experts" so your company doesn't look like all the others. The team effort assures that you'll communicate the right information and the company's unique abilities to the client.

Comprehensive Industry Knowledge Is Vital

That approach, however, is not enough. The educational and consultative marketing approach cannot be completely achieved unless the entire marketing department understands telemarketing from A to Z. Salespeople should be trained in more than how to bring the programs in the door. They must learn how to help in the development and implementation of those programs. Salespeople need to first learn telemarketing and more about the company they are representing. Before they can truly work in your marketing environment, they need to be a part of the operation for a while. That means that your internal people will play a part in marketing training. It just doesn't work properly any other way.

Your upper-level administrative and operations people—president, vice presidents, operations manager, account and program managers—will have to spend more time during the initial stages of developing the salespeople and helping them close accounts. But the long-term benefits far outweigh the disadvantages of that involvement.

So the answer is not to just hire a good salesperson with a lot of sales background and unleash that person on the world. If you hire a person with a sterling track record working for Rayovac and making $86,000 selling batteries, don't assume that you can just say "Go get us business." You are bringing that person out of the OEM industry and into the service business. They are two different worlds. That person can go out and sell, but may not be able to educate the prospect about telemarketing and do the entire selling and marketing job.

We've had salespeople work for us who would have been willing to bring in business by promising the client the moon, knowing that the closest we could come to that was to offer them a good lunar map and a peek through a telescope!

We have made the mistake of not properly training good *sales*people to be tele-*marketers* . . . and we learned from those mistakes.

> **EXAMPLE:** Several years ago, we hired a guy who had built the entertainment coupon market for a major region of this country. He had been a school teacher for several years and was a natural educator. He had very close relationships with key executives at many ad agencies. He had been in the advertising and promotions industry. But he hadn't been in telemarketing.
>
> We hired him and didn't support him with the right effort because we were in too much of a hurry to get him "productive." He was lost when he went out to meet people. He couldn't answer many pointed questions. He didn't understand the industry well enough to use his natural talents properly. He was largely reduced to selling the buzz words, the brochure, the company's capacity, and the track record.
>
> That wasn't his fault. It was ours, and it was a mistake we made in spite of our own experiences.

Companies that don't correct that kind of mistake may run the risk of bringing in hundreds of tests, but get only a handful of rollouts. It's not solely because some programs work and some don't. That alone won't account for those kinds of numbers. It's because they sold programs which *they* weren't qualified to execute, didn't fairly evaluate for program potential, or rushed into rather than taking the time to develop it properly.

Note: *A telemarketing company can't make it in this business only on the basis of short tests, and a good salesperson will solve many of those problems before the program even comes to the door.*

The sales skills are important. The ability to sell the "sizzle" of the company's systems and operations *is* valuable. But the "steak" is the ability to design, develop, implement, and execute the client's program cost-effectively for ongoing success. The sizzle may get prospects to test with you. . . . The quality of the steak and the taste that you leave in the clients' mouths will determine whether or not they come back to you for their next meal!

Key Point: *Committing more time and resources to educating new salespeople before you unleash them in the marketplace will serve them well when they go belly-to-belly with a client.*

The Difference Between a Trained Marketer and a Simple Salesperson

Entrepreneurs usually take one of two approaches in handling the marketing area. Either they have no sales and marketing people and continue to do it all themselves, or they tend to find and hire decent salespeople with a little telemarketing background and assume they will make good marketers with very little training. Each approach comes from the feeling that they don't have the cash or time to give comprehensive training.

As the company grows and they can no longer handle the marketing alone, the entrepreneurs usually go to the second approach. They bring on the salespeople and hope *they* can go out and be marketers with very little training. Then the problems start appearing.

When confronted with a new or unknown issue in a sales call, the new and inadequately trained salesperson has a few choices:

1. Say "Gee, that's really beyond my range of expertise, and I really don't know. Let me call back to the home office and find out."
2. Avoid answering the question by stalling or changing the subject.
3. Talk around the subject and make up an answer. (That's known as faking it. It's called the B.S. technique and the letters don't stand for Bachelor of Science!)

Each of those approaches carries its own particular discomfort for salespeople:

Choice #3 (which is too often the route taken) gives salespeople a very slim chance to guess right on something they don't know about. Salespeople know that, and no matter what the apparent bravado with which it is presented, they are shaking underneath. And scared salespeople don't do their jobs well.

Choice #2: (which the vast majority of salespeople use when they don't make choice number three) fails to answer the request for information. They know that and the client knows that. And salespeople are always concerned that the question *will* be asked again—at which point they usually resort to choice number three.

Choice #1: (which is all too rarely used) reveals the ignorance of the salesperson and eliminates the opportunity to immediately close the account. Yet it is by far the best choice, given that the salesperson has the ability to fall back on the "team selling" approach. The other choices will eventually reveal the stupidity and duplicity of the salesperson and will severely reduce the chance of *ever* closing the account.

That's where the major differences between a trained marketer and the ordinary salesperson are revealed.

- The trained marketers are more secure in the knowledge they *do* have.
- They will recognize the importance of admitting when they lack particular bits of information.
- They recognize that their job is *more* than bringing business to the door.
- They know that they must play an integral role in the development of the client's program.
- They know that doing the true marketing job includes being able to accurately and honestly answer the client's questions, even if that means delaying asking for the order.
- They know that when they *do* ask for the account, they will have *earned* the right to ask for it.

Deal with the Marketing Realities

Your sales and marketing people need to have a realistic time line for their earnings expectations. The realistic time lines include the allowance—since a person who doesn't know telemarketing cannot sell consultatively—for some time that is dedicated to training before the salesperson will be allowed to go out and get commission-producing accounts.

If the outside sales force is not hired with that understanding, serious problems can result.

> **EXAMPLE:** I once worked with a guy who would hire people and promise them $200,000-a-year opportunities in commissions, along with the assurance that there would be "stacks of real easy leads to close". Then the guy left, and the company I was working for asked me to take over for the man who had left. I hadn't hired the guy. He just got stuck with cleaning up the mess that had been left! The salespeople had been hired with ridiculous hype and unreasonable promises.
>
> I knew he wanted the salespeople to:
>
> - be working on a qualitative basis;
> - be consultatively educating the client and teaching them telemarketing;
> - honestly tell the client the most effective ways to run the program, even if that resulted in lower initial volumes;
> - give the client the best advice on the ways the program could be most productive and cost effective—such as letting a client know that they should test a "no premium" offer even if they had decided to spend the extra money for the premium. The client needed to know that the premium tended to cheapen the offer when it was made by phone, and that there was an excellent chance that the cost/reward ratio would not pay out; and,
> - teach and sell both the importance and the disadvantages of the backend performance. (If, for example, the client was experienced in direct mail but new to telemarketing, the client needed to know that the backend for telemarketing-generated orders would always perform less well than the backend for the "self-generated" orders of direct mail.)

The outside salesperson must also be reminded that all good rollouts begin with tests, and those tests probably consume a relatively large amount of time before a program rolls out. They need to know that very large rollouts normally proceed in stages of successive development, with interim tests each time the program is expanded. That might mean several tests and two to three years of work before a program reaches its full-volume potential. The true marketer will understand and appreciate that, in the long run, such an approach will produce much greater earnings.

> **EXAMPLE:** Our largest clients all started with small tests. The first big client started with a 100-hour test, with a series of tests each time we expanded the program. We developed the program at a pace that would allow us to grow the

client's program successfully. It was 1 1/2 years before we got past the 50,000-a-month call level. Then we were able to fully roll them out. That slow but sure approach helped the client grow not only their program, but their overall company. And they stayed with us because we helped them be successful. That initial 100-hour test resulted in a long-term relationship at high monthly volume levels.

Key Point: *The real success of being able to develop the client's program to its maximum potential rarely comes overnight.*

If you hire salespeople at a $50,000 salary and promise them big commission bucks overnight if they go out and get big business in the door immediately, you're asking for eventual problems for everyone concerned. Those salespeople are going to rush out and try to close big rollouts. You will then see tests that aren't properly structured or don't fit with your areas of expertise. If you don't paint an accurate picture, the salesperson is not going to be interested in suggesting multiple-phase tests and doing the full consultative job.

Outbound telemarketing companies need to do that job comprehensively if they are to develop long-term relationships with the clients and, thus, affect the long-term health of the industry. That approach is also important for the development and satisfaction of the individual salespeople. Industry-wide, it's not uncommon for only a small percentage of the big accounts to be full-boat commission accounts.

Since the salespeople lacked the full training or ability, they couldn't close the business and earn the full commission. The best they could do was lead qualify it and bring it to the door; someone internally had to design the program and close the account. And most of the big house accounts *started out* as house accounts, because the salespeople didn't know how to bring them in or how to develop the small accounts into large ones.

If you know you're putting on a new salesperson, you may be telling them the truth if you say: "After you are with us and the tests you bring in begin to roll out, you'll develop a base of producing business. If you do a good job of selling the client right and developing the relationship with them, a few years from now, you could be looking at a six-figure income."

If you are paying a base in the area of $50,000 plus commission, and the salesperson does a good job, that's a reasonable statement. But the odds of that person hitting six figures the first year aren't good—and certainly not if the person does not have deep telemarketing experience and some established contacts.

It's important to tell people when you hire them that they can expect to sacrifice some short-term income during the learning process. But let them know that those short-term sacrifices will put them into a much better position for long-term earnings. They have to understand that they won't earn full-boat commissions if all they can do is qualify leads and get them to talk to the company so their business can be designed, developed, and closed by someone else. They need to know that full-boat commissions come from doing the *full* job. If they really understand that concept, they are much more likely to be willing to take the 60 to 90 days that will be required to really learn the company's operations and the full marketing job. When they realize that the initial sacrifices will result in more commissions, they will be much more eager to learn the information and skills required to get the full job done.

SETTING MARKETING COMPENSATION GUIDELINES

With the fundamental issues covered, the development of marketing compensation guidelines is the next issue. Again, there are a number of questions to answer in determining the best guidelines for your company.

8 Questions to Ask in Determining Marketing Compensation

1. What are the financial objectives of your company?
   - Hours
   - Hourly Rate
   - Profitability
2. What type of sales mix do you want?
   - Business-based
   - Consumer-based
   - Applications (survey, lead generation, sales, etc.)
   - Industry mix (computers, food services, travel, insurance, etc.)
3. What size outside sales staff do you have or need?
4. What type of sales organization?
   - Full client service orientation
   - Strictly sales orientation
5. Are your sales force (or your company's attitude toward) earnings primarily:
   - Salary with a small commission incentive,
   - Lower salary with a greater percentage coming from higher commissions?
6. Will commissions be based on gross margin or on revenue?
7. What is your total salary administration plan, and how—if at all—will if affect or be affected by your sales and marketing compensation plan?
8. What marketing compensation (plans and total earnings potential) is offered by similar or competing firms?

With answers to those questions and a clear determination of your marketing needs, the specifics of the marketing compensation plan can be tailored to your telemarketing company. There are, however, certain additional guidelines that should be considered in designing that plan.

15 Marketing Compensation Guidelines

1. Make sure that incentives drive the plan, and that the incentives are based on achieving the desired results of the company's financial plan; remember, not all business is equal in value. For example, if you want the bulk of the sales efforts to occur in the daytime business-to-business area, then place higher commission value on that type of business.

2. Compensation plans should not exceed one year, and should be adjusted annually.

3. Commissions should be paid on new business only, or should be progressively and significantly lower on repeat or "ad infinitum" business.

4. Sales quotas should be established that would result in earnings higher than the salesperson's financial minimum needs, but still realistically achievable.

5. The plan should enable you to offer higher commissions for exceptional levels of productivity.

6. Territories or sales boundaries should be established if there is to be a multiple-person sales force.

7. Clear definition should be made of "house accounts" and "commissionable accounts," especially as you move into new market areas and new niches.

8. Clearly define all commission payments, including reduced commissions for business brought in at less-than-standard hourly rates or at lower-than-targeted margins.

9. Specifically determine and define all commission accounting (cutoff dates, etc.).

10. Include recognition incentives as well as compensation incentives.

11. Make provisions for special bonuses during the year.

12. Make sure the commission plan is flexible enough to incorporate changes necessitated by varying business conditions.

13. Travel and entertainment policies must be established if expenses are to be reimbursed.

14. Make sure the plan is completed and announced prior to the start of the sales year. (No surprises!)

15. Make sure the final plan and all agreements under the plan are signed.

HOW TO HANDLE PRICE COMPETITION

Another marketing issue is price competition. It is a part of the business a telemarketer has to live with. You may not like price competitors. You may not appreciate or respect them. But they aren't going to go away. How they are handled can have a major impact on your rate of growth and your profitability.

Many companies panic and drop their prices immediately in the face of competition, because they just don't understand the business well enough. Yet some accounts get frightened and worried when they hear rates as low as $22 or $23 an hour. *They* are uncomfortable about giving work to a low hourly rate company, but they are also hesitant to pass them up. They like cost savings, but they want quality. If you develop strong relationships with your clients, they will give you every chance they can when you are caught in a price-competition situation, or "Price Competes."

You must maintain your strong convictions when you face a price compete. Look back at your pricing and remind yourself how and why it was developed. Remember that your price structure is an integral part of your business plan, and that maintaining price integrity is extremely important in properly executing that plan. Redo the numbers on the program to determine what price you can afford to work with in relation to the importance of getting or keeping the account. If the net effect of altering your price structure will be detrimental to the ongoing and long-term health of your company, be prepared to walk away from the new business. Make sure you clearly plan your strategy and respond with strength and consistency.

A Successful Strategy Against a Price Compete

Since each situation is different, this is a difficult area to try to set hard and fast rules. Perhaps an actual price compete example can best explain the concept of maintaining strength through effective strategy.

> **EXAMPLE:** A relatively new company wanted to grow their business. After doing their market analysis, they chose to expand their involvement in a particular market segment where they were already very experienced. One of the clients they identified was already involved in telemarketing and was expanding their program.
>
> The new company made a proposal and a very strong presentation for some of the client's volume. They recommended a test on a substantial number of hours, with the rollout dependant upon their ability to produce and be cost effective. The client responded favorably and gave a tentative commitment to take some of the volume that had been targeted for an older telemarketing company that had been handling the bulk of the client's volume.
>
> The older company reacted to the news by trying to price compete. They made an impressive corporate-style presentation, talking about how they were doing things in new and different and better ways. They presented evidence of many new ergonomic and technological improvements. They talked about recent results in relatively small numbers of hours that were improved over the old numbers. Then they undercut the new company's prices by $3 to $4. They left the meeting with the client, confident that they had beaten the new company and prevented them from getting any of the client's business.
>
> But they had underestimated the competition. The new company had antici-pated the price compete. They knew the client had a policy against placing all their business with anyone vendor. And they knew that—in a price battle—they would get the final rebuttal. Instead of initially going after the clients at a low price compete rate, they had gone in and gotten the commitments at normal pricing. In their presentations to the clients they had focused on quality services at competi-tive prices. Opening at standard rates had left enough room to negotiate against the price compete, provide quality service, and still be profitable. And they had done it by anticipating the older company's coming back with a lower rate. They knew that starting to low would have meant having to go to unprofitable rates later to secure the business.
>
> The new company's price response to the client remained consistent with their initial presentation. They said they wouldn't cheapen themselves by dropping down to the undercut price, because neither they nor anyone else could provide excellent telemarketing service for the client's product at the older company's

undercut rate. They acknowledged that price *was* important, but that they felt the client believed in knowledge and quality service. They pulled out their own copy of the client's credit card and pointed out that *they* could go many places other than the *client's* locations for lower prices, but they wanted excellent quality and went with the best.

They said that, because they realized that there was competition, they were willing to drop their price somewhat, but left it $1 above the level of the older company's price. The final question was: "For a buck an hour, don't you want the additional telemarketing knowledge and the extra quality that we will bring?"

The new company had made a powerful presentation and walked away with 50/50 test split at rates a dollar an hour higher than the old company had negotiated. They had gotten those tests at prices that could be profitable. And they had gotten what they had most wanted: the opportunity to test against the older company, to beat them in head-to-head battle, to gain the volume of the rollout, to improve their reputation, and to get a good reference.

The new company went on to win the test and, as a result, the ensuing rollouts. And they had done it smartly. Instead of trying to get all the business, they simply gained the fair test that any good vendor is entitled to. They hadn't undercut the competition's prices to get the business. They had gained the opportunity through fair competition for their fair share at fair prices. An important battle had been won because of superior knowledge combined with excellent strategy.

That example demonstrates the importance of well-planned and well-executed marketing strategy. Marketplace advantages are developed in small steps during the process of doing business.

Build Strength Through Proper Positioning

Part of winning the battles with competitors involves getting enough recognition to have a chance to enter the battles. Just because you're not the most well-known telemarketer in the country doesn't mean you can't grow your business, so long as you are knowledgeable and adroit in your positioning. You can look at it as a marketing effort. If you stay alert and creative, almost everything you do *well* can be used as an effective part of the marketing effort, in some way and at some point.

When marketing is considered in this country, most people think of building market share in a new area or of increasing the share in established market segments. Yet an important part of marketing is the work you do just to develop "market awareness" to become known, with "brand-name identification."

If you are going to embark on a large marketing plan but aren't quite ready to start the effort, it doesn't make sense to spend all of the time and money on the actual marketing program itself. The first thing you want to accomplish is to put yourself in a *position* to go out and sell. You can do that very inexpensively by proper use of public relations. That doesn't mean that you have to spend a fortune on a huge marketing team and 40,000 mailpieces. You do need, however, to know how to get information disseminated throughout your industry.

Proper positioning requires effective action followed by effective PR. It's analogous to the use of direct mail to position yourself for your sales call. A well-placed publicity release or announcement can help put you in a position—or at least give the marketplace the *perception* that you are in a position—to grow more rapidly or more effectively than you previously were able to do. If you prepare the strategy and the wording of that announcement in such a way that it hints or teases at future growth and development, you have set yourself up to follow that announcement at a later date with another about the expansion of that strategy.

Keep yourself in the eye of the marketplace and have them wondering what you will be doing next. The very fact that you have gotten them wondering means that they perceive you as being a growing and developing organization, rather than one that is static.

Key Point: *When you make strategically placed announcements that are based upon your plans and actions for growth, your future growth will be perceived in the marketplace as a natural result of excellent planning and management.*

Note: *That perception will be true, yet positioning yourself in the marketplace so the perception is created is an important part of the overall strategy.*

Caution: *Public relations has to be based on reality in order to work over the long term.*

> **EXAMPLE:** One telemarketing agency opened a new shop with 600 phone stations and heavy automation . . . and started telling everyone that they were as big as anyone around. They were—almost—positioned properly. The short-coming was, in terms of building credibility, that they had cut out a lot of important steps.
>
> First, the company was basically a one-man show. The guy had 600 phone stations but was only filling 30 to 40 of them every day. Sooner or later, anyone in that situation has to have real growth or the investors will pull the plug. Having hundreds of empty phone stations doesn't pay the bills, and doesn't justify that kind of claim.
>
> Apparently, the guy didn't understand the difference between PR and BS.

It's not sufficient just to open up with a strategy that causes people to *assume* you are well-positioned. It gets back to the fundamentals. Who *is* your market? Who *is* your competition? What's your *niche* in the market? Unless you have the wherewithal, the knowledge, and the expertise to get the job done well, you'll find yourself in serious trouble very quickly. You've got to be able to back up your positioning statements with action and results.

Strategic In-House Positioning

While this approach is from a service agency perspective, any in-house operation is really an internal service bureau. Even the in-house operation has to position itself within that organization if it wants to grow. The way to do that in-house is not to run to the top management and say "Let's go to 200 phones," because what they're going to look at is how your plans will impact the current marketing strategies and marketing mix.

The in-house operation should establish a small and controlled environment where it can excel on everything it touches. If that is done effectively, the company will initiate the action and ask the in-house shop to grow. It's somewhat like the strategy of a service agency. Instead of convincing everyone to give you volume now, you show the marketplace how effectively you can produce and how ready you are to grow.

It is different in that you are working with a "captive" client. But it's not different at all in that you want your client to give you more business. That goal is accomplished by first testing, then fine-tuning and demonstrating the capacity to provide high-quality, volume production. It's still a service business. If you do your job well and you're making money, you're going to get more business.

Remember: *The best advertising and best positioning for any service business is word of mouth from happy clients. Advertising and PR expenditures simply help create more interest in what your references will say. Growth only occurs when opportunity is met with preparation.*

MASTERING THE NEGATIVE SELL

The more successful you become, the more likely you are to have to turn away business. It's not just because you are more likely to (at least for some period of time) hit your capacity. It's also because the more successful you are, the more you will be asked to do. Again, this is equally true for the in-house operation or the service bureau. Some of the programs you are offered will not be right for telemarketing. Some will not be right for your expertise. Some will not come when your situation allows you to take them.

It's hard for a start up company to turn any business down. So you try to take every account, unless you know that you will get into the account, fail, have to bail out, and be in a negative cash flow situation because you put yourself into the extra expense of the program. If you know you're going to fail, it makes no sense to take the program. Yet, even though you may not want to, there are times when you will probably take almost any account. That's just survival.

"Gut Check" Time

Once your immediate survival is not the issue—although it may not be a conscious decision—there is a tendency to begin to *negative sell*. It carries some uncomfortable feelings even if you have the ability to do it well, because it's always hard to turn down opportunities for the right kind of business for your company.

Note: *The ability to practice the art of the negative sell with reasonable comfort comes when you have reached a point in your growth process that you really can't take on that additional business and deliver the kind of quality you have set as your standard.*

There are times when you *could* handle the extra volume, but the business is wrong for you. Maybe it's a program that simply doesn't fit into your business plan or your area of expertise. Maybe the program itself is questionable, or the restrictions being put on the program make for a very low likelihood that you will succeed on the program.

Whatever the reason, you know that you should turn it down. That's when your character and your intent are tested. That's a time your real principles and values are tested. That's when you find out your real level of commitment and find out your real inner feelings about the value of turning down business. That's "gut check" time. And if you compromise your knowledge, beliefs, values, and principles, the choice will wind up haunting you. Somewhere, some way, you will have backlash from the decision. And whether it's internal or external, it will affect your business.

The Negative Sell As Marketing Strategy

When you start turning away business, you are implicitly practicing the art of the negative sell. Beyond that, once you are making it and you *know* you are going to continue to make it, the negative sell becomes a part of your marketing strategy . . . but you need to be very careful. We've met only a few people who truly excel at the *art* and *science* of the negative sell.

> **EXAMPLE:** One person who is a *master* at the negative sell is Gary West, of West Telemarketing. For the vast majority of the time he was running his first inbound business, he did something that was the reverse of the industry norm. He didn't travel to trade shows or speak or write articles. It was a conscious choice he had made. It was a negative-sell strategy. When he did go to his first trade show, you might have thought that Howard Hughes had shown up. At first, people were whispering and asking who he was. Gary had been a mystery man with an unparalleled reputation for brilliance, innovation, and excellence. And the reputation is justified. Suddenly he was there, and the excitement was tremendous.

We also have had some personal experience on the subject of the negative sell, and its long-range benefits.

> **EXAMPLE:** In 1982 we had an opportunity to pick up some business that was ideal for telemarketing, was ideal for our expertise, and would have been great for our growth. We got a request to make 170,000 outbound calls in four weeks on a rollover certificate of deposit program for one of the nation's largest banks. We also felt confident that if we did a good job on that program, we would have the inside track on a very large new program that industry rumor indicated the client would be starting a few months later.
>
> However I felt I had no choice but to turn the volume away. I just couldn't justify taking the business because of the situation the company was in.
>
> At the same time the certificate program opportunity came up, we were involved in complete restructuring after we had called a couple of thousand names for the wrong clients because of intermixed labels. As much as we wanted and needed the program, we had to put our house in order first.
>
> Our response to the request to take the program had to be "We can't do it!" You can be sure it hurt, on a personal basis. But it didn't hurt our reputation. In fact, it helped. It enhanced our reputation for insisting on providing excellent service.

That's something more companies need to understand. While the immediate feeling is sometimes difficult to handle, the long-term benefits more than make up for the short-term frustration.

Practice the Art with Tact and Integrity

If the business is right for you, then—however real your reservations—it's not wise to just say "I'm sorry, but I'm sold out."

Instead, we prefer to say something like:

> We could take the business and probably do a fair job, but at this time we don't feel we can do the kind of job that we would want to do to justify your confidence in us. We believe we could take the program and have a fair shot at being competitive with most of the industry, but that's not going to make us happy. We want to be more than that. We want to be what we've been to date—consistently ahead of the competition.
>
> Frankly, we would much rather be telling you 'Sure, we have 1,500 phones, and we can dedicate 50 of them to your project.' And we are confident that *if* we could have the right management teams on those 50 phones, you would see us outproducing all the competition. But, at this time, we don't believe it's fair to *you* for us to take the job.
>
> If we tried to do your program now, we would be scattering our efforts and wind up learning the program at your expense. That would be unfair. We would have to compromise our standards of excellence. We don't want to work that way, and we hope you can appreciate that.
>
> However, we will be able to handle that kind of volume in a few months, so please don't forget us. When we can do *right* by you, we would *love* to have you as a client.

If the client really insists on us working the program, there is still a possibility for taking the volume, but the client will have to understand the costs. If the client is willing to pay properly for it, we might dedicate the time and new facility required for the program. But it's all a matter of structure and management depth and finances. If the client is:

- willing to pay the additional costs involved in that rapid-growth structuring; and
- willing to wait a little longer than planned to start the program,

then we *might* be able to take the project.

However, if the money isn't in the program to get the right management talent and develop it quickly enough, or if we have just gone through such a heavy growth period that we can't get and develop the right talent quickly and effectively enough to meet the clients needs and maintain our standards, then—as much as it hurts—we will *still* have to take a pass on the business.

TODAY'S MARKETING BATTLE LINE: MANUAL VS. AUTOMATED TELEMARKETING

We cannot—in good conscience—discuss managing outbound telemarketing growth and the marketing of telemarketing services without addressing the question of automation. In the course of operating a growing company, the possibilities of automation will be considered by most companies. In the process of marketing, the reality of automation as a force in the industry cannot be avoided.

Real Automation Advantages

Automation does offer some very real benefits. The single greatest advantage is the ability of an automated operation to capture, compile, organize, report, and manage data.

- Automation brings important capabilities to the game any time you have to manage a large data base—more than name, address, city, state, zip code, account number and phone number.
- Any time you need more than that basic information before or during the call, being able to bring it to the screen is a real plus.
- Automation is a virtual requisite for business-to-business telemarketing applications with large data bases on buying histories, inventories, stock records, and frequent price changes.

The manual shop is not as fast, and it can't extend its capabilities beyond a certain point without overtaxing the system. The manual shop can handle the basic control and manipulation of data, but that's about it. Exotic and complex data base analysis brings the manual shop to a grinding halt.

Note: *The competitive edge that automation provides in this area will become increasingly important as the industry matures and the requirements of the clients become more complex. The need for automation will be dramatically greater in the 1990's than it was in the 1980's.*

Automation Is Valuable . . . But Not a Cure-All

Telemarketing is a dual-focus industry. It is a data base management industry, and it is a people-intensive industry. Both of those areas must be considered when the automation question is addressed. For inbound telemarketing, the answer is clear: automation is required to do the job correctly. The degree to which data base management must be weighed in answering your outbound automation question depends largely on your client and program mix.

- Some programs need to be handled manually if they are to be profitable for the client.
- For others, their data base complexity requires automated operation.

When you deal with data base management, deciding which way to go isn't as easy as it might first seem. Automation can bring many benefits, but it is not a cure-all. Many creative things can be done on a manual basis that will provide many of the advantages of automation without the higher costs. And some of the claimed benefits of automation simply don't hold up under close scrutiny.

Being able to manage the data base is important. But that issue cannot be considered in a vacuum. The reality is that:

- Given an average data base, good people will prove time and time again that they can do the job and sell the program.
- Given a great data base, bad people who are poorly trained and motivated will create dangerous problems.

Telemarketing is still a *people* industry from top line to bottom ranks. And, more than anything else, it's the *people* who make the difference. That factor—which often is not adequately considered in making the automation decision—must not be overlooked.

Critical Factor: *Whether the decision is to be automated or to be manual, the people issues must be resolved. The industry is first and foremost a* people-intensive *business.*

Perceived Automation Advantages Should be Questioned

While automation offers some real advantages, its perceived advantages are sometimes questionable. Some of the most effective management information can be gathered just as well in a manual environment. It is true that the more sophisticated and complex data management programs are more likely to need an automated system, and that some consumer programs and a high percentage of business-to-business projects demand automation. However, good manual operations can easily handle all the data that is needed for many business programs and for a wide variety of consumer programs.

Tip: *Many people think that very little data base management can be done manually. Yet a great deal of data can be very effectively manipulated on a manual basis.*

Real Answers to the Question of Increased Productivity

Some people insist that automation will automatically bring about increased productivity, and claims have been made that automated shops can expect to outproduce manual operations by as much as 42%. Of course, there *are* programs where the automated shops outproduce the manuals.

We have already indicated that, on a complex number-crunching program, a manual shop can't do what a really good automated firm is capable of doing. If the comparison is being made in that area, the claim may have some validity.

There are some other types of programs where automation will be a clear productivity winner, such as a special upgrade credit card offer that was made on a pre-approved and free basis to all of a well-known retailer's base credit card holders. It's difficult to match the strength of automation where it's basically a matter of calling the prospect and saying: "Mr. Smith, we would like to offer you the new upgrade card free of charge and with no credit application to fill out. Would you like it? Good! Thanks. Goodbye."

On a program like that, with a predictive dialer, about all the TSR has to do is answer the call as it is directed to them, say a few words, press the "Yes" button, and go to the next sale. Because of the short presentation, the minimal information to be taken, the high conversion rate, and the predictive dialer, a manual shop can't make as many calls per hour on that type of program. In those cases, the manual shop *can't* legitimately compete.

But a manual operation *can* outproduce an automated firm on many programs. The higher productivity and the cost-effectiveness part of the automated claims doesn't always wash.

Many automated firms stand up and scream about how they can always outproduce the manual shops. *But they don't!* They just don't. Not the *good* manuals. On a wide range of programs, the argument that automated outproduces manual is a fallacy, unless the operation inherently doesn't understand how to properly manage a group of phone people in the first place.

Where those claims resulted from tests against some old-style in-house shops, it's not a valid claim. The vast majority of those shops never compared favorably in productivity against a good service agency. If they tested it in a business-to-consumer shop that was getting seven calls an hour, and a predictive dialer increased that to 10, then—in itself—it's nothing to get excited about.

A well-run manual shop completes 9 to 14 calls per hour—on a typical consumer program—depending upon the program at hand, the product being sold, the length of the script, and the response factor. So, just because automation increased calls on a typical consumer program from 7 to 10, that doesn't necessarily tell the whole story—or even a very good one. Anyone looking at those claims needs to say "Wait a minute! Somebody said that automation delivers more productivity . . . but said who, and in what situation? Did I prove it on *my* program?"

Maybe someday it will turn out that automation is *unequivocally* the best and only way to go. Today that's not a clear fact, especially when cost effectiveness is considered. Somebody has to prove to major clients who have less complex programs why they should pay an automated shop more for the same productivity they can get for less in a manual shop.

Additionally, much of the claims for greater productivity are based on the use of a predictive dialer. Even when there *is* an increase in productivity, it doesn't necessarily justify versus the sometimes disproportionately higher costs. And, today, in all cases, when a predictive dialer pushes through a call for which no live operator is available, the technology either places the call recipient "in que" or hangs up on him. This is a big-time negative and not good for the telemarketing industry!

Much of the furor that has been raised about computerization of telemarketing operation automatically resulting in greater productivity is based on smoke and mirrors. The only meaningful answers come through direct head-to-head comparison, program to program, of the productivity of the manual versus the automated shop. And, again, beware of the downsides of predictive dialers.

The Impact of the Marketing Battle

It is clear that the automated firms did not make their strategic operational and marketing decisions arbitrarily or from sheer ignorance. They took the route of increased automation with dramatically reduced floor management supervision ratios, to save costs and be more price-competitive with the manual shops.

The automated shops dropped their early price structure because they weren't cost-competitive with the best manual companies. They couldn't really outproduce the manual shops. But they *could* give a cleaner environment and manage data better. First, the automated shops were able to sell through the cost effectiveness by selling the additional data management. But when the increased productivity wasn't there to go with the increased data capabilities, they had to drop their rates to be competitive.

Today's marketing game is too often one where the winners are the ones who do the best job of convincing the client that their approach—either automated or manual—is the way to go. That's unfortunate because, frankly, there is so much misinformation and partial information in the marketplace. And, with the relative youth of the industry, many clients in the marketplace aren't yet fully prepared with accurate and sound information to make those decisions.

If a client is new to the industry, the claims from both sides can be very persuasive, at least until the client tests manual versus automated. Then the client is likely to be even more confused, because the results probably won't look anything like they were led to believe. That only weakens the credibility of the industry and aggravates the problem of confusion in the marketplace.

Some clients are afraid of manual shops. Others are afraid of those that are automated. Many of the big clients have a tough choice between the two.

The clients who have the toughest choice are the ones who know that the automated system may not be as well managed at the people level. And while they feel safer about the knowledge levels and operational skills of the manual shop, they are concerned whether the manual shops can provide sufficient management of the data.

The real problem is that there is *no one*, today, who can do *both* automated and manual telemarketing as well as they could be done.

A Conflict to Be Resolved

Obviously, certain automated firms are very knowledgeable, and certain manual firms are not. But from an on-line, operational management standpoint, most automated firms are many years behind in hands-on, grassroots telemarketing experience. However, they do have the edge on the knowledge of how to use the bells and whistles, and they've developed effective strategies to bring in client business that way. Because their automation can cover a multitude of sins, the firms that started out automated have yet to be fully challenged to meet their capabilities at the real grass roots level of telemarketing.

The automated shops' strengths have made the really good manual shops think even smarter in order to compete, not just in the marketing area, but in internal operations, as well. Yet most manual shops lack sufficient understanding of the potential value of automation and its effective use.

Result: *Most of the operational expertise lies in the manual firms, and most of the technological expertise lies in the automated organizations.*

That will continue to be the case until the more knowledgeable manual competitors wake up and hear the marketplace loudly and clearly saying: "By and large, we want automation," and until the automated firms gain more hands-on experience.

Even worse than the division of expertise, neither side of the competition—manual *or* automated—has been willing, or in some cases able to tell the open market the whole truth. One of today's biggest marketing challenges is to get rid of the misinformation and untrue and unethical marketing tactics sometimes employed by some service agencies.

Solution and Recommendation: *The only honest answer is for the automated shops to admit that automation alone is not the final answer, and for the manual shops to acknowledge that there is more to doing the complete job than can be done manually.*

When that happens, we will be able to move into an era of new and better marketing, one where the victor will provide the client with precisely the type and level of service that is really needed, cost-effectively, and at a price the client can afford.

31 KEYS TO DEVELOPING AND DIRECTING THE MARKETING EFFORT

- Sometimes the fundamentals seems too simple, but the core strategies of every winning team is built upon them.
- The in-house unit has many of the same marketing concerns as the service agency, particularly at the consultative level of dealing with product managers.
- The relationship between the in-house operation and the product divisions is—as it should be for a service agency and its clients—a partnership in progress, and it is absolutely essential for the telemarketing arm to be able to consultative advise the product divisions.
- Telemarketing services should be sold with honest promises that are consistent with the company's overall image and based on the company's capability to fulfill the promises.
- In developing the plans to accomplish those objectives, you should recognize that—in telemarketing—the operation truly drives what the sales and marketing department can offer to the market. The keys that should guide the marketing function are what *kind* of business to bring in and how to *best* to do it.
- The company should take steps to assure that its salespeople become truly knowledgeable about the entire process of telemarketing, the company they represent, the market being developed, and the companies within that market.
- Quality marketing means developing quality client relationships, by giving an honest marketing story that is followed by the creation of quality programs that generate good cost-effective production.
- The marketplace knows that "*The* Marketer" exists only as the *whole* company, its makeup, its levels of knowledge and productivity, and the image it leaves with the client.

- There are four core parts to the marketing effort: market analysis, marketing goals, strategies and tactics, and controls.
- The three most commonly used marketing thrusts are insertion, extension, and attack.
- As seductive as the alternatives might seem, abandoning the core of your marketing strategy and the marketing niche you have established often fails to bring the joys and rewards that were anticipated.
- Rather than developing tunnel vision by becoming overly concerned about a particular competitor, if you keep focused on how you can best manage and grow your *own* business, you will have much greater success.
- Whatever your overall strategy and target market, remember to *not* to put a lot of energy and money into going after the market segments that aren't the meat and potatoes of your business.
- Advertising doesn't create long-range image in this business. *Performance* does! Good word of mouth travels fast, and the only thing that travels faster is bad word of mouth.
- The telemarketing industry begs for a marketing approach that is educational and consultative. You have to make sure that you educate the client about your business and how you work.
- If this is to remain a healthy industry, some of the industry's marketers must stop confusing the marketplace with a lot of hyerbolic promises. Instead, more *smart marketing* proposals are needed.
- Running readily controllable 5–10 phone tests should be part of your parameters before attempting a full rollout. You need to go slowly and surely, not just because it's safer for your company, but because it's better for the client.
- Smart marketing concerns itself with more than just bringing in business. The positioning you establish in the marketplace is very important, and it should never be abused.
- Training only in telemarketing theory is not sufficient to communicate a deep level of understanding to the outside salespeople about what the company does and how it does it. They need to live through each phase of the whole process, observing and experiencing the hands-on reality of how the company functions.
- Committing more time and resources to educating new salespeople *before* you unleash them in the marketplace will serve them well when they go belly-to-belly with a client.
- Your outside salespeople must have an understanding of realistic time lines for their earnings expectations, including allowance for time to really learn the business and time for the proper gradual development of accounts.
- Make sure that incentives drive the marketing compensation plan, and that the incentives are based on achieving the desired results of the company's financial plan.
- Strive to maintain your strong convictions in the face of price competition.
- If the net effect of altering your price structure will be detrimental to the ongoing

and long-term health of your company, be prepared to walk away from the new business.

- Marketplace advantages are developed in small steps during the process of doing business, and the street-smart strategy of fighting the competition—even more than concentrating on the marketplace needs—may be the key to winning price competition battles.

- Effective public relations are an important part of the marketing plan. If you stay alert and creative, almost everything you do *well* can be used as an effective part of the marketing effort.

- The negative sell becomes an important part of marketing as your business grows, but it needs to be practiced with art and diplomacy.

- Today's marketing game is too often one where the "winners" are the ones who do the best job of convincing the client that their approach—either automated or manual—is the way to go.

- Most of the telemarketing operational expertise lies in the manual firms, and most of the technological expertise lies in the automated organizations. The real problem is that there is *no one,* today, who can do *both* as well as they could be done.

- One of today's biggest marketing challenges is to get rid of the misinformation and, sometimes, downright untrue and unethical marketing tactics employed by some service agencies.

- The telemarketers who are true marketing professionals—and those who can join them in this larger perception—will be the leaders in the development of a new and more profitable markets.

Abe Lincoln said:
'You can fool all of the people some of the time,
and some of the people all of the time,
but you can't fool all of the people all of the time.'
Good marketing means not trying to fool
***any* of the clients *any* of the time.**
—*Steven A. Idelman*

Remember that the client is the most important
factor in any business. If you don't think so, try to
get along without them for a while.

—*Napoleon Hill*

Chapter **8**

How to Manage and Develop the Telemarketing Client

Developing good client relationships is important whether you are in-house or a service agency. Just because the in-house operation's client is a part of the same company, that doesn't mean that the continuing relationship can or should be assumed or taken for granted. As an in-house operation, your growth and success depend on the commitment of your company's internal management. And that may vacillate from time to time, because you are constantly being challenged.

More than 300 Service Bureaus are knocking on your door trying to prove that they can do a better job. They sell against your weaknesses:

- that your company should use them as a control group;
- that they will save your company aggravation and capital investment;
- that they have greater flexibility to grow or shrink the program as needed.

Result: *The in-house bank is vulnerable to competition from the service agencies.*

Additionally, the lack of experience and understanding of the non-telemarketing personnel may create problems ranging from lingering resistance to outright hostility. In many cases, the in-house shop is also faced with "hidden agenda" competition from old-line, conservative field sales personnel. So long as the rest of the company looks upon the in-house telemarketing effort with reservation the in-house telemarketing effort cannot achieve its full potential. Winning the cooperation and confidence of those resistant and doubting elements must take a high priority.

HOW TO DEVELOP THE CLIENT RELATIONSHIP

Getting a client or clients to give you enough volume to pay the bills means short-term survival. Long-term survival results from developing a reputation for quality service with your clients rather than just selling services. Sustained growth comes from the establishment and nurturing of mutually advantageous relationships with your clientele.

Why? Because long-term contracts are the "Fantasy Land" of the service bureau business! Like other Fantasy Lands, they do exist in a few places, but they are few and far between. And between the serenity of those Fantasy Lands, there's a harsh reality. Your next opportunity is dependant on your past productivity and the satisfaction you have been able to create for the client.

Happy clients are still the bottom line. To have a happy client, you need to do two things. You need to manage the client's program well, and you need to manage the client well. Although those are two interlocked areas of management, they are also two separate functions.

Good management of the client's program includes a knowledgeable, sensible, and practical initial program design, effective development, and continuing quality execution and development. Good management of the program results in the achievement of optimum program productivity. If the program itself is also a good concept and a good application for telemarketing, it should result in cost-effective production for the client. But that's not enough if you are aiming for long-term growth.

Good management of the client can create strong relationships with mutual trust and respect that lead to ongoing opportunities for both the client and the telemarketing vendor. Whether that vendor is an in-house shop or a service bureau, it is that harmonic and dynamic partnership that brings innovation and increased opportunity for both stability and growth.

Recommendation: *In a sense, you should treat your client as you would treat your children: love them and appreciate them for what they are, educate them, and help them grow.*

Avoid Hyperbole

The proper management of the client starts with your company's marketing effort. Unfortunately, much of the marketing thrust in today's telemarketing is more fluff than substance. And it all sounds much the same, no matter what the quality of the end product. Our TSR's are the best. Our program development is the best. Our "everything" is the best. Our telemarketing ads and brochures say the same thing—"We're the best." We need to get away from comparison and into consultation.

The problem is that we all tend to do it, even when our intentions are the best.

EXAMPLE: In 1985, when he was still president of the firm, Steve came out with an ad that said: "WATS Marketing Outbound Pales the Competition. Enough said." His real intent with the ad was to *avoid* hyperbole. Yet, as he pointed out in a speech to the 1985 ATA Convention (when he was still with WATS), the ad was . . . in its own way . . . as hyperbolic as all the rest!

Too many companies try to say the equivalent of "No matter what your needs are, we can serve them." That approach may bring in business, at least at the test level. But it won't necessarily assure a reasonable likelihood of executing in accordance with the promises made to the client. If you can't execute at a level that is reasonably close to the promises made at the sales level, it's unlikely that you will be afforded the opportunity to roll out the program.

Remember: *A service agency cannot make it in telemarketing on the basis of tests only.*

Base Your Relationship on Continuing Results

Real success in telemarketing comes from establishing long-term, interactive business relationships with your clientele. Long-term client commitments are developed by making the relationships mutually beneficial ones.

Unlike most industries in which companies are rewarded with long-term contracts after having done a good job over a short-term trial, telemarketers are always on a short string. There simply is no such thing as long-term contracts. You are always hoping to get the new tests and hoping that you can maintain a continuing rollout, but you know the client may take the program in-house at any time. That's the nature of the service agency business and the reality of telemarketing.

Key Point: *There's really* one *thing that keeps you the business you have and continues to generate the references and referrals you need to pick up new accounts:* good recent results.

You're only as good and secure as your last call, and that situation will continue unless there's a drastic change in the way telemarketing works.

Almost nobody signs long-term contracts, so you've got to work on developing and maintaining long-term relationships and keeping people happy.

> **EXAMPLE:** For years we knocked the socks off a Fortune 500 telemarketing client's in-house efforts. In many industries, that would have virtually guaranteed getting a contract for the entire production at least by the time the relationship entered into a second year. Was there ever a possibility of our getting the entire account on a long-term basis? No. In fact, there was a policy against it.
>
> In a sense, we went into competition against ourselves by helping the client company establish their in-house operations. That might seem senseless, but in reality it was a practical act of self defense. By making sure they had a viable in-house operation, we assured that their control group was their own in-house bank. That meant that, if we could continue to do an excellent job, the *bulk* of the rollout—which was as much as we could ever hope to get—would continue go to us.

Be Patient and Make Your Client Your Partner

We have said before that the telemarketing industry needs to do a more accurate and comprehensive job of dealing with the client. In fact, this industry begs for an approach that is educational and consultative. At some point, we *have* to make sure that we educate the client about our business and how we work.

- We have to let them know exactly what we need from them and when we need it.
- We need to explain why we do things a certain way and what it accomplishes for the client.
- Individually, we need to explain how we work differently from our competition.

A vital part of doing that is letting our clients and our potential clients know exactly what we need from them and when we need it. We need to get them to understand: the importance of maintaining continuity of management teams who do the analysis and interface with the vendor. They must understand the importance of giving consistent and accurate backend data. They must accept our expertise in our field, and to listen to our input about *telemarketing* techniques, such as how to target lists. We must get the client to *accept* the validity of our expertise and our input.

When the client truly understands how you work, why you work that way, and what it does for them, they can truly be partners with you in helping make their programs successful.. They'll understand:

- what is going to happen,
- why it needs to happen, and
- what the realistic expectations can be.

Key Point: *When the client truly understand how we work, why we work that way, and what it does for them, they can work* with *us in a cooperative endeavor that will help make their programs successful and all of our futures brighter.*

HOW TO MAINTAIN RATE INTEGRITY

A part of maintaining both the educational approach and consistent management practices is not being afraid to educate your clients and let them know why you should be paid a fair rate. The rate the client pays for your work determines what funds you have available to hire, train and maintain people. If the client wants only a cut-rate job-shop operation, and you want to be more than that, then walk away from the business. If may hurt at the moment, but maintaining price integrity will help you to grow in a manner that is consistent with your philosophy and your plans.

Tip: *Show the clients more than* what *your rate is; show them* why *it is . . . and needs to be . . . your rate.*

Handling Volume Discount Requests

As you grow, requests from large clients for volume discounts can be expected. Dealing with them can really be frustrating, because you want the volume to help you grow, but giving a rate discount to get the additional volume may cut too deeply into your margin to make it workable.

EXAMPLE: One of your current clients calls and says, "I have good news. We have given you 10,000 calls, and you've done a good job. I'm going to give you 30 times that many calls!" You are delighted until you hear the kicker: We want those 300,000 calls out in 30 days, and we've been paying $28 per hour for the 10,000 calls. This is a great opportunity for you, so what's our decreased price?"

To be honest and fair with the client, with the changes that are required to handle the volume, you might have to turn the volume away. Or you may have to look at your client and say, "Believe it or not, I'm going to have to charge you about 20% more!"

That's hardly the answer the client expects! But it's a realistic answer. Why? Because taking on that additional volume in a very short period would mean not being able to *grow under control.*

You would have to recruit a lot of labor quickly. Because you can't spread some of the labor here and some of it there and allow that labor six months to internalize the required knowledge, you have to train *all* of them on the program *now.* You need especially good people who can internalize the program quickly, or the client takes the risk of having crummy people and crummy results on the program. You probably can't get that many good people overnight at your normal hourly rate, so you may have to increase your wages—either short-term or permanently—to entice the additional labor market to come in.

Although the client is offering you substantially more calls, it would require you to put disproportionately higher expenses on the books.

If you can't take the additional hours without disproportionately increasing your costs, giving a volume discount probably makes very little sense. You need to understand that fact, and you need to get the client to appreciate it.

Make Sense to The Client

While being able to handle large-volume discount requests is essential to the growing telemarketing company, it is not unique in the business world. Other industries going through rapid growth periods have had to face the same challenge, and you can learn from their experiences.

EXAMPLE: In the early stages of growth of Sony, the giant Japanese corporation, Akio Morita (its co-founder) was on a selling trip in the United States. One buyer asked for price quotations for pocket-sized transistor radios in quantities of 5,000, 10,000, 30,000, 50,000, and 100,000. While the request seemed very promising, Sony's total production capacity for the radios was less than 10,000 a month at the time. An order for 50,000 or 100,000 would have required an immediate—and risky—major investment for expansion.

After analyzing the situation, Mr. Morita returned to the buyer with the quotes. The price for 5,000 units would be at the regular price. An order of 10,000 units would offer a discounted price. Between 10,000 and 30,000 units, the price per unit would gradually get higher. At 50,000 units, the price would be *higher* than the *normal* 5,000-unit price . . . and at 100,000 units, it would be *much* higher!

Morita then explained to the stunned buyer the reasons for the seemingly illogical price structure. Without hesitation, he explained precisely the situation he was in, what he would have to do to meet the higher-quantity orders, and the additional costs and risks he would have to assume. After a brief pause to consider the explanation, the buyer placed his order for 10,000 units. It was a price and a volume that both of them could live with!

We know how hard that is to do, because we've had to turn down business and we've had to explain that type situation to our clients. But a part of managing telemarketing growth involves properly managing and educating clients about price structure.

Key Point: *If we make sense to our clients, they'll respond and grow with us.*

However, clients won't respond in the way you want if you are satisfied to be just a big "job shop" that executes calls. You have to help make the clients' programs healthy and correct problems as they arise. You have to really pick a program apart, analyze it, and actively recommend changes for improvement. Then you have to get the client to understand the cost of doing that and the value of paying the price to support it. If you do that, the client will be willing to pay the price.

It's a very simple concept that works.

CREATING A GROWTH ATMOSPHERE WITH THE TELEMARKETING CLIENT

Developing an atmosphere of growth with your internal staff is not sufficient. You also need to create that growth attitude in the marketplace. As you make plans to grow, you need to keep your client informed of those plans.

The clients know that what you can do alone in a 10- to 50-phone shop, you can't do alone in a much larger operation. The clients also know that it holds just as true in the management of the account as it does in the management of the floor operation. As a result, the clients will be willing to go along with many of the changes that growth brings. However, you must make sure that your clients know that *your* growth will not cause *them* to suffer.

Earn the Client's Trust

A major part of making the telemarketing client comfortable with your growth is to have them experience no problems as a result of it. Unfortunately, there are times in any business that something happens and the ball gets dropped.

As you grow, you will make mistakes on the sales floor and in the executive suite. They may be caused by your growth problems, or they may be completely separate from them. In either case, the clients see that:

- You are growing, and
- A mistake has been made.

You can't assume that the clients will not put the two facts together and come to fear that the two are linked and that your growth is costing them.

Some of those mistakes will be serious enough to threaten to undermine or destroy all of the hard work you have done to create a business relationship that can continue to prosper. At the times of highest tension—when you know you caused the problem—your actions likely will determine the future course of the relationship.

It has been said that there is some situation which occurs which will test . . . and either cement or destroy . . . any relationship. If you are fortunate enough to have only one such situation, make sure you are prepared to meet the challenge and turn it into an opportunity. If you are faced—as most of us are—with more than one such challenge, you have to face each one as if it were the only one, and face each one with integrity. If you don't, the challenge may be your last.

EXAMPLE: In the chapter on structuring, we described how, in July, 1982, we made the mistake of mixing the lists of a major publishing firm and a major travel card company. We called 1,000 of the magazine's renewal customers for the travel card company, and 1,000 of the travel card company's list for the magazine renewal. Before we closed down the operation for the 48 hours required to re-inventory and reorganize the materials department so the mistake could not be repeated, we had to do the hardest part of the job of correcting our mistake. We had to tell the clients.

I was shaking as I prepared to make the call, because I knew there was a chance that both clients would tell us to bring their programs to a complete halt and pull the programs *permanently*. Because of their importance to the company's survival at that point, that would have meant a *much* longer shutdown than 48 hours. But I refused to try to hide the error.

I called and told them what had happened, told them they would not be billed for that time, and begged their understanding and forgiveness. Although I was just hoping they would tolerate the mistake and allow us to continue, I was very pleasantly surprised.

The clients told me that they appreciated my telling them, and that it was nice working with people who would be as open and honest as we had been. They asked us to please get back to work as quickly as possible and to try to make up the lost volume. We were both relieved and grateful.

Not only were they good clients then. The relationships with them grew and became more profitable through the years. They didn't forget what we did to admit and correct our mistakes, and we'll never forget what they said.

Key Point: *Developing good client relationships includes admitting your mistakes, even if you have to admit them at the risk of losing your client.*

When you are honest about the mistakes you make, most clients will be reasonable and give you a fair chance. All of them will appreciate your honesty. You have to be prepared to lose money in the short term in exchange for maintaining your principles, your reputation, and your long-term health. If you're not willing to do that, your clients will find you very difficult to trust, and maintaining the client's trust is essential in creating a growth relationship.

Keep the Client Informed and Involved

When you are trying to build a growth atmosphere with the client, it's not enough to say "We're growing by leaps and bounds." You have to take steps to create the explicit feeling in the marketplace that you are growing, and the feeling that the clients should help you in that growth process. They need to know how you are going to grow. The client simply can't be expected to feel that you're "somehow" going to grow overnight from 40 phones to 700, especially if your basic philosophies focus on quality service.

Caution: *If the clients don't understand how you will accomplish growth, they will be concerned that your quest for additional volume may result in a reduction in management quality and sales results.*

Let the clients know how you will grow and how you will maintain quality as you grow. Tell the marketplace that story in a way that will both reassure and excite them. The more fully you can create the plan and the structure *ahead* of growth, the easier it is for the clients to feel comfortable that you will be able to handle the growth without neglecting their programs.

It has a powerful impact when you can send your current and proposed clients a full organizational chart, showing fully developed teams in place that can readily handle additional volume. Of course, that will not do the job by itself. If your previous track record is one of mediocrity, the marketplace will only perceive that you are capable of producing greater volumes of mediocrity. But if your reputation as an excellent organization has been developed, the perception that you are organizationally well positioned for growth can be extremely valuable.

If your biggest clients get the idea that you are going after every other account in the country that is similar to theirs, will they feel they should go out and test every other telemarketing unit? Not if they can feel secure that your company is the one best suited to provide the information and expertise that will make them successful. If they feel that, they will stay with you.

Key Point: *When the clients are confident that you can maintain your standards as you grow, they will chose your company to help them grow their programs.*

How to Delegate Account Management

Sometime during the development of that deep organizational structure, the CEO/founder must turn over some of the account management responsibility to others in the telemarketing company. The existing staff is simply unable to handle all of the account management and maintenance of client relationships. How you handle the client communication and the delegation of account management duties becomes critical to the continued quality of the relationship.

How do you make that transition? Don't just call and say "Hi. Here's Pete. He'll handle your account from now on." Invest a few dollars in taking the new account manager to meet the client. Let them get accustomed to and comfortable with each other. Make sure the communication patterns, frequency of contact, and personalized style that the client has become accustomed to are continued. If you forsee a personality clash between the account manager and the client, transfer the client to another person in your organization. It's more expensive and it takes more time, but the results will prove the wisdom of the strategy.

MAINTAINING THE CLIENT RELATIONSHIP

Building a productive and partnership-oriented growth relationship with the client is only the beginning. As difficult as establishing the solid foundation of that relationship will be, growing and maintaining the relationship is not a process that continues automatically and without care. Any partnership is subject to tensions and to low ebbs. Making sure those natural parts of a relationship don't grow into problems that seriously damage the relationship requires continual nurturing and attention.

Maintain Personal Involvement

As a company continues to expand from a very small operation to a much larger one, more and more of the day-to-day involvement in the operational and support services has to be delegated by the top people to employees who have been developed and can assume greater responsibility. Hiring and training often are the first to be delegated. Operational floor management usually comes soon after. Then, progressively, the process moves into the account management area. If the company grows large enough, the day eventually arrives when the top one or two people have to give up much of the day-to-day coordination with, and management of, the client.

After delegating that day-to-day responsibility to the account managers, the top person in the company needs to stay involved. That person needs to oversee the quality control of account management by *personally interviewing* those clients. And the sporadic contact with the client that usually is maintained is not enough. It's important that the President/CEO makes a point to talk in depth with the client at least every three months. He or she needs to interview the client and determine:

- how the communications and contact are going;
- how responsively and responsibly individual account managers handle the client's account and programs;
- how the company is doing its job;
- what the company is doing well;
- what the company is not doing well;
- how the client feels about the total relationship; and
- what *more* the company can do

A big secret to the successful maintenance and continuing development of the client relationship is asking those questions and the many more that will come naturally during those interviews. The clients will provide the most important and meaningful evaluations the company can get. They will also offer suggestions about how to improve both the company and its working relationship with them.

And it's not a question of how much the leaders of companies trust their people. It's not a personal issue. It's a business matter. There simply is no substitute for having the leader of the company be the backstop in this quality assurance area.

Extend the Quality of Your Performance

On a couple of occasions we have been asked: "What is the the biggest secret to maintaining telemarketing growth?" The "secret" was best explained by a client in answer to a question during one of Steve's client interviews.

Steve asked: "Why do *we* keep growing your volume, and why do you not use other vendors as much as you used to?"

The client's answer was: "Steve, no matter who I'm working with in your company, they take the same approach to working with us. You and your firm aren't satisfied to just be a big job shop and execute the calls. You really pick a program apart, analyze that program, and you proactively recommend changes for the better. You've helped make our programs healthy when they've been near the brink of disaster. And your company does that better than *anyone* we have worked with."

To us, that's the best kind of praise. And it's the kind of praise you can earn.

- Go beyond relying on your personal skills and develop people who will also insist on being *proactive* with your clients and with their programs.
- Develop people who will honestly and knowledgeably advise the clients of how you can help them, and of how they can help you.
- Keep *improving* the quality of your performance, but also *develop* people who can *extend* the quality of your performance through every job they do and through every action they take.

When you do that, the clients will continue to be well managed and served by an organization that can't help but grow.

Key Point: Help *your* clients *grow, and your clients will help* you *grow!*

17 KEYS TO MANAGING AND DEVELOPING THE CLIENT

- While client management and development might seem more important to the service agency, it is also vital to the in-house telemarketer. An in-house operation's growth and success depend on the commitment of your company's internal management.
- Unlike most industries in which companies are rewarded with long-term contracts after having done a good job over a short-term trial, telemarketers are always on a short string. Real success in telemarketing comes from establishing long-term, interactive business relationships with your clientele.
- Good management of the client results in strong relationships with mutual trust and respect that lead to the creation of ongoing opportunities for both the client and the telemarketing vendor.

- If you continually fall far short of those sales promises on the test execution, you will develop a reputation that will soon limit much more than your opportunity to grow; it will threaten your survival.
- There's really *one* thing that keeps you the business you have and continues to generate the references and referrals you need to pick up new accounts: *good recent results.* You're only as good and secure as your last call.
- The telemarketing industry begs for a client management approach that is educational and consultative.
- When the client understands how you work, why you work that way, and what it does for them, they can truly be partners with you in helping make their programs successful.
- Large-volume programs can dramatically help you grow, but if you can't take the additional hours without disproportionately increasing your costs, giving a rate discount to get the additional volume may cut too deeply into your margin to make it workable.
- A part of managing telemarketing growth involves properly managing and educating your clients about your price structure. Show the clients more than *what* your rate is; show them why that is . . . and needs to be . . . your rate. If you make sense to your clients, they'll respond and grow with you.
- In addition to developing an atmosphere of growth with your internal staff, you need to create that growth attitude with your clients and in the general marketplace.
- You must make sure that your clients know that *your* growth will not cause *them* to suffer.
- You have to take steps to create the explicit feeling in the marketplace that you are growing, and the feeling that the client should help you in that growth process.
- Developing good client relationships includes admitting your mistakes, even if you have to admit them at the risk of losing your client.
- How you handle the client communication and the delegation of account management duties is critical to the continued quality of the relationship.
- After delegating that day-to-day responsibility to the account managers, the top person in the company needs to stay involved. That person needs to oversee the quality control of account management by *personally interviewing* those clients.
- Develop people who will honestly and knowledgeably advise the clients how you can help them and how they can help you.
- Help your *clients* grow, and your clients will help *you* grow.

Good counselors lack no clients.

—Shakespeare

If you keep your nose to the grindstone too long,
you reach a point where all you can think about is
the grindstone and your sore old nose.

—John Laird

Chapter 9

Coping with the Downsides of Growth

A young man was working with his father to build their new house. They were working to level the earth at the bottom of a large, deep hole that eventually was to become the basement. Since it had rained quite heavily the night before, they were struggling through a large area of deep mud.

As the young man tried to get better footing, he sank his right foot into the mud up to the top of his thigh-high wading boots. Trying to disengage himself from the mire, he lost his balance and fell onto his back into one of the wettest, muddiest areas of what would someday be a beautiful family room.

When he cried out in frustration, his father said: "Wayne, don't get so discouraged. I know it's hard now, but think of how nice it will be this Christmas when we're sitting right where you are now, in front of a roaring fire. Can you picture that, Wayne?"

The young man's reply? "Yeah but the way it feels now, I can see myself sitting in front of that beautiful roaring fireplace at Christmas . . . *still* up to my butt in mud!"

Sometimes when we get into difficult immediate situations, we can lose perspective about the potential long-range rewards for the efforts we are giving. And it *is* hard to see beyond the immediate trying situation when it seems it will never end.

AVOIDING EXPLOSIVE GROWTH

The idea of growth is extremely attractive. It conjures images of:

- increased opportunity
- increased recognition
- increased profits

Those images can be quite seductive, and their realization can be very satisfying. Yet, while each of those expectations is potentially very realistic, that is not the whole story. The actual experience of reaching them can present a far different picture and pose a much-less-pleasing reality.

In spite of good business and financial planning, structuring ahead of growth and alert marketing, your most wonderful plans may get blown away by the demands of the marketplace. As pleasant as the additional business might be, the demands it places on your time and resources can create frustration, concern, and fatigue. Rapid growth can easily explode the fantasy and fry the participants. At those times, your motto could very well be "When you're up to your ass in alligators, it's hard to remember that the initial objective was to drain the swamp!"

Major problems can arise when the growth comes in a manner that is not planned for . . . at least at the time it happens. Then it may be explosive growth. In telemarketing, explosive growth takes the form of rapid increases in call volumes, for which your advance plans, structure and resources are inadequate to allow you to conduct the expanded business in a manner consistent with your standards of excellence.

The strain from explosive growth can affect more than the quality of your production. It may also mean that the growth cannot be handled without demands that are well beyond desired levels being made on your people and your resources. When that happens, explosive growth can become destructive.

The Costs and the Questions That Must Be Asked

As hard as you may try to avoid it, there may be times when you will find yourself having to manage explosive growth because is already too late to avoid. In that situation, your company probably is not sufficiently structured and your people are not adequately developed to handle the growth gracefully. If one very large account expands dramatically, or if you are growing with many accounts coming in at the same time, you're likely to disappoint your clients and yourself—at least for some period of time—by falling short of your standards. If you haven't structured and planned ahead of the growth sufficiently to be able to quickly add the required facilities and to tap the required management people, something's got to give. That "give" probably will be in your productivity and/or your quality.

Explosive growth rapidly confronts you with the questions of how well you have planned and structured.

- How well have we planned for this type of growth?
- Can we simply expand our existing structure or must we restructure?
- How well develop is our work force?
- How many people do we need to do the job right?
- How many people do we have to do the job?
- Are they the right kind of people, with the required skill levels to meet this challenge?
- What new steps must be taken to assure that we have enough trained and talented people?

- Are our systems and our operating environment (either automated or manual) equal to the task at hand?
- Can we get the additional facility in place quickly enough to handle the expansion?
- Will the growth require going to additional locations and new labor markets?
- How adroit are we at managing decentralized operations?
- How will this activity affect our ongoing productivity?
- How quickly can we make the necessary changes and additions?
- What will be the cost of taking the steps required to meet the challenge?
- Do we have enough retained earnings and financial resources to accommodate the growth properly?
- What will be the effect on our profitability?

If you haven't planned and structured far enough ahead, you may be surprised and severely disappointed with your answers to the questions.

If your financial situation is not extremely strong, the problems that are exposed by explosive growth may be impossible to manage. You may have to go out and buy the management talent you need. You may have to go out and get additional fixed plant space, furnish it, and install all of the phone equipment and facilities required to support the operation.

Note: *Even if you have the money required to handle massive growth, if you haven't structured far enough ahead of that growth, you may not get everything done in time.*

A Test of Your Abilities

The first downside of explosive growth is the immediate challenge of integrating the additional volume into your existing work load. These are the times that test your abilities. These factors will affect how readily that growth can be managed.

- The structure of the company,
- Its financial condition,
- The number of talented, dedicated, trained people available
- The type of programs causing the growth,
- The size of those programs,
- The number of clients involved

EXAMPLE: For our first few years, we managed to maintain rapid but controlled growth. Then we took on a huge consumer telecommunications program for a Fortune 500 client, and we underwent explosive growth. It required gearing up within a few months for more than a 50% increase in our size at the time.

- It added a tremendous amount of evening and weekend calling. We very quickly had to structure up for approximately 200 extra evening and weekend phones, and ultimately for around 300 more.

- It also gave us substantial volume of new daytime calling in addition to our very small existing daytime base. We also had to add the people to man and manage approximately 100 additional daytime phones.
- Supporting the expansion brought by the program required a great deal of expansion of facility, general personnel and management staff—including a facility manager for an entirely new branch facility in a new labor market, an assistant facility manager for the daytime operations, and an assistant director of operations.

The client's program was also complex and intricate and created a lot of headaches and frustrations . . . but it was still only *one account*. That was the saving grace that allowed us to handle the massive growth caused by the program.

Because the tremendous growth came from a single account, we only needed to assign one account management team. Although the account management team needed many more people than a 40-phone program would have, it required no where near what would have been needed for five separate 40-phone projects. We didn't have to put together the several additional account management teams, the several additional program development teams, and the several additional program test teams that would normally have been required to add on that number of phones. One of each could handle the single project.

The comparatively lower staffing requirement for a single program was most significant at the level of knowledgeable upper management. The economies and efficiencies of scale of the large program saved us. Otherwise, we would have had much greater demands and more serious problems in adding top management. We could not have taken on that much additional volume that quickly if it had come from several different programs.

In taking on that kind of a challenge, you have to ask yourself the penetrating questions and consider all of the potential problems *before* you commit to the new volume. You may find that you are not structured far enough ahead to do it without some fast and furious action, yet be close enough to take on the project with a high level of confidence that your ability and resources will bring success on the project. If that is not the case, you have to pass on the opportunity. You may feel like kicking yourself for having to let the volume go by, but that would be less painful than destroying your reputation or destroying the company.

Taking on a program of that magnitude almost certainly means violating some of the principles of growth management that we have recommended. The question is whether you are well enough grounded to stretch the growth management rules—and your resources—to the limit. . . . but not so significantly that taking it on would be a mistake.

EXAMPLE: We did violate some growth management principles in taking on the project. In fact we learned some of those principles as a result. Still, the decision was a sound one.

We had turned away business repeatedly when it represented too much of a cost to get the organization ready for it. We would have been willing to do it again, but it was a situation of the right opportunity at the right time causing us to extend a little further than we normally might have preferred.

- Although our volume was among the top five outbound shops in the country, it was down from a few months earlier.
- We had made a point of keeping the organization lean and on its toes, but of not overtaxing our capabilities. As a result, we still had a good reservoir of talent and resources to tap.
- We had lost a 60-phone evening account and had more reserve facility than we really wanted.
- Taking on the opportunity for productivity and revenue increases fit in with some additional priorities and mandates that were created by changes going on with our parent corporation.

While the new project was both a unique challenge and a wonderful opportunity, we would have had to turn it down if it had come two or three years earlier. We would not have been prepared, and we would have had no choice.

It was a real stretch, and we went through some trying times. But for all the difficult situational downsides that resulted from the added volume, it pushed us into doing some of the things we wanted to do but had delayed doing. In fact, in some areas, it forced us create stability out of instability . . . just to make the project successful.

REMEMBER TO "DANCE WITH THE LADY WHAT BRUNG YA"

Situations do arise for which there are no realistic possibilities to do the full advance structuring that will be required. A program's size, complexity or urgency may mean that you have to extend beyond your comfort levels. When it happens, it is all too easy to lose sight of the existing clients. As tempting as the situation might seem, succumbing to the temptation will almost surely invite problems.

In addition to "keeping your head on straight," it is essential to keep the entire organization clearly focused. Your people may be overly impressed by the size and prestige of the new account. Their natural tendency is to focus the vast majority of their energy and attention on something that is new and fresh. And the rallying of efforts and encouragement of them to do well on the new program may have some downside effects that you had neither intended nor anticipated.

EXAMPLE: We were willing to do all of the hard work for the huge telecommunications program opportunity because we knew that succeeding on the project would bring:

- increased image in the marketplace
- additional opportunities, and
- an incredible amount of long term stability.

At no point, however, was top management willing to pay the opportunity cost of having our other existing programs suffer because of the demands of the new program. The staff was warned in advance. They were strongly reminded that the reduction of attention or intensity on our existing client's programs could *not* be allowed to happen.

Our existing clients—who had helped get us to the point of being entitled to bid on such a significant program—were promised that the new growth would be dealt with *while* making sure their programs were not neglected. In fact, I told everyone, both internally and externally, that the day I saw those existing accounts get second-class treatment would be the day I would "kick ass."

I understood that the staff might see the situation as a developing opportunity to work with the prestigious giant corporations of the world, and focus too much of their attention on the new project rather than on the accounts that had brought us to the position of resources and respect that allowed us to take advantage of the opportunity. They were told not to believe that the new program would be around forever. I reminded them that, no matter how well they did, the nature of the account meant that it would be a relatively short-term project. And I reminded them of the obligation and the responsibility we felt we had for the existing accounts that were the "meat and potatoes" of our business.

Others were put in charge as account managers not only of the new project, but also of some of the accounts I had been managing. That put me in the position of being able to remain neutral and assure that all accounts got their fair share of attention. Then, if their focus was overdone one way or another, I could correct the problem from a neutral position.

And that "over focus" did happen. We began to overdo it on the telecommunications project, for reasons that were understandable.

- The size of the account required a large management team and one of the strongest people in the company as the account executive.
- Those assigned to the account felt that it was the entry point into an entirely new corporate direction.

Result: *Many of the people working the new program began to lose sight of the realistic importance of the account, and the older accounts began to suffer.*

To make sure I would get a first hand view of the progress after the new account had been in place for a short time, I had scheduled myself to fill in on the new account for a key player who was to be on vacation. When I stepped into that hands-on role, I discovered that the older accounts were not getting the attention they deserved, and the new project was not being managed according to all of our company guidelines and philosophies.

- Numbers on the new account were being managed at the cost of our caring properly about the employees.
- People were being sent home for the day in large numbers, day after day, for low production.

- TSRs were afraid to take earned time off for fear of negative reactions from management.

When I found out that some employees were even afraid to go to the doctor when it was necessary, I was flaming angry.

Warning: *Any opportunity cost that is paid at the expense of alienating your grassroots people and your loyal and long-standing clients is completely and totally unacceptable.*

The new program *was* difficult and demanding, but *we* were not treating the TSRs in a manner consistent with the company's long-held, underlying philosophy. And our older clients were not receiving the kind of attention they had been promised.

The opportunity cost we were on the verge of paying was the loss of faith and confidence of our people. And it was *our* fault—not the new client's.

Key Point: *When you take on challenges of a new magnitude, operational mistakes and errors in decision will happen, no matter how thoroughly you believe you are prepared.*

The kind of change that comes with such dramatic growth creates difficult situations for everyone involved. The keys to keeping those problems from overwhelming the operation are:

(1) Identify in which areas and in what situations the mistakes are most likely to occur.
(2) Make people aware of what they need to do to reduce the probability of those mistakes occurring.
(3) Create a checks-and-balances system to prevent any errors that do happen from going on undetected.
(4) Take rapid and firm corrective actions when the mistakes are found.

Restores the Commitment . . . and Make the Corrections

When you consider almost any significant business decision, you have to weigh the opportunity costs. You first have to decide which opportunity costs you are capable of paying. Then you have to decide which ones you are willing to pay.

Note: *It is impossible to avoid opportunity costs. They are a part of the business, and they are not going to go away.*

If the cost is too great, you either find a way to resolve the problem or pass on paying the cost. You simply have to prepare as best you can, do your best to make the right decisions, and take action. You also have to be prepared to make any necessary corrections along the way. If—throughout the process—you remain consistent with your guiding philosophy, you will rarely go wrong.

EXAMPLE: Under no circumstances were we willing to accept a continuation of the operational management approach we had discovered. Although we had—however unintentionally—compromised our principles, it would not be allowed to continue.

First, I called the new client and explained the problem. I also explained the need for:

- a short moratorium on productivity demands,
- different parameters that would allow us to restore some control and sanity to the program, and
- the opportunity to restore some humanity to the management of the people.

Then I explained that the job might be done in a slightly different way than the client had originally planned. But I promised that the ultimate results would meet their projections.

The client was wonderful. They understood the importance of the changes and graciously agreed to let us put them into effect.

The staff was immediately reprimanded and corrected, without exception and almost without mercy. Some of the staff thought I was a madman, and they weren't far off in that perception.

The staff was reminded of the commitment that had been made to the clients and of the basic philosophies of the company that had been violated. The offenders were reprimanded in no underterm terms and, in some cases, I wasn't very nice about it.

Fortunately, the staff understood that my reactionary display was an honest demonstration of a deeply felt commitment to the other clients and the employees who had helped bring us to where we were. *Everyone* on the staff dove into the trenches. We put in new control systems, and we removed those managers and supervisors who were unwilling to make the full commitment to success *through* excellence.

The telecommunications project was the largest program and the primary activity in house for 16 months, and the members of our organization were constantly reminded that they had the responsibility to "dance with the lady what brung them." They met that responsibility, and they danced beautifully.

No one remained willing to sacrifice the quality of our performance on the other accounts. *All* of the accounts received full effort, attention, and commitment to excellence. The objectives were met for the telecommunications client *and* for the other clients.

Key Point: *The commitment to excellence cannot be made selectively or preferentially. If it is to be made and kept, actions to fulfill that commitment must consistently be carried out for* every *client.*

Remember: *Making mistakes will happen in every organization. The most important part is in keeping them to a minimum, taking immediate, decisive action to repair the problems, and re-establishing levels of performance that match your commitment to excellence.*

THREE MARKETING NIGHTMARES

Another area of downsides that comes with explosive growth is one of mixed blessings. It is the constant struggle to maintain the delicate balance between your capacity and your marketing effort. With too little marketing effort, your excess production capacity can kill you. But if you have a greater marketing effort than you can support, it can kill the marketers.

There are two primary situations to deal with in this area during the rapid growth process:

(1) Adding significant volumes so quickly that you are sold out and the commission-earning marketing salespeople can't close business opportunities that they have developed;

(2) Dealing with the negative impact of losing—either through problems or through completion of the project—a very large volume account that created your rapid growth.

Sold Out . . . and Nothing to Sell

The first problem—the demoralizing effect that being sold out has on the marketing salespeople—can, in large part, be avoided by planning well ahead in your marketing efforts and taking the gradual advance actions that keep you ahead of growth. Yet there is a limit to how far ahead of growth you can structure and develop facility.

Yellow Flag: *You are headed for trouble if you conduct a marketing effort that is larger than you are capable of supporting operationally.*

It makes no sense to add three or four marketers to help you grow if they are are going to be frustrated *because* they do a good job. If you can't keep pace with them internally, you have no good choices. You can't afford to take on the projects and fail to execute the job in the volumes your people have sold.

- That will embarrass the marketers, and you will probably lose good people.
- If you turn down the business to avoid doing a bad job, you've forced the marketing person and the client to pay high opportunity costs by spending so much of their time and energy in planning a program you ultimately turn away.

Either way is a "no win" situation.

> **EXAMPLE:** One of the most frustrating situations I've ever experienced was when one of our marketers really applied himself and did a good job of learning the full marketing job. During the period of time he was learning, he didn't bring in any business. During that time we grew like crazy, but it was almost all house business. The marketer fully learned his lessons and then went out in the marketplace.
>
> Suddenly he had three big deals at one time. He had been dreaming about earning those big commissions and he had gotten to the point that he had three

really tasty opportunities for us. And they weren't a matter of getting them proposals. He had really done the job, and the new clients just wanted us to send them the contracts.

But we had to turn *all three* of them down because we just didn't have the capacity to handle them! He had been too successful, too soon—at least in relation to our projections. We had the physical plant to handle them, but our people were stretched to the limit. If we had taken on the projects, we would have burned out our *people* and wound up hurting the efforts for *both* the existing *and* the new projects. As hard as it was, the only choice we could make was to turn down the business, knowing it might cut the heart out of the salesman who had worked so hard to get those accounts.

Having to turn down accounts that the salesperson is ready to sign is very different than simply declining to respond to an RFP. If you simply decline to bid on an RFP, the client usually will understand and respect your decision. However, if you actively develop the client's interest and then draw back, you probably won't get another chance with that client.

When you are sold out for an extended period of time, the sales force winds up being demoralized. They know that no matter what they pick up or want to work on, the company can't take it on and do a good job. The marketing force feels useless and limited when you have so severely taxed your resources that you can't take on new commitments. While turning away those accounts may be good for the business as a whole, it is destructive to the attitude and ongoing productivity of your marketing team. They are commission-earning salespeople, yet they have been given a negative incentive. Telling them to work on something that can come in 12 months later doesn't really help.

Key Point: *You always have to balance your marketing effort and your growth capacity.*

Resolving the Problem . . . and Creating Two More

You can put out a marketing effort that is larger than your *existing* capacity. But you simply can't justify creating a marketing thrust that you know will generate commitments beyond your *ability* to expand. Still, it is difficult to draw distinct lines between where marketing ends and execution starts. Sometimes the sales force or the marketplace surprises you with more business than you had anticipated or planned for and you find yourself sold out. Most of those kinds of problems can be prevented if you:

- Stay alert enough to see the problem coming.
- Redirect and refocus your people toward the kinds of business that you will be able to fit in to your situation.
    —If you are primarily consumer-oriented, new daytime business can provide excellent incremental profits.
    —If you are a daytime operation, you probably have phones available at night.

You can generally keep the marketers on if you work to refocus your marketing thrust, because "sold out" should still mean that you have at least some test phones and/or some phones available during another part of the day.

EXAMPLE: We saw an approaching problem of reaching our capacity in evening/ weekend calling. To prevent the "sold out . . . nothing to sell" problem with the marketers, we began to take steps to redirect the marketing efforts several months before we expected to reach that point.

We had primarily been an evening and weekend consumer program operation, and we had a lot of phones available during the daytime hours. But we also had a good deal of successful experience with daytime business programs, so we knew the operational end of the business would pose no problems for us.

We talked with our marketing people as soon as we recognized the potential problem. We explained the situation we were faced with and the solution to the problem. We also gave them both reason to become an active part of the solution:

- We gave them the responsibility of bringing in business-to-business accounts for the daytime.
- We pointed out that the daytime business carried higher hourly rates.
- We offered them a higher commission rate on that business.
- We created special incentive programs that included trips and special cash bonuses.

Those were the right things to do. But we failed to do one other thing. We didn't support the new thrust with education and hands-on field management training on how to go after those business-to-business markets. Left to their instincts, the marketing people chose not to go for the daytime business. It was a tougher market to learn, get into, and sell.

Like most people, they were resistant to change. And, as happens to anyone who resists change when change is required to succeed, they failed to bring in the daytime business.

The responsibility for the failure was partly theirs. But, ultimately, their failure was our responsibility. We had the right idea, but we didn't do all of what was needed to assure success in the new thrust. We failed to provide the *educational* and *training support* that would have made them comfortable enough to tackle the project.

Key Point: *When you create a new marketing thrust, it's not enough to do the* planning *for the effort. You have to make sure the marketing salespeople have the* knowledge *and the* willingness *to execute your plan.*

When you start that new thrust, it's important that you:

- Explain to the marketers exactly what the problem is and what they need to do to help resolve it.
- Communicate to the marketers the kind of programs that you will be able to accept.
- Let the marketers know that you can take on new accounts that can be grown over a three- or four-month period.
- Train the marketers—with both classroom and field training—on the new market segment and what is required to penetrate it.

- Offer special incentives for securing accounts of the newly targeted type.
- Begin the early development of the staff that will be needed for the programs when they are ready for rollout.

If you take all the steps, you have an excellent chance for success. However, missing even one step may cause problems.

In the previous example, we addressed the downsides of not having the marketers buy into the plan. When they *do* buy into it, you will have a different problem if you fail to prepare for their success.

> **EXAMPLE:** You faced the upcoming problem in plenty of time, made your plans, and did the complete job of selling the marketing salespeople on your new marketing thrust. They were excited about the challenge and went after the new opportunity with a thorough understanding of the requirements for entering the new markets. They were successful in bringing in the amount of daytime business you wanted, and they did it within the time frames you had asked for.
>
> However, because you were concerned about whether or not the salespeople would be successful in the new thrust, you delayed taking the internal steps required to develop the personnel that are needed for the new business. Now you have created another serious problem.
>
> You decide that—since you don't have time for proper development of the required staff—to temporarily shift some of your existing management personnel to the new daytime schedule. However, you have already been running lean in your operation, since you have been growing toward capacity.
>
> You soon see deteriorating results on some of your evening programs. Because they have to be promoted before they are fully prepared, the new operational people—the ones who took the place of the experienced managers who went to the daytime projects—are not able to maintain the same kind of quality as you normally produce.
>
> **Result:** *Your existing clients suffered because you have not prepared far enough ahead of growth.*
>
> **Remember:** *Staying ahead of growth includes creating no marketing effort that you expect will generate commitments beyond your* ability *to expand in all areas.*

It is sound strategy to control the types and sizes of programs the marketers bring in to fill unused capacity. But the strategy must go beyond getting the business in. You have to go beyond the up-front marketing strategy and put in place the actions that will allow you time to gradually develop the additional operational personnel, support staff and facility required to handle that volume when it comes in the door.

What to Do When Nothing Else Works

There probably will be times when you are sold out even though you have done a good job of managing your growth. It is not an ideal situation. But there are worse situations. You may have to say: "All of our phones are sold out on both days and nights. We've stretched our people a thin as we can afford to, and we need to take some time to solidify what we have. We just don't have any new commission opportunities for you for the next few months."

While that is not a pleasant situation, it is not the worst of worlds. Recognize the pluses of your position.

- You have accomplished the short-term growth that you hoped for.
- Since you are working at capacity your incremental margin gains should put you in an enviable profit position.
- You can gain some image in the marketplace by respectfully declining to bid on projects brought to you.

Still, you can't ignore the effects on your sales and marketing people. Much of how you handle it will depend on *how* you sold out.

- If it is all the salesperson's accounts that have maxed you out, that salesperson needed to recognize that is a part of the game. It's a good time to point out what a great job has been done in selling out the capacity and to offer congratulations for the big commission income that has been earned. The salesperson needs to realize that it is a time of reaping the rewards of a job well done.
- If a high percentage for the business is house accounts, it might be wise to say "As you know, we are sold out. We appreciate what you have done to help us reach this point. Since you don't have the opportunity to earn additional income for the next little bit, here is a special cash bonus. This is a good time to update yourself on the operation by coming in to the facility and getting personally involved, as a part of your continuing telemarketing education or to begin developing some new and different markets."

The second approach obviously works best with the newer salespeople.

But what if you have sold out almost entirely with house business and a salesperson who has been with you for two or three years is responsible for little or none of your business?

That probably is a good time to suggest that the salesperson "consider a career change."

Three Dangers In Growing with a Large-Volume Client

The second of the marketing downsides is really a set of problems. They come from the dangers of basing the growth of your business on only one or two large clients and the negative impact of losing a very large volume account.

While there are many benefits in having a few large accounts, there are also three major dangers.

- First (and least important if you handle the client well) is that the large accounts are the ones that draw the competition and make you a bigger target to shoot at.

- Second, your reliance on the big client as a critical factor in your profitability means that you are always subject to serious price renegotiation, especially at contract renewal time.
- The third danger, as a result, is the biggest one: the problems caused if the big client that helped you grow goes away.

When the Major Growth Volume Goes Away . . .

Whether you have grown the account gradually and over a long period of time, or you have taken it on as a huge account that caused explosive growth, losing that client hurts. If that account is a very major part of your business or if it is one very large program, it hurts even more. If you have grown with that one very large client as your only client, losing the account does more than nick you a little bit when it goes away. It cuts past the skin and into the aorta.

That kind of loss creates a marketing problem that takes more than mirrors and an intensive marketing effort to resolve. Even if the marketing department does resolve the problem by quickly replacing the lost volume, it may create new operational problems.

> **EXAMPLE:** You have just gotten past the worst of the problems that a period of explosive growth has caused. Life is just returning to a reasonable pace, and you see no major reason—and have *no* desire—to gear up for another major growth and development spurt. You finally are comfortable that you can handle the number of phones that you have, and you would like a short rest and recuperation period for everyone in the company.
>
> And then you are shaken back to reality by one of outbound telemarketing's harshest and most difficult downsides.
>
> Your primary client informs you that the program you have helped build from 15 to 220 phones is going to go to their new in-house telemarketing facility. The client thanks you for the work you have done in developing the account, making it so productive, and simplifying its operation. They ask that you keep some phones active on their account as a comparison/control unit for their own operation.
>
> Although you try to keep more of the calls, they simply point out that they have helped you grow from 30 to 250 phones in less than a year. They won't budge, and you know you are 90 days away from losing 200 phones on a program that fills 220 of your 250 phones.
>
> You go to your marketing department, explain the situation, and give them three months' notice that the program is going to go away. They respond to the challenge and turn up the burners. Because your salespeople are very good (and because you have proven your capability to the marketplace), you bring in the replacement volume for 175 of those 200 phones within the 90 days.
>
> However, since your dramatic growth came at the hands of one big program, and you have to replace it with six smaller programs, you are into another round of problems.
>
> You had only one management team handling the large program. Now you need separate teams to handle each of the six smaller new accounts. Also, the new

programs are unproven and more complex, so they are going to require steeper management ratios than were needed for the other program. Unfortunately, you have been so occupied in taking care of the problems caused by the original rapid growth that you have not developed the necessary people.

Suddenly, you find yourself forced right back into an explosive growth situation, even though you aren't adding higher volume or extra phones.

When you grow rapidly with a single client's large program, you pay a heavy opportunity cost in marshalling all your growth resources to meet that program's demands. It costs you the opportunity to get a number of new clients that could make you a healthier company overall—with your eggs spread into more than one basket.

STRESS, FATIGUE AND OVERLOAD

In an industry without long-term contracts, *not* being able to bring in new accounts is—at best—nerve wracking, and—at worst—may be a kiss of death. To bring in those account, you sometimes simply *must* stretch your resources.

If you have five perfect new accounts that come in at the same time but you are short on the number of developed personnel you would like to have to handle them, something has to give. Either you accept the business and stretch your existing personnel to the max, or you have to pass on at least some of the five accounts.

Result: *You and your people will often get called upon to deliver efforts and performances that are well beyond the normal call of duty.*

There are some upsides to that.

• Some people will learn and develop very quickly.
• If those people are properly managed, motivated, and inspired, you will gain a great deal of camaraderie and positive emotion within the daily activities of the company.
• If you can pull it off, you'll develop a high level of commitment to getting the job done.

Growth brings more achievement, more accomplishment, a bigger company, and more money. It also brings challenges—such as "How am I going to do it all?" Then, with hard work and long hours, you manage to find a way to get everything done and still not blow your promises to your clientele.

You may think that your people are already playing at or near to the highest possible level of intensity. Yet it is amazing to see the additional amounts of strength, commitment, and additional effort that develop when everyone's back is against the wall. That's the test of how effectively you have developed, defined, and disseminated the company's philosophies and values. That's when you find out if the people are willing to live the concept of "doing whatever it takes to get the job done."

Still, constantly working in that way is an abnormal and unhealthy intensity level. It is a level that neither *can* nor *should* be maintained for any great length of time. As productive as it might be in short bursts, it will become destructive if you try to keep people operating at or beyond their limits for extensive periods.

If you try to push to the limits all the time, you will see more than damage to your programs. You'll begin to see significant damage to your entire organization.

- Attitudes start to creep.
- People start to wonder "What am I doing—and is it worth it?"

Those are realistic questions. When the push is unrelenting, days melt into nights and back into days. Weekends become the same as weekdays. Days off, when they come, are too short to provide sufficient rest and recuperation. Your people lose their professional edge and their personal satisfaction.

The Neverending Struggle

The largest single downside of managing growth in outbound telemarketing has to be that if it is done properly, the exercise *never ends*. Well-managed growth leads to more growth which needs to be managed well . . . which, when managed well, creates more growth, which needs to be managed well. . . .

Growth can definitely make you appreciate the simpler things in life.

But the cost that is paid is your mental and physical well-being. When you work seven days a week with an honest 70- to 80-hour average work week, that pace effectively eliminates any kind of quality in your personal life. Hopefully, your personal relationships are strong, everyone involved understands what is happening, and everyone survives the strain.

When you work that kind of a pace, you simply don't have the time needed for rest and relaxation. You begin to *live* the old adage "All work and no play makes Johnny a dull boy." You lose variety in your life. You also start to lose perspective and start to develop tunnel vision. You're so busy that you begin to lose any kind of an edge, and you lose your ability to focus and dedicate your thought processes.

Going Beyond The Limits

You have definitely exceeded the limits when the signs of *real* "brain fade" starts to set in: you start to feel like you would rather be a pressure-sensitive label . . . or a microchip . . . or a golf ball . . . or . . .

When you reach that point, it's like being a race car that is designed and tuned for high speeds. You can race at very fast speeds for a while, but you can't go forever at "pedal to the floor," red-line limits.

If you constantly keep the gas pedal pushed to the floor, something bad is eventually going to happen. The constant stress will cause your engine to blow. Or your suspension to fail. Or your cooling system to overheat. Or your tires to fail. Something will happen that will require much more extensive repairs than can be accomplished during a short-pit stop.

Key Point: *If machinery made of steel can break down under the constant stress of running at full capacity, then* people *are sure to have the same problems.*

A high adrenaline level can be maintained for only so long. Then it burns itself out.

The Effects of Pushing Too Far

Some of the things that make your people the company's most valuable resources—their hearts and brains and emotions—are the very things that make them some of the most fragile components of your operation. If the explosive growth requires you to push your people at those abnormal levels for too long, they *will* start to burn out. Mistakes caused by mental and physical fatigue will begin to be made. Tempers will begin to flare. Interpersonal conflict, caused by tired and frayed emotions, will erupt.

People may say: "You're amazing! How do you do it?" But you may be crying inside of yourself, saying: "I don't know *how* we do it, but I *don't want* to do it! Not any more!" If you push too far, you ultimately reach a point where you burn out . . . whether you recognize it or not. And when your people begin to hit that burnout point, your organization suffers for it. And if your organization suffers, your clients suffer.

The clients begin to pay in ways they may never really see. Instead of having that sharp analytical and creative edge in developing and upgrading the programs, each of the people on the staff begins to get very adept at juggling five or six things all the time. They lose track of their commitment to quality and become production machines, turning out volumes and volumes of work.

If you don't recognize it, if you allow it to continue, you'll lose your competitive edge. You are no longer positioned to grow. Even the *idea* of company growth is painful, let alone the *thought* of having to *manage* it.

This whole issue is the personal downside of rapid growth, and it is *the* biggest one. You can go through all the financial downsides, the marketing downsides, structural downsides and all the rest. But if your *people* exceed their limits, the rest of the problems can do nothing but get worse. When people reach the point that the burden of responsibility exceeds their ability to carry on, *everything* collapses. If that happens, all your gains are lost.

Key Point: *Constantly pushing yourself and your people past the limits is not a mistake that is worth making . . . and may not be one that can be corrected.*

In an industry that is as fast-paced and demanding as outbound telemarketing, it's all too easy to push past the limits, especially when you are focusing on all of the problems and requirements of managing explosive growth. You need to schedule in some rest stops. You must make sure you recognize the early warning signs of the problem and take the necessary corrective steps . . . or just take some time off . . . before it's too late.

A strapping young man once challenged his grandfather to an all-morning wood chopping contest. He was both surprised and amused when the old man took him up on it. Both worked hard for a while. Then the grandfather stopped, walked a short distance away, and sat down with his axe. His grandson saw the opportunity and increased the pace of his work. Throughout the course of the morning, the scene was repeated: the old man occasionally stopping and walking away for a few minutes, with the young man always chopping feverishly at the wood. At the end of the morning, they compared the amount of wood they had cut. The old man had won!

The young man was stunned. He protested that he had worked through-out the morning while his grandfather had taken several breaks, and he didn't understand how he could have lost. He asked: "How could you possibly have won?"

The old man answered "Son, I spent that time honing my axe. No time is lost if it's spent sharpening your tools."

There are times in the process of managing growth—especially explosive growth —that you may feel that business is so pressing that you have to work around the clock. It may call for that kind of effort on occasion. But you may become so tired and frustrated that you find your judgment is slipping and your effectiveness is faltering. When that happens, it is important that you take the time you need to rest and "sharpen your tools."

Consider the Alternatives

During the times of stress caused by rapid or explosive growth, it's easy to lose sight of the gains being made and the victories being won. Sometimes, the best thing you can do to deal with the situation is to consider the alternatives.

The lack of growth also has very definite downsides to it.

- When you are not growing, you aren't providing new opportunities to your talented people, and that talent may go elsewhere. That will make it harder to grow when the opportunities come.
- The lack of growth may mean that you are not able to add to your cash reserves as quickly, with the resulting restrictions on being able to take advantage of opportunities that arise.
- You may find that you are attracting very little attention or recognition for what you are doing, and that may make it even harder to grow in the future.
- If you have had desires to build the company, you may experience a great deal of frustration over the lack of growth.
- In a non-growth situation, you don't have the same kinds of opportunities to stretch yourself, and you may not have the same sense of achievement when you walk out the door at the end of the day.

All things considered, the downsides of growth really may be quite manageable after all!

28 KEYS TO RECOGNIZING AND SURVIVING THE DOWNSIDES OF GROWTH

- Dangerous, explosive growth happens when you have rapid increases in call volumes, for which your advance plans, structure and resources are inadequate to allow you to maintain your standards of excellence.

- As hard as we try to avoid it, there are times that we all find ourselves having to manage explosive growth because is already too late to avoid.
- If you haven't structured and planned ahead of the growth sufficiently to be able to quickly add the required facilities and to tap the required management people, something's got to give. That "give" probably will be your productivity and/or your quality.
- The immediate challenge of integrating massive additional volume into your existing workload is a time and situation that will test your abilities.
- Before you commit to large new volumes of calls, consider all of the potential problems and ask yourself penetrating questions about the company's ability to handle the strain.
- The rallying of efforts and encouragement of your people to do well on large new programs needs to be balanced by the reminder that there can be no reduction of attention or intensity on your existing client's programs.
- Any opportunity cost that is paid at the expense of alienating your grassroots people and your loyal and longstanding clients is completely and totally unacceptable.
- When you take on challenges of a new magnitude, operational mistakes and errors in decision will happen, no matter how thoroughly you believe you are prepared.
- When mistakes occur, you must take immediate, decisive action to repair the problems and re-establish levels of performance that match your commitment to excellence.
- A significant downside that comes with rapid growth is the constant struggle to maintain the delicate balance between your capacity and your marketing effort.
- When you are sold out for an extended period of time, the marketing force tends to feel useless, limited, and frustrated.
- You can put forth a marketing effort that is larger than your *existing* capacity. You simply can't justify creating a marketing thrust that you know will generate commitments beyond your *ability* to expand.
- When you are approaching capacity, you can generally keep the marketers active if you work to refocus your marketing thrust. Generally, being sold out still means that you have at least some test phones and/or some phones available to load during another part of the day.
- When you create a new marketing thrust, it's not enough to do the *planning* for the effort. You have to make sure the marketing salespeople have the *knowledge* and the *willingness* to execute your plan.
- Staying ahead of growth includes creating no marketing effort that you expect will generate commitments beyond your *ability* to expand in all areas.
- The problems caused if the big client that helped you grow goes away are a serious downside of growth. If you lose one of those large accounts, you may be in *deep* trouble.
- Even if you can replace one big program that caused your dramatic growth, you may have to replace it with several smaller programs. If you do, you are likely to be headed into another round of growth-management problems.

- As valuable as the large client is to the rapid growth of an outbound telemarketing business, you pay a heavy opportunity cost in marshalling all your growth resources to meet that one account's demands.
- It almost takes a gift from heaven raining down upon you to replace a very large volume project in anything resembling a convenient and timely manner.
- The people in outbound telemarketing will often get called upon to deliver efforts and performances that are well beyond the normal call of duty.
- The single largest downside of managing growth in outbound telemarketing has to be that if it is done properly, the exercise *never ends*. There is no break.
- If you try to push to the limits all the time, you will see more than damage to your programs. You'll begin to see significant damage to your entire organization.
- If machinery made of *steel* can break down under the constant stress of running at full capacity, then *people* are sure to have the same problems.
- When the people have pushed beyond the limits for too long a period, they lose that sharp analytical and creative edge they need to develop and upgrade the programs that are vital to success in outbound telemarketing.
- Sometimes, when we get into difficult immediate situations, we can lose perspective about the potential long-range rewards for the efforts we are giving. And it *is* hard to see beyond the immediate trying situation when it seems that it will never end.
- Constantly pushing yourself and your people past the limits is not a mistake that is worth making. If they reach the point that the burden of responsibility exceeds their ability to carry on, *everything* will collapse.
- It is important to take regular breaks from the fast-paced demands of managing growth. No time is lost if it's spent sharpening your tools.
- When the alternatives to growth are considered, the downsides of growth really may be quite manageable after all!

On the day of victory, no one is tired.

—Arab proverb

There is no medicine like hope, no incentive so
great, no tonic so powerful as the
expectation of something better tomorrow
— *Orlson S. Marden*

Chapter 10

The Challenges of Telemarketing's Future

Telemarketing is in the process of moving into a new maturity, one that will determine its capacity to effect profound changes in the marketing strategies of every astute marketing direct, president, and chairman of Corporate America. Our tomorrows look extremely bright. "The future is what we make it" is certainly true in our industry. An exciting and thriving future can be achieved, but we must meet a number of challenges—as an industry—to realize the promising predictions for telemarketing's potential.

THE MARKETING CHALLENGES

In the chapter on marketing, we mentioned that today's victors in marketing game are the ones who can best convince the client that their approach to telemarketing—either automated or manual—is the way to go. If very sophisticated data base management is a requisite of a program, a manual shop just can't do the things an automated shop can. Yet too many automated firms *claim* their automation makes them more productive on *all* programs, and too many manual shops will tell you that they can crunch and manage *all* the data you can think of. All this information is out there, and not everybody is telling the *truth*. That represents a serious problem for telemarketing that needs to be addressed in the very near future.

The problem is that we have two different philosophies which are opposed to each other at the level of the *essence* of the business. But the two sides don't have to be at war. Neither side should exclude the tools and expertise of the other.

Key to Improvement: *Each side—the manual and the automated—needs to* learn *from the other to improve what each can bring to the party.*

If we do that, we can create a better situation for the industry and for the marketplace.

Combining the Tools and the Experience

When an outbound company marries a truly excellent and comprehensive automation package with deeper levels of supervision and true expertise in handling the grassroots end of telemarketing, then they will be able to *kick the dickens* out of *any* manual or automated shop that exists in today's environment. They will be a little more expensive per hour than today's automated firms, but they will be able to outproduce the current standards of the industry—not just in calls per hour, but in the real meat of the business: conversion rate, SPH, and cost per sale.

When that happens, both the automated and the manual shops will feel the pressure. And *both* types of companies will be scouring the hills to find the people and the systems that can help them meet the new competitive standards.

The ultimate solution may be for outbound shops to be partly manual and partly automated, if they are to serve a wide variety of markets.

Reality: *The fact is that some programs work best for the client with automation, while others are still most effective when run manually.*

If a firm's choice is to be automated, perhaps it should still dedicate 20% of the facility to being manual. And if a firm opts for the manual approach, perhaps it should automate 20% of its operation. With that kind of a combination, a telemarketing company could really educate the client without carrying an overriding prejudice in its argument of automated versus manual. Then either kind of firm has the ability to test any given program in both environments to see which works better for the client.

Even if the client doesn't buy off on that kind of a dual test, a service bureau that is part manual and part automated will have the opportunity to develop the knowledge of how best to manage in both environments. And we need to marry good people management to good data management. That marriage violates a lot of principles of managing growth, which makes it a unique challenge of the future.

The Challenge of Achieving Quality Education

In addition to the automation challenge, telemarketing has two other particularly important challenges for the future. Both deal with the issue of quality. The first challenge deals with improving the quality of telemarketing's management personnel.

In the chapter on people issues, we addressed some of the problems with hiring and developing good people. People with a traditional business background do not generally perceive telemarketing as a "career" industry. They are uncomfortable with the untraditional work hours. The lack of a system to educate, train and develop key telemarketing management personnel makes it difficult to hire excellent people who are developed through the traditional educational process.

Reality Report: *Today's degrees in telemarketing come from the School of Hard Knocks and on-the-job training, and the people who move into management usually lack the kind of background and education required to properly prepare them to run the organization.*

In telemarketing, we still have to rely too much upon on-the-job training and home grown talent. That situation is not healthy for the future of the industry. But until telemarketing becomes a full course of studies in our educational institutions, we *have* to put out those additional costs, the additional training, and the focused developmental attention to help overcome the problems.

If we are to develop the kind of long-term, quality situations that the projections for our future indicate we will need, the education crisis has to be solved. We need to encourage:

- the development of formalized telemarketing training programs
- the development of more night courses and degree programs in our educational institutions

And those programs—to be truly effective—should not be limited to classroom environments, but rather should involve live, *hands-on* telemarketing experience, as well.

TELEMARKETING'S IMAGE AND THE CHALLENGE OF ENFORCED REGULATION

To accomplish those objectives, we will have to deal with the second "quality" challenge of the future: the need to improve the quality of our efforts so we can improve the overall image and acceptance of telemarketing.

A Reduction in Turnover

A part of establishing that acceptance in the educational arena is making dramatic improvements in the turnover rate in the industry. We have to become *much more* selective in recruiting and hiring people whose profiles would *lessen* the possibilities of turnover. Getting some courses or programs on telemarketing established in our colleges and educational institutions will be a valuable step forward. But, by itself, it isn't the answer.

The Stumbling Block: *If the perception of the young people of this country is that telemarketing is an undependable provider that can be relied upon only for transitory jobs and little likelihood of career opportunity or development, they won't enroll in those courses, no matter how good they are.*

We can do all the PR work we want. But unless we address our retention rates and bring measurable improvement, the word-of-mouth advertising about telemarketing's "meat market" atmosphere will doom those promotional efforts to failure.

Improved Quality Control

We also have to make sure that our internal quality control is more effective. And that means more than the quality assurance within the individual firms for which we are responsible. What an individual can do alone in a 30- to 50-phone shop can't be done alone in a much larger operation. In the same way, as our industry undergoes the tremendous growth that is anticipated for the future, we cannot—as individual firms—maintain the quality assurance that we need as an industry. We have to manage quality as an *entire industry,* if it is at all possible.

Helping the Industry Grow Under Control

We have addressed a great deal about managing the growth of individual telemarketing *firms.* Now let's look at some of those ideas with the focus on the growth of the industry.

The *industry* can simply grow for growth's sake, or we can *choose* controlled growth. Growth for growth's sake assumes that bigger is better and, ultimately, that biggest is best. But biggest isn't best if growth comes without regard for the continuance of standards of excellence, or for the development of people resources, or for the long-range profit performance of the *industry.*

Key Point: *If telemarketing's growth starts to cost too much—in terms of the essence of the industry—then the growth could become an uncontrolled cancer.*

We have to open our eyes to the need for growth that is planned for and anticipated, and for which the telemarketing *industry* has the necessary financial and human resources. We cannot allow telemarketing's growth to cause harm to the clients or to the public. Nor can we afford to have that growth decrease margins so much that the industry becomes financially unhealthy. This requires that the industry plans, focuses, and budgets its efforts and execution. Quality growth requires having the ability to say "no" to a client or company when that business is not right for the public or the industry. We must ask ourselves—as an industry—"How do we grow *and* maintain *and* improve our standards of excellence?"

Regulation Will Happen

Outbound phone shops make calls representing major names in Corporate America. In effect, they are selling a commodity. And as much as we don't want to admit it, outbound phone shops do cause a good deal of stress to buyers and prospective buyers. It can be reduced dramatically through ethical and knowledgeable telemarketing procedures, but that stress does occur. There's the interruption factor, the pressure to make a decision, and the backend stress. In the case of less-than-ethical telemarketers, *they* cause outright *harm.* They may cause loss of unavailable cash flow. That's the case even if the cost of the product or service is only $49.95. Who says that $50 isn't just as important to that buyer as $5000 is to someone who buys sugar options from a phone room operation?

If we are not sensitive to that reality, it will come back to haunt us.

People who sell options, commodities, stocks, bonds, and other types of products are required to pass a test and become licensed. The assumption behind those laws is that training, testing, licensing, and the potential for punishment of offenses will reduce the probability of the buying public being exposed to misrepresentation or fraudulent tactics.

Unavoidable Reality: *History has shown that the larger an industry gets, the greater the possibility for abuse and for reactive legislation.*

We have to be very aware of, and careful about, this situation. We don't want to get caught in a situation that winds up throwing a monkey wrench into the ability of the industry to operate.

This is an extremely serious subject. Perhaps this story can better put it into perspective. Perhaps you've heard of "the three great lies, but you might not have heard the *business* version of the three great lies.

1. "The check is in the mail."
2. "We are the best, no matter what your needs."
3. "Hi! I'm from the government . . . and I'm here to *help* you."

THE CHALLENGE OF SELF-REGULATION

We are in an industry that has a serious need to mature in its efforts to police itself.

Prediction: *If self-regulation is done properly, we can largely forestall regulation by legislation. If we don't, there's going to be unnecessary and overly restrictive legislation passed that will take the regulation of the business out of our hands.*

Maybe not tomorrow, and maybe not next month, but somewhere down the line, someone will get hit for improper telemarketing procedures, and it will stimulate overly restrictive legislative action on a very large scale. But if we can show that we are *proactively* taking meaningful action to self-regulate, we can reduce the negative impact of that kind of legislation.

We need to make sure we don't face a licensing process that requires a person to go through 12 months of study to become a licensed TRS. That would be devastating. We're in an industry that is constantly under attack by certain segments of the press as being high-pressure, misleading, and an invasion of privacy. There *is* an element in the telemarketing industry that is guilty of those tactics. According to widely published accounts, the estimated yearly amount of fraudulent activities in telemarketing reached $1,000,000,000 in 1988. That's a *billion* dollars. And every true case brought to the public's attention affects the entire industry through guilt by association.

The industry has tried to approach this issue. The Direct Marketing Association has created TPS, the Telephone Preference Service, to help companies remove from their lists the names of people who have requested that they not receive solicitation calls. That's a step in the right direction, but we need to do more.

If we're glad we're in the business, why should we be ashamed to say "Let us know if you don't want to receive a phone call"? There are many possible approaches. Maybe we're afraid that if we advertise, people who would never otherwise put their name on the list will do it. Maybe we're afraid that if we talk about it too much, we'll come under too much scrutiny by the public and by governmental bodies.

Under any circumstances, as provisions are made to allow more of the public to add their names to "do not call" lists and as some states pass more restrictive legislation, there will probably be some list shrinkage. That's going to happen with or without self-regulation. There are similar situations. The bells and whistles of automation will help cut the less-ethical and less-skilled firms out of the marketplace. But the public doesn't hear the bells and whistles.

Face the Music: *The public perception of telemarketing is shaped by the approach and actions—good, bad, or indifferent—of the grassroots TSR when that phone rings, whether that TSR works for an automated or manual firm.*

Self-Regulation with Enforcement

Much of our industry's organized attempts to correct its own problems have been little more than lip service. We are not saying that to criticize those who have tried; it's just the reality of the situation. As good as TPS is, it doesn't *require* anyone to do anything. Without some kind of enforceable regulations and standards, the results of the efforts will be mediocre at best. Until we have *requirement-based* self-regulation, it will not carry deep enough into the industry to be effective.

The most successfully regulated industries have been ones who structured the regulatory systems themselves. AT&T did it by creating the most advanced research facilities in the world, obsoleting their own products and services with new and better ones, and creating their own competition. Finally, they were the ones who suggested the outlines for government regulation of the industry, including regulation of how much they could charge and how high a profit margin they could make. Would it have happened anyway? Almost assuredly. Would those regulations have been as acceptable to the industry if they had simply fought all internal and external regulation? Not at all likely.

There are other good examples.

- The Chicago Board of Trade
- The New York Stock Exchange

They are self-regulated industries. They report to an even higher authority called the Securities and Exchange Commission, which they helped create.

An industry that was hurt, though not decimated, by its failure to self-regulate was the auto industry. The automakers waited for the EPA and other agencies to force them into regulations for emissions, fuel efficiency, and safety before they began to take significant action. Yes, some of that was caused by extraordinary situations in the marketplace and in the economy. But the real problem was that the automakers had been unwilling to look beyond the short-term and take action to prepare for a better offensive strategy through self-regulation.

The Japanese were able to step into the marketplace much more readily and with much more impact than they otherwise could have, because they had already taken the steps that would allow them to drive in through the gaping hole left by the American auto industry. The Japanese had developed other areas of strategic advantage, but the lack of attention to emission, economy and safety by the American automakers was the area that paved their way into the consciousness of the American public.

Key Point: *We need to be willing to look beyond the short-term and take action to prepare for a better offensive strategy. We need to be better prepared to take our destiny into our own hands.*

A Proposal for Self-Regulation

In July, 1986, Steve made a presentation to the Iowa Telemarketing Conference in Des Moines. In that presentation, he first proposed a situation in which a *firm* doing outbound telemarketing would be required go through a process to become a licensed or certified telemarketer. To be clear, the suggestion was to license the *firm,* not the individual sales representative. The firm, to be licensed, would have to be willing to answer questions such as where they operate, how long they have been in business, the kinds of solicitation they do, etc. Those are basics.

They would also be required to submit a minimum of three typical scripts they have created, letting them substitute "the ABC company" for the client's name. The scripts would be judged *not* for creativity or sales effectiveness, but for adherence to prescribed standards of ethics. In addition, the firm would present an outline or synopsis of their hiring and training process. This could be submitted in a general proposal form that gives away no proprietary procedures. The firm would also have to agree to "on location" spot reviews by the board who reviews the firms for the initial and renewal licensing or certification.

Some of those proposals might seem agreeable and some might seem disagreeable. Some people in the industry may feel they're all disagreeable. But we need to initiate self-regulation action before the possibility of self-regulation is taken out of our hands.

Suggestion: *We should give serious consideration to establishing self-regulating bodies and procedures that can bring—at the very least—some measurable control and enforceable standards to the industry.*

While we might not *all* like the structures and standards that would result from our combined efforts, waiting for legislation to be enacted will result in rules and guidelines that *none* of us like. Some laws with which very few telemarketers are happy are already being enacted in some states.

It will *not* work if a government or legal panel makes the telemarketing rules. It *can* work if the panel or board overseeing the certification is one composed of real experts in the industry. (Of course, we could argue for months about who the experts are!)

But something has to be done, *if* we are going to protect the buying public *and* our own industry. Decisions will have to be made about what standards are to be followed, what panel guidelines should be, how to encourage participation, and how to enforce the standards.

The Key Regulatory Problem: *So long as there is no formal body in charge of requirement-based regulations and standards, the results of any self-regulatory efforts will be destined for failure.*

Everyone in the industry knows there is concern about what will happen, from a regulatory standpoint. A lot of people discuss it and just keep going on with business as usual. Others have actually gotten out of telemarketing rather than be caught in what they perceive to be the approaching death of the industry through governmental regulations that may effectively *outlaw* outbound telemarketing. Some of the companies in the industry aren't particularly concerned because they feel they barely would be affected, no matter what regulations might come down. Perhaps they are right. What if they are not?

The Need for Cooperation and Action

What we are advocating is not collusion or non-competition. It is simply the suggestion that reasonable cooperation in setting standards and systems for self-regulation can create results that are much superior—in the long view—for the public and for the companies involved in the industry. Trying to avoid or fight any form of regulation will ultimately fail. It's a case of self-discipline and self-regulation arising from enlightened self-interest.

We must begin *now* to study the examples and the methods of those industries which have managed the development of the successful regulation of their industries. Then we need to take *action* based on those successful precedents.

This is not nearly as critical for inbound telemarketers as it is for the outbound side of the business. Yet the inbound side *could* suffer from that same "guilt by association." If the inbound *and* outbound sides of telemarketing join together on this issue, there will be even greater probability of successfully meeting the challenge.

Prediction: *If we fail to meet the challenge, there will be much more restrictive tele-marketing legislation enacted than is required to effectively protect the public and police the industry.*

We have to do something to educate the public in how to tell good telemarketing companies from bad ones, yet that approach is fraught with pitfalls and possible image backlash. There's always the view to be taken of "Why make something that isn't a major issue in the public's mind that important? Let's just ignore it." It's not an easy issue, and there are no easy answers. Yet it is an important issue and one of the primary challenges of the industry.

Most importantly, it should no longer be referred to as a challenge of the future. On these issues, the future is here, NOW!

TROUBLE, CRISIS, AND OPPORTUNITY

Telemarketing is a growth industry. And the bigger the industry, the more we need leadership, and the stronger the leadership needs to be. Telemarketing is, and will remain, a unique field with its own set of rules and requirements. The industry will be carried into full recognition and power by a new breed of telemarketing managers with the expertise to balance traditional business values and the special requirements of the fast-paced, high-quality production, innovative growth environment that *is* today's tele-marketing.

When the Chinese symbols for "Trouble" and "Crisis" are combined in the Chinese language, the new symbol represents "Opportunity." Perhaps we can take a clue from the wisdom of the Chinese. So long as we can look at any trouble or crisis that arises in our companies and in our industry and see new and challenging opportunities that can lead us to a better future, then that future will be bright for all of us.

When we meet crisis with determination and innovation, we can create wonderful new opportunities. It depends on our ability to see beyond the immediate obstacles to the promise beyond them. In 1879, a fire destroyed the University of Notre Dame. After the fire, Father Sorin (Notre Dame's founder) was seen walking around in the rubble and rummaging through the ashes with a stick. The people who were nearby thought he was looking through the ruins of his dream, hoping to find something to remember it by. When they went to console him and asked what he was looking for, Father Sorin said: "I'm laying out a new foundation. Hand me a shovel!"

If we are active and innovative in meeting the challenges of telemarketing, we can prevent the fires that could destroy our industry. We can expand upon the foundation built by our industry's early pioneers, and step out boldly to make the aggressive plans today that will lead us to bigger and brighter tomorrows.

The challenges and the opportunities of the future that must be met include the industry's extended needs for vision, ingenuity, and creativity. The industry needs people who will challenge current barriers and lay the new foundations that will bring telemarketing to a higher and better level of productivity and respect.

We need to dream the dreams of what the industry can be. We need the vision and imagination to preceive what the industry could become. We need to be innovative in finding new ways to better service existing markets and to create new ones. And we need more people with the leadership and the courage to step out and challenge each one of us in the telemarketing industry to create a stronger and better telemarketing future.

We hope to see you among that group of talented and committed people.

**Accept the challenges
so that you may feel
the exhilaration of victory.**

George S. Patton

because

**Where there is no vision,
the people perish.**

Proverbs XXIX, 18

and

**The credit belongs to the man who is actually in the arena;
whose face is marred by dust and sweat and blood;
who strives valiantly; who errs and comes short again and again;
who knows the great enthusiasms, the great devotions,
and spends himself in a worthy cause;
who at the best, knows the triumph of high achievement;
and who, at the worst, if he fails,
at least fails while daring greatly,
so that his place shall never be with those
cold and timid souls
who know neither victory nor defeat.**

—Teddy Roosevelt

Appendix *A*

Sample Marketing Plan

Marketing Plan Elements

- Plan Overview (Definition)
- Background/Business Review
  - Market Maturity
  - Competitive Overview
- Marketing Strategy/Objectives
  - Advertising and Promotional
    - Copy Objective
    - Media
      - Media Effectiveness
      - Promotion Objectives
  - Budget, Advertising and Promotions
  - Market Share
- Business Building Opportunities
  - Identify Customers
  - Develop Client Test
- Financial Impact
- Testing Marketing Plan
  - Test Business Case
  - Verify Market
  - Test Level of Acceptance

ABC Telemarketing, Inc. Survey Telemarketing Marketing Plan

Overview

The survey telemarketing business represents a growth revenue area for ABC. With the utilization of daytime hours, fixed costs will not appreciably increase. Thus, it is believed that we can increase profitability without having to reach a large-volume production environment.

Background/Business Review

The telephone still represents the most cost-effective method to gather data for many businesses and polls.
The basic advantages are:

- Higher response rate
- Faster sampling
- Less expensive questionnaire
- Quick, changeable questionnaire

Market Maturity

The survey market is developing. For many years, only the large companies recognized and could afford to capture the information. This was performed in several different manners, including the use of internal staff or data-gathering companies.

With the stress towards increased customer service, the need to know more about the buying habits and after-sell satisfaction of customers has become a "must" in remaining competitive. There is a definite early-market phase for this business. Like any industry that has large players, the opportunities exist in targeted industries and with smaller customers.

Blending our agency approach and the need in smaller companies, the potential should support long-term growth. Remember, telemarketing is one step in the process of gathering customer information. The recognition of needed customer feedback will drive the maturing of this market.

Competitive Overview

The major players who have dominated the survey markets are:

- Donnelley (prior to being acquired by D & B)
- Dunn and Bradstreet
- Nielson
- Gallup

As these companies have grown, they have proven the telemarketing survey concept to industries. The demand has spread from advertising and promotional needs to such areas as customer satisfaction, product preference, and lead generation.

Marketing Strategy/Objectives

Marketing Objectives

The Marketing objectives are:

- To identify an industry
- To target a service
- To build a success story

Marketing Strategy

The marketing strategy is to acquire a small survey telemarketing company that has a client base and operates with a profitable revenue stream. With the existing client base, the goal then will be to increase the direct sale effort to maximize the revenue growth in that industry.

With the success story in a particular industry, we can expand to other industries by focusing on small companies, then growing our revenues from each particular industry. By spreading the services to multiple industries, we should protect financial downsides from seasonal, recessional, and industry downturns.

Advertising and Promotional

Target three industry specific trade magazines that have strong BPA Audits for their circulation and decision makers reached.

Copy Objective Will Be:

1. Uniformly identify ABC as a brand.
2. Establish service effectiveness for customers by using testimonials.
3. Sell the customer benefits

Media

1. Utilization of trade magazines
2. Exhibiting at trade shows
3. Sponsorship in executive associations

Budget

See attached exhibit for budget.

Market Share

The objective is to acquire an existing company that has no less than 2% market share. With infusion of capital, this can grow at a rate of 25% per year for 5 years.

Business Building Opportunities

The planned venture is central to the overall growth in ABC's base business, as well as cross fertilization of our base business into new accounts.

- Sell existing services to companies that will use the survey services.
- Also sell surveys to base customers.

Financial Impact

The financial impact can be seen in the attached pro forma. It reflects a first-year revenue of $16 million with a pre-tax income of $2.3 million.

Testing Market Plan

The steps in testing this plan are:

1. Determine if an acquisition is possible
2. Determine the lapse time on acquisition
3. Verify customer base (part of due diligence)
4. Utilize telemarketing and test ads to determine market size
5. Test for service acceptance

ABC Telemarketing, Inc. Marketing Budget 1989

Marketing Expenses	1st qtr	2nd qtr	3rd qtr	4th qtr
Media & Publicity	$10,000	$15,000	$5,000	$2,500
Promotions	$0	$0	$5,000	$7,500
Research	$25,000	$0	$0	$0
Special Sponsorships	$0	$2,500	$0	$0
Brochures	$0	$23,000	$0	$0
Total Marketing Expenses	$35,000	$40,500	$10,000	$10,000
Selling Expenses:				
Salaries	$25,000	$25,000	$25,000	$25,000
Travel & Entertainment	$2,500	$3,000	$4,500	$1,000
Commissions	$5,000	$15,000	$17,500	$25,000
Trade Shows	$0	$12,500	$0	$3,500
Total Selling Expenses	$32,500	$55,500	$47,000	$54,500
Total Marketing Budget	$67,500	$96,000	$57,000	$64,500
% of Sales	13.5%	19.2%	5.7%	2.2%
Projected Cost Per Billed Hour	$3.38	$4.80	$1.43	$0.54

ABC Telemarketing, Inc. Pro Forma Income Statement 1989 (000's)

	1st Qtr.	2nd Qtr.	3rd Qtr.	4th Qtr.	Total
Revenues	$1,000	$2,000	$5,000	$8,000	$16,000
Variable Cost	$ 720	$1,440	$3,600	$5,760	$11,520
Gross Margin	$ 280	$ 560	$1,400	$2,240	$ 4,480
Fixed Cost	$ 350	$ 425	$ 600	$ 750	$ 2,125
Net Income Before Debt	($ 70)	$ 135	$ 800	$1,490	$ 2,355

Marketing Budget 19 ____

Marketing Expenses	1st qtr	2nd qtr	3rd qtr	4th qtr
Media & Publicity				
Promotions				
Research				
Special Sponsorships				
Brochures				
Total Marketing Expenses				
Selling Expenses:				
Salaries				
Travel & Entertainment				
Commissions				
Trade Shows				
Total Selling Expenses				
Total Marketing Budget				
% of Sales				
Projected Cost Per Billed Hour				

Pro Forma Income Statement 19 ____ (000's)

	1st Qtr.	2nd Qtr.	3rd Qtr.	4th Qtr.	Total
Revenues					
Variable Cost					
Gross Margin					
Fixed Cost					
Net Income Before Debt					

Appendix B

Pro Forma Statement

The pro forma statement is a very interesting tool and serves at least two contradicting purposes:

- To qualify the belief of a business venture.
- To sell financial sources on the viability of the venture.

The composition of the statement is more important than the actual numbers. The pro forma statement serves to illustrate:

- Quality of earnings
- Understanding of cost components.
- Understanding of the telemarketing business.

This tool normally will lead into explaining at a high level what telemarketing can achieve now and in the future. Remember, financial people must believe that your knowledge, skills, and financial ability have credibility before they will have confidence in the projected results.

Used for:

- Standard presentation
- An educational tool (i.e., per billed hour)
- Actual or industry as cross validation

ABC Telemarketing Pro Forma Income Statement 1989

Hours 500,000
Rate $30

		Per Billed Hour
Revenue:		
Sales	$15,000,000	$30.00
Sales-Other	$ 250,000	$ 0.50
Total Revenue	$15,250,000	$30.50
Variable Cost:		
Payroll	$ 6,000,000	$12.00
Telephone	$ 2,500,000	$ 5.00
Other	$ 500,000	$ 1.00
Total Variable Cost	$ 9,000,000	$18.00
Gross Profit	$ 6,250,000	$12.50
Fixed Cost:		
Payroll-Executive	$ 500,000	$ 1.00
Payroll-Other	$ 1,250,000	$ 2.50
Advertising-Help Wanted	$ 250,000	$ .50
Depreciation	$ 400,000	$ 0.80
Facility Rent	$ 300,000	$ 0.60
Equipment Rent	$ 200,000	$ 0.40
Other	$ 1,350,000	$ 2.70
Total Fixed Costs	$ 4,250,000	$ 8.50
Debt Service	$ 250,000	$ 0.50
Net Income Before Taxes	$ 1,750,000	$ 3.50

Appendix C

Sample Financial Plan

ABC Telemarketing, Inc. Financial Plan 1989

Overview

The purpose of this plan is to define the financial plan for ABC Telemarketing. ABC is being started to meet the market needs for outbound telemarketing in the Consumer Club Membership industry.

Business Overview

The consumer club membership industry traditionally has relied upon direct marketing activities to grow its business. The competition for new consumer members has created significant increases in acquisition costs from all of the more passive, less interactive, direct marketing media.

The key to growing consumer memberships cost-effectively today is to increase the utilization of live, interactive, persuasive Outbound Consumer Telemarketing as an acquisition tool. This approach will present Consumer Club Membership marketing companies the greatest opportunities for growth. The cost of generating the memberships becomes the key for selecting the approach (in-house or outside agency) to outbound telemarketing.

Today, Consumer Club Membership marketing companies use the following marketing methods with projected costs per new member:

Direct mail	$ 20.40*
Television response	$100.00
In-house telemarketing	$ 38.00
* not enough volume	

ABC will be able to supply a high volume of new members at $28.00 per net paid member. The revenue to ABC will average $25.00 per hour.

See pro forma income statement.

Capitalization Plan

ABC will be capitalized:

Equity	$ 900,000
Family Investment	$ 525,000
Lease and Long Term Debt	$1,800,000

Funds Usage

ABC will need to support a first-year capital budget of $2,450,000 and accounts receivable growth of $5,800,000. See exhibits for capital budget and pro forma cash flow.

The shortfall will be $2,575,000. It can be supported through a revolving line of credit pledging accounts receivable. This would be less costly than factoring receivables.

Financial Plan

The financial plan for a telemarketing firm is often overlooked or stops short of explaining key factors:

> Capitalization of business (start-up capital)
> Debt repayment
> Cash budgeting
> Growth capital requirements

Like many industries, telemarketing is driven by the highly motivated sales oriented person or the operationally focused manager. The financial projection is often used in place of the financial plan, when in real terms, the financial projection is just part of the overall plan needed to support the business purpose.

Key Elements of a Telemarketing Firm's Business Plan

Capitalization methods

> Equity (owner's cash)
> Bank loans
> Other debt
>> Venture capital
>> Relatives
>> Friends
>> Personal loans
> Public offerings

Short-term debt
    Revolving lines of credit
    Trade debts
    Selling accounts receivable
Debt repayment
Accounts receivable
    Working capital needs
    Granting credit
    Collections
    Seasonal influences
    Ratio of number of days sales to net receivables
Cash budget
    Forecasting
    Reality check
Pro forma income statement
Pro forma cash flow statement
Capital budget

ABC Telemarketing, Inc. Capital Budget 1989 (000's)

Leasehold Improvements:		
Deposits		$ 15
Phone Workstations (700 phones @ 450)		$ 315
Facility Build Out		$ 320
		$ 650
Lease-Purchases		
Automation ($2,500 per Workstation)		$1,750
Office Equipment		$ 50
		$1,800
Total Capital Expenditures		$2,450
Assumptions		
Billable Hours		
1st Qtr	40,000	
2nd Qtr	80,000	
3rd Qtr	200,000	
4th Qtr	320,000	
Total	640,000	
Hourly Rate	$25.00	
Variable	$18.00	
Capital Budget	$2,450,000	

ABC Telemarketing, Inc. Pro Forma Income Statement 1989 (000's)

	1st Qtr.	2nd Qtr.	3rd Qtr.	4th Qtr.	Total
Revenues	$1,000	$2,000	$5,000	$8,000	$16,000
Variable Cost	$ 720	$1,440	$3,600	$5,760	$11,520
Gross Margin	$ 280	$ 560	$1,400	$2,240	$ 4,480
Fixed Cost	$ 350	$ 425	$ 600	$ 750	$ 2,125
Net Income Before Debt	($ 70)	$ 135	$ 800	$1,490	$ 2,355

ABC Telemarketing, Inc. Pro Forma Cash Flow Needs 1989 (000's)

Source Of Funds	1st Qtr.	2nd Qtr.	3rd Qtr.	4th Qtr.	Total
Net Operations	($ 70)	$ 135	$ 800	$1,490	$2,355
Depreciation	$ 15	$ 20	$ 25	$ 30	$ 90
Trade Debt Increase	$ 100	$ 45	($ 30)	$ 80	$ 195
Provision/Billing Losses	$ 20	$ 20	$ 20	$ 20	$ 80
Changes in Prepaids	($ 50)	$ 10	$ 10	$ 15	($ 15)
Personal Investments	$ 500	$ 100	$ 250	$ 50	$ 900
Family Investments	$ 125	$ 125	$ 150	$ 125	$ 525
Total Sources	$ 640	$ 455	$1,225	$1,810	$4,130
Use of Funds:					
Acct. Recvble. Increase	$ 800	$1,500	$1,000	$2,500	$5,800
Capital Expenditures	$ 375	$ 125	$ 150	$ 0	$ 650
Capital Leases	$ 45	$ 70	$ 70	$ 70	$ 255
Total Uses	$1,220	$1,695	$1,220	$2,570	$6,705
Gross Funds Available	($ 580)	($1,240)	$ 5	($ 760)	($2,575)
Debt Service @ 10% Annual	$ 15	$ 30	$ 30	$ 20	$ 95
Net Funds Available	($ 595)	($1,270)	($ 25)	($ 780)	($2,670)

ABC Telemarketing, Inc. Balance Sheet Review

The challenge of any person reviewing a balance sheet is to understand it. Many ratios can give indications of liquidity, profitability, and financial effectiveness. However, a ratio must be compared to an industry standard or to previous financial periods before it can be utilized effectively.

Financial ratios are no more than indicators of a business at one point in time. They are just like the balance sheet, a financial snapshot. A financial ratio does not tell what has happened unless it is compared with another point in time, nor does it necessarily reveal what will occur in the future. Still, financial ratios are very useful tools, and they should be used in conjunction with other financial measurements.

Liquidity

Liquidity testing is a quick way to determine how long you can stay in business before needing more formal financing. In telemarketing, the Quick Ratio approach is preferred over the Current Ratio approach.

The Quick Ratio: Highly liquid assets (easily converted to cash: i.e., cash, investments, and receivables) divided by the current liabilities.

This approach allows you to determine, if you liquidated today, whether or not you could pay off all current liabilities. Depending upon the circumstances, you may prefer to reduce accounts receivable by 75%. Why? Because, if the company was liquidated, the receivables would bring less than face value for a quick conversion to cash. There are other factors, as well, such as age and quality of customers, that could impact the value of the receivables.

Very important to remember: Other than cash and certain types of investments (like CDs, for example), the market value of the company's assets will be different from book value.

The Current Ratio is a broader view achieved by looking at all current assets divided by current liabilities. Again, this is an indication that if you were to liquidate current assets at book value, could you pay short-term debt?

Profitability (Measured by Rates of Return)

Even though multiple ratios can be used to view the profitability, the most effective tools are:

- Rate of return on net worth
- Rate of return on total assets

These reflect the percentage return from your growing investment and from the use of assets purchased.

Rate of Return on Net Worth

Divide the net income after provision for taxes by the stockholders' equity (before current earning). This can easily be compared to alternate investment opportunities and previous years' performance.

Rate of Return on Total Assets

Divide the net income after provision for taxes by the total assets. This indicator tells how well your assets are performing compared to last year, or compared to industry standards.

Financial Effectiveness

Most of the following ratios are related to sales. They establish goals that are action-oriented and measurable by events versus financial results. As an example, when we talk about *days in collection,* the size of the receivables is not the controlling criteria. The key point becomes how many days' worth of sales are in the receivables. The days in collection ratio does not hinder business growth; however, it gives the telemarketing firm's finance department a target to maintain, for example, a collection cycle that allows a buildup of only "x" number days sales of receivables.

Days in Collection

As mentioned above, the days in collection ratio is a useful tool for helping your finance department maintain a growth situation. It is calculated by taking 365 days divided by the receivable turns yearly.

Turns of Accounts Receivable

This ratio on an annualized basis tells how many times the receivables turn over. The formula is credit sales divided by average receivables balance.

Accounts Payable Turns

This is a quick indicator of cash and cash flow management. When comparing the payables to financed debt, the ratio lets you see how well you use trade debt financing. If the ratio (accounts payable ÷ financed debt) is too low (i.e., 2 to 1), bankers become very concerned with your ability to pay or to stay in business. Therefore, the goal is not to have the lowest possible ratio; it is to have a mix with debt financing that allows the interest-free use of money.

Fixed Asset Turns

This ratio is *sales divided by fixed assets* not as useful in telemarketing as in some other industries. By the very nature of our business, we do not build strong fixed assets. In a fast-growing environment, it is good to see if you are spending money for items such as leasehold improvements too far ahead of growth. The appropriate comparative basis are previous years.

Net Worth

The formula is sales divided by net worth.

The net worth ratio is a good indicator for a growth situation. When compared to previous periods, the net worth ratio can show if the incremental growth has been profitable. In a smaller telemarketing firm, restating net income by having partners withdrawals added back reflects more accurately the profitability of growth.

ABC Telemarketing, Inc.
Balance Sheet Ratios

Liquidity:

Quick Ratio	.92%
Current Ratio	.96%

Financial Effectiveness:

Receivables	5.18
Days in Collection	70.5 Days
Accounts Payable	7.62
Fixed Assets	1.64
Net Worth	8.64

Profitability:

Rate of Return on Net Worth	82%
Rate of Return on Total Assets	5%

ABC Telemarketing, Inc.
Balance Sheet
January 14, 1989

ASSETS
Current Assets:

Cash	$97,800
Accounts Receivable	$1,545,000
Less: Allowance for Bad Debts	($55,000)
Misc. Accounts Receivable	$45,000
Prepayments and Other	$37,500
Total Current Assets	$1,670,300

Fixed Assets:

Operating Equipment	$1,750,000
Leasehold Improvements	$320,000
Other Equipment	$50,000
Furniture and Fixtures	$315,000
Total Fixed Assets:	$2,435,000

Other Assets:

Deposits	$15,000
Organization Costs	$25,000
Total Other Assets:	$40,000
Total Assets	$4,145,300

Liabilities & Stockholdes' Equity

Current Liabilities:

Accounts Payable	$525,000
Accrued Payroll and Other	$750,000
Profit Sharing Accrual	$265,000
Note Payable to Bank	$150,000
Current Portion of Leases	$27,450
Current Portion of Long-Term Note	$15,000
Total Curent Liabilities	$1,732,450

Long Term Liabilities:

Obligations Under Leases	$1,250,000
Long Term Note	$700,000
Total Long-Term Liabilities	$1,950,000
Total Liabilities	$3,682,450

Stockholders' Equity

Common Stock, $1 Par Value; 5000 Shares	$5,000
Paid-in Capital	$250,000
Retained Earnings	$207,850
Total Equity	$462,850
Total Liabilities & Stockholders' Equity	$4,145,300

Appendix *E*

Revised Financial Analysis

1. Projected Cash Flow

    The projected cash flow statement allows a telemarketing firm to revise on a daily, weekly, and monthly basis the projected cash needs. It is not intended to show profitability nor a complete "Source and Use" of funds. A projected cash flow statement:
    - Gives advance notice for borrowing needs
    - Establishes collection goals
    - Facilitates prioritization of expenditures

2. Profitability Projections

    Profitability projections take on many forms. Too often, the normal operating statements are used to project profitability. You will find that the emphasis ends up being on statement presentation and accuracy of numbers versus an honest thought process of events and financial conclusions. In telemarketing, the most effective profitability projection is a statement that reflects what your goals are for:
    - Billed hours
    - Hourly rate
    - Variable cost
    - Fixed cost

    The report becomes very simple in nature. However, it can be a powerhouse in defining how to market telemarketing more profitably on a short-term basis.

ABC Telemarketing, Inc. Projected Cash Flow October Thru December

	October	November	December
Payrolls	$500,000	$600,000	$300,000
Taxes	$145,000	$180,000	$90,000
Phone	$120,000	$140,000	$70,000
Rent	$56,000	$56,000	$56,000
Utilities	$12,000	$12,000	$12,000
Debt Service	$16,500	$16,500	$16,500
Misc Dissbursements	$58,000	$125,000	$62,000
Capital Investments		$150,000	
Total Disbursements	$907,500	$1,279,500	$606,500
Expected Collections	$795,000	$1,100,000	$1,450,000
Surplus (Deficit)	$112,500	$179,500	($843,500)

ABC Telemarketing, Inc. Projected Profitability October Thru December

	October	November	December	Y-T-D
Hour	110,000	97,000	85,000	950,000
Hourly Rate	$30.00	$28.50	$27.25	$26.00
Revenue	$3,300,000	$2,764,500	$2,316,250	$24,700,000
Variable Cost @ $18.25	$2,007,500	$1,770,250	$1,551,250	$17,337,500
Gross Margin	$1,292,500	$994,250	$765,000	$7,362,500
Fixed Cost	$550,000	$525,000	500,000	$6,340,000
Net Profit Before Taxes	$742,500	$469,250	$265,000	$1,022,500
Per Billed Hour	$6.75	$4.84	$3.12	$1.08
Percentage of Sales	22.5%	17.0%	11.4%	4.1%

Appendix *F*

Financial Model Worksheets

Financial modeling is a testing technique for management to determine profitability using run rates and/or assumptions. The key again is to understand the cost relationships and to determine if the assumptions are "real-life."

Financial and organizational/operational standards exist in many industries. However, telemarketing information is not as readily available, which makes comparisons difficult. That places importance on knowing your costs and how to manage them relative to your revenue at any point in time and over the course of time.

Another useful financial modeling tool is break-even analysis. This is a very quick way to determine the number of hours of production necessary to break even (to keep the doors open). It makes more sense to do break-even analysis on both a monthly and a quarterly basis.

a. Model A: This model illustrates what costs can be if you want to achieve 10% pre-tax margin.

   This model reflects a yearly view of what fixed costs can be if you want a 10% pre-tax margin with a set run rate for variable cost. Even though the following example for Model A was created on a spreadsheet, the formulas next to each line item enable you to calculate manually.

b. Model B: This model illustrates what pre-tax margin can be with budgeted fixed cost.

   Model B differs from Model A in that you forecast line-item fixed cost expenses. From this point, you use the variable cost run rate at different revenue levels to determine the pre-tax margin.

c. Model C: This model illustrates the actual operational output needed to break
even.

   In telemarketing pricing, your business profitability is a must. This may
sound elementary; however, many businesses fail to understand when expansion
is going to be needed.

   Validating projected financial results to operational abilities can be simple and
allow for a realistic buildup of staff to meet client needs.

ABC Telemarketing, Inc. Model A 1989

Assumptions:			
A-Hours	500,000		
B-Hourly Rate	$30.00	$27.50	$25.00
C-Target Margin	10%		
D-Variable Cost	$18.50		
E-Fixed Costs	?	Monthly ?	Annualized ?
Question:			
What can fixed costs be to obtain a 10% pre-tax margin?			
Hourly Rate	$30.00	$27.50	$25.00
Revenue (A×B)	$15,000,000	$13,750,000	$12,500,000
Variable Cost (A×D)	9,250,000	9,250,000	9,250,000
Pre Tax Margin (Revenue×10%)	$1,500,000	$1,375,000	$1,250,000
Fixed Cost (Rev - Margin)	$4,250,000	$3,125,000	$2,000,000

ABC Telemarketing, Inc. Pre Tax Margin - Model B 1989

Assumptions:			
A-Hours	500,000		
B-Hourly Rate	$30.00	$27.50	$25.00
C-Target Margin	?		
D-Variable Cost	$18.50		
E-Fixed Costs	$350,000	$4,200,000	
	Monthly	Annualized	
Question:			
What will the pre-tax margin be with budgeted fixed costs?			
Hourly Rate	$30.00	$27.50	$25.00
Revenue (A×B)	$15,000,000	$13,750,000	$12,500,000
Variable Cost (A×D)	$9,250,000	$9,250,000	$9,250,000
Fixed Cost (E)	$4,200,000	$4,200,000	$4,200,000
Pre Tax Margin (Rev-VC-FC)	$1,550,000	$300,000	($950,000)
Pre Tax Margin %	10.3%	2.2%	−7.6%

ABC Telemarketing, Inc.
Fixed Cost Approach -
Model B 1989

	Total
Fixed Costs	
Salaries & Wages	$1,890,000
Fixed Fringe Benefits	$230,000
Advertising-Help Wanted	$125,000
Auto	$25,000
Adv-Mktg	$75,000
Commissions	$65,000
Contributions	$10,000
Conventions	$25,000
Depreciation	$300,000
Dues & Sub	$10,000
Travel & Entertainment	$150,000
Insurance	$35,000
Professional Fees	$150,000
Facility Rents	$400,000
Repairs & Maintenance	$135,000
Fixed Telephone	$500,000
Utilities	$75,000
Total Fixed Costs	$4,200,000

ABC Telemarketing, Inc.
Breakeven Analysis -
Model C 1989

	Total
Fixed Costs	
Salaries & Wages	$1,890,000
Fixed Fringe Benefits	$230,000
Advertising-Help Wanted	$125,000
Auto	$25,000
Adv-Mktg	$75,000
Commissions	$65,000
Contributions	$10,000
Conventions	$25,000
Depreciation	$300,000
Dues & Sub	$10,000
Travel & Entertainment	$150,000
Insurance	$35,000
Professional Fees	$150,000
Facility Rents	$400,000
Repairs & Maintenance	$135,000
Fixed Telephone	$500,000
Utilities	$75,000
Total Fixed Costs	$4,200,000
Variable Costs	$18.50
Rate Per Hour	$30.00
Sales	$10,956,521
Break-even Hours	365,217

Appendix G

Suggested Organizational Needs

Introduction/Explanation

Following is a chart of suggested organizational needs, by function, for small, medium, and large telemarketing companies.

Suggested Needs	Small	Medium	Large
Personnel functions			
— Recruiting	X	X	X
— Regulatory Compliance	X	X	X
— Printed Employee Handbook		X	X
— Orientation Package		X	X
— Record Retention	X	X	X
— Benefits Coordinator			X
— Salary Administration Plan		X	X
— Mgt. Incentive Programs			
— Long Term		X	X
— Short Term	X	X	X
— Payroll Processing	X	X	X
— Record Retention Program	X	X	X
— Training			
— Full Initial Training			
— TSR Positions	X	X	X
— All Other Positions	X	X	X
— Ongoing Advanced Training	X	X	X

Suggested Needs	Small	Medium	Large
— Employee Communication/Relations Vehicles			
— Employee Focus Groups	X	X	X
— Company Sponsored Events (Picnics/Parties/Teams)	X	X	X
— Company Newsletter	*	X	X
Insurance Relationships			
— General	X	X	X
— Liability	X	X	X
— Workmen's Compensation	X	X	X
Evaluation Program			
— In-House	X	X	X
— Outside Evaluation		X	X
Accounting Relationships			
— In-House			
— Internal Financials		X	X
— Controls	X	X	X
— Management Reporting		X	X
— Public Accountant			
— Tax	X	X	X
— Audit		X	X
— Legal Relationships	X	X	X
— Job Descriptions		X	X
— Travel & Entertainment Policies		X	X
— Regulatory Information			
— Federal	X	X	X
— State	X	X	X
— EEOC	X	X	X
— Industry Trade Association	X	X	X
— Banking Relationships	X	X	X
— Utilities	X	X	X
— Facility			
— Phone Room Space	X	X	X
— Administrative Space	X	X	X
— Breakrooms	X	X	X
— Bathrooms	X	X	X
— Storage	X	X	X
— Vendors			
— Printing	X	X	X
— Data Processing			
— Labels	X	X	X
— Telephone Look-ups	X	X	X
— Federal Express	X	X	X
— U P S		X	X
— Courier Service		X	X
— Office Supplies	X	X	X
— Telephone			
— Long Distance Service	X	X	X
— Local Bell Company	X	X	X

Suggested Needs	Small	Medium	Large
— Repair & Maintenence	X	X	X
— Newspaper	X	X	X
— Labor Market Information			
— Age distribution for area	X	X	X
— Unemployment rate & type	*	X	X
— Transportation availability	*	X	X
— Competitive forces	*	X	X

* Only if you want to grow.

Appendix *H*

Expansion Capability

Expansion Capability Formula

Assumptions:
  Number of telemarketing hours
  Number of shifts per month
  Number of hours per shift
  Maximum facility utilization = 80%
  Average facility size (phones) = 80 phones

Formula

Phones × Shifts × Hours Per Shift × Facility Utilization % = Hours

$$\text{Phones} = \frac{\text{Hours}}{(\text{Shifts} \times \text{Hours Per Shift}) \times \text{Facility Utilization \%}}$$

$$\text{Facilities} = \frac{\text{Phones}}{(\text{Average Facility Size})}$$

Expansion Capability Project Chart

Assumptions:
  100 Hours Per Phone
  100 Phones Per Facility
  90% Phones Filled

Hours Per Month	Number of Facilities
0–9,000	1
9,001–18,000	2
18,001–27,000	3
27,001–36,000	4
36,001–45,000	5

Financing a
Telemarketing Business

Arranging financing for a start-up business is difficult. The experiences of business failures during the 1980s have created an even greater problem for telemarketing firms when talking with bankers. The traditional banker wants collateral, collateral, collateral! Securing Small Business Administration (SBA) loans is not always a viable alternative, since most SBA loans are guaranteed by the government and use private funds.

What most telemarketing start-up companies, and some expanding companies, find is an unwilling banker who may be convinced to lend on a short-term basis. It is not unusual that receivables and personal assets must be pledged. So it is extremely important to have financial projections that reflect:

- Your knowledge of the industry
- Financial ability to repay
- Contracted business

Remember, from the banker's perspective, a service-based company has few assets to liquidate.

The following summaries explain some of the more common financial methods. These brief summaries are not intended to be all inclusive. However, as long as there are creative people, there will be creative financing.

Equity Personal Cash and Assets

This is the most common method of financing, either in part or in total, especially to enter business.

Pro's

- No qualifying
- No pledging assets
- No debt
- No interest expense

Con's

- Uses personal funds
- Limits rapid expansion
- Isolates personal risk

Partnership

A partnership can be a good financing vehicle. The partner's involvement in day-to-day business can be passive or active.

Pro's

- Can increase borrowing power
- No debt
- No interest expense
- Spreads risk
- Could bring needed skill levels into company
- Inexpensive to set up
- Good tax vehicle

Con's

- Could bring "bad" partner to company
- Easy to end
- Generally can give up too high a percentage of ownership for a start-up company.

Bank Loans

Bank loans can be short-term or long-term. The most common difficulty in arranging bank loans normally centers around the security required by the lender.

Line Of Credit

A common short-term financing tool is a line of credit. The agreement normally is short-term (1–2 years) with floating interest rates above prime. A maximum is set on the dollar amount the line of credit can reach. The basis is a percentage of receivables or a limited dollar amount. As an example, the bank might lend you $1,000,000 at 2 points above prime or the lower of 75% of all receivables under 60 days old. It is possible that your receivables would not be high enough to cover $1,000,000. Therefore, you would be able to borrow only what the receivables would cover.

Term Notes

Term notes differ from the line of credit in that they are set for a certain number of months at a per-month payment. The advantage is to spread repayment out over a set number of months and use future cash flow to repay debt.

Bank Financing

Pro's

- Do not necessarily utilize all personal funds
- Can match future cash flows with repayments

Con's

- Slow to secure and finalize
- Can be unavailable when needed
- Interest expense can be high
- Personal assets normally part of security

Venture Capital

The amount of venture capital available for service-based companies grew significantly in the 1980s. Prior to then, venture capital was more common in manufacturing and technology. Venture capital normally involves ownership (equity) with debt.

Pro's

- Resource of capital
- Can be a source for revenue

Con's

- Normally gives up major portion of ownership
- Can be closely monitored
- Venture partner can be very *un*knowledgeable of business

Relatives and Friends

In many cases, relatives and friends represent a legitimate source of inexpensive capital. These are the people who know you best and, hopefully, trust you enough to lend money. Also, this form of financing can take the form of equity and/or loans.

Pro's

- Can be an inexpensive source
- Easy and quick
- Often unsecured

Con's

- Family and friends can make bad business partners
- Can be limited resources

Personal Loans

Personal loans (from yourself) are very similar to equity investments. The primary difference is that the intent is not to leave the money in the company.

Pro's

- Quick access
- Flexible terms
- Low cost to company

Con's

- Ties up personal assets
- Not as secure as other debts

Trade Debts

Trade debts financing is a recognized, informal method to gain short-term financing. It is simply using your vendor's money to generate cash flow.

Pro's

- Usually no interest
- No formal agreement
- No security used

Con's

- Potential ill will with vendors
- Can lose important vendors
- Can increase pricing
- Can reduce level of service to the company

Public Offering

Selling stock at a public offering, while a useful and realistic possibility for a firm with an extensive track record, is most often a pipe dream for a start-up telemarketing company.

Pro's

- Equity funding
- Spreads risk

Con's

- Loss of ownership
- Expensive to "go public"
- Can change management

Accounts Receivable

In telemarketing, accounts receivable is the key asset that financial people use to secure loans. The receivables do not yield face value. The quality, size, age and average number of accounts will determine the cost associated in selling the receivables. If the receivables are sold without recourse, meaning that the buyer of the receivables will suffer any or all bad debts, the discount factor is 20%–30%. In most cases, the receivables are sold with recourse, and normally will be charged back by the bank when an invoice is 90 days old.

Commercial Paper

Some banks will lend money on the receivables with the invoices not only being the security, but with the actual client payment going directly to the lender. This arrangement is referred to as *a lock box agreement*. The idea is the bank has all rights to the payment, which will be at face value of the invoice.

Pro's

- Quick cash
- Turns accounts receivables

Con's

- Discount charges
- Collection efforts can eliminate client
- Uncollectable and "old" receivables come back

Factoring

Factoring receivables has its roots in many industries, but it has moved very slowly into telemarketing. A service-based invoice is not really desirable by factors.

Pro's

- Quick money
- Turns accounts receivables

Con's

- Usually very expensive
- Minimum amount
- Uncollectable and "old" receivables come back
- Normally there is a minimum amount placed on hold for settlement problems.

Leases

Leases are classified into two groups:

1. True lease, in which the asset ownership is with the lessor.
2. Lease-purchase, in which the ownership is with the lessee.

Pro's

- Little money needed up front
- Pay for only use of money
- Tax deductible

Con's

- Can be trapped into a long-term agreement
- May limit asset selection
- Lease rates can be higher

Rentals

The primary difference between rentals and leases is that ownership does not pass to the renter. It is an effective way to utilize cash flow without creating longer-term debt.

Pro's

- No cash up front
- Usually can terminate easily
- Does not show on balance sheet
- Use only the amount of time you desire
- Tax deductible

Con's

- Cost more over a longer term
- No ownership, thus does not show as an asset
- Cannot always find exactly what you need

Sale-Lease Backs

This is a form of leasing that allows a start-up or growing company to acquire needed assets. The lender receives all tax benefits and cash-flow advantages associated with the lease asset.

Pro's

- Quick
- Better interest rates because of tax benefits being passed to the lender
- Low monthly notes can be achieved with balloon payment of residuals at end of lease

Con's

- Asset does not show on books
- May want use of asset longer than lease

Linked Financing

Linked financing is simply using the credit of another company or person as collateral for loans or supplies

Pro's

- It is a source of cash
- Quick

Con's

- Rates are in excess of prime
- Heavy collection efforts
- Financial information becomes known to suppliers and customers

Letters of Credit

This financial instrument guarantees payment to a vendor based on submission of proof of shipment. It is a way to purchase without paying in advance.

Pro's

- No money up front
- Low cost

Con's

- Have to have credit approval ahead of time
- Ties up credit
- A fee is charged whether used or not

Working Capital

For a start-up firm, working capital is one of the items that is financed either through equity or debt. The growing telemarketing concern uses the excess cash flow to finance growth. It is the easiest method of financing.

Pro's

- No interest paid
- No qualifying for credit
- Quick
- No debt

Con's

- Can keep company cash poor
- Does not match long-term revenue and financing
- Can limit growth rate

Grants

Another source of financing that emerged during the 1980's is grant money from local, state, and federal funds. With the country moving from an industrial base to service base, high unemployment in the cities and rural areas have caused government agencies to begin funding businesses that will bring jobs to an area.

Pro's

- No cost
- No repayment
- No debt

Con's

- Tied to a community for a certain amount of time
- Size of grant is in relationship to jobs, not to business needs
- Lengthy to qualify
- Non-business criteria used for approval

Low-Interest Development Loans

This financial device is very similar to grants, except there is a repayment of debt.

Pro's

- Low-cost interest
- Very broad in application
- Longer debt repayment
- Tax incentives

Con's

– Tied to a community for a certain amount of time
– Size of loan tied to jobs
– Lengthy to qualify
– Non-business criteria used to approve

Bonds

Local bonds are source of low-cost financing; however, bonds are generally reserved for "hard" asset financing.

Pro's

– Interest rates low
– Long repayment schedule

Con's

– Hard to qualify
– Restrictions on use of funds
– Tied to community

Financing a Telemarketing Business
Types of Financing

Type of Financing	Short Term	Long Term
Equity (Personal Cash)	X	X
Partnerships		X
Bank Loans	X	
Lines of Credit		X
Term Notes		X
Venture Capital		X
Relatives and Friends	X	
Personal Loans	X	
Trade Debts	X	
Public Offering		X
Accounts Receivable		
Commercial	X	
Factoring	X	
Leases		X
Rentals	X	
Sale-Lease Backs		X
Link Financing	X	
Letters of Credit	X	
Working Capital	X	
Grants	X	
Low Interest Development		X
Bonds		X

Appendix *J*

Pros and Cons for Automation

Pros and Cons for Automation in a Telemarketing Firm

General	Pro	Con
1) Heavy upfront capital costs.		X
2) Can (and usually does) change the way you operate		X
3) Changes physical workstation.		X
4) Change training time.	X	
5) Introduces new skills.		X
6) Reduction of paper process.	X	
7) Improved accuracy.	X	
8) Client reporting.		
– Accuracy	X	
– Timeliness	X	
– Reports		
– Standard	X	
– Customized		X
9) Downtime from computer problems.		X
10) Converting back to manual on a temporary basis is difficult.		X
11) Reduced paper flow cost.	X	
List Management		
1) Control over list/Data base management.	X	
2) Flexible record selection		
– Responsive to weather, special events, etc.	X	

General	Pro		Con
– Logically related multiple criteria.	X		
3) List extract			
– Performance information	X		
– Zip Code	X		
4) Summary Merge/Purge	X		
5) History			
– Access	X		
– Resolve Conflicts	X		
– Comparative standards for future	X		
6) Call back control	X		
7) Objective measurement of list performance.	X		
TSR Performance Measurement			
1) Quantification of TSR performance	X		
– Calls Per Hour			
– Sales Per Hour			
2) Management reports	X		
3) Selective sales tracking	X		
4) Sales cycle each evening	X		
5) Staffing programs for weighted TSR performance	X		
6) Human interface to computer	X	*and*	X
7) Possible increased productivity.	X		
Script Management			
1) Script changes			X
2) Implementation of script changes	X		
3) Control of correct script	X		
4) Responsiveness to selling objections	X		X
5) Technical skill needed			X
6) Amount of time needed to develop script			X
7) Ability to select appropriate answers	X		
8) Access to reference material	X		

Index